RELIGION
&
THEOLOGY

A guide to current
reference resources

This book is dedicated to

THE AUSTRALIAN AND NEW ZEALAND THEOLOGICAL LIBRARY ASSOCIATION

with affection and gratitude

RELIGION & THEOLOGY

A guide to current reference resources

Lawrence D. McIntosh

Centre for Information Studies
Charles Sturt University - Riverina
Wagga Wagga New South Wales

National Library of Australia cataloguing-in-publication data

McIntosh, Lawrence, 1928- .

Religion and theology: a guide to current reference resources.

Includes index.
ISBN 0 949060 37 2
1. Religion - Bibliography. 2. Theology - Bibliography. I. Charles Sturt University
- Riverina. Centre for Information Studies. II. Title.

016.2

ISBN: 0-949060-37-2

1st ed. published 1997

Centre for Information Studies
Locked Bag 660
Wagga Wagga 2678 Australia
Fax: (069) 332733

Contents

Preface   vii

Acknowledgments   ix

Introduction: A Guide to the *Guide*   xi

Abbreviations   xv

Part 1   **General reference resources**   1
Part 2   **Subject reference resources**   33

Chapters
2   Religions in the world   35
3   Judaism   47
4   Christianity: Church history   61
5   Christianity: Churches in the world   93
6   The Bible and related literature   117
7   Christian theology   157
8   Christian worship, liturgy, preaching and church music 167
9   Spirituality   179
10   Religious and theological education   183
11   Religious art and architecture   187
12   Pastoral care and counselling   195
13   Philosophy and ethics   199
14   Religious and theological periodicals   207

           Author and editor index   219
           Title index   227
           Subject index   243

Preface

THE MATTERS OF RELIGION AND THEOLOGY

This guide is designed to introduce students, teachers, librarians and others to current reference resources in the fields of religion, religions and theology.

Obviously the choice of items for inclusion reflects the compiler's understanding of the meaning of these terms and so definitions are in order. But what definition of religion could hold good for each and every living faith, for monotheistic and polytheistic religions and for religions without identifiable gods at all? Is there one definition that would satisfy an Australian Aboriginal, a liberal Jew, an undogmatic Buddhist, a spiritual vagabond of the New Age? Certain theory-laden abstractions, psychological and sociological, are available but, at least for our purposes, it seems best to proceed phenomenologically and to note some of the characteristics and patterns of the religious life.

Religious experience involves an awareness that one's life is informed by a force which is other than human, which transcends human existence. People may speak of this power as God, or a pantheon of gods, as some *mysterium tremendum*. Whatever symbolism is used to describe this object of faith, religious experience derives from a belief in the reality of a power that confronts us as the Other, that gives to life its ultimate meaning and orders its ultimate priorities.

Belief is affirmed and confirmed within a community of faith that adopts common interpretations of this transcendental reality. Concomitantly, members accept distinctive ways of looking at the world and of living within it. So we speak of religions, acknowledging that they are ancient and modern, Eastern and Western, institutionalised and non-structured, world-rejecting and world-affirming. Their appearance in the modern world ranges from the tranquillity of contemplative groupings to the religiously-charged vitality of militant fundamentalisms.

Religious people describe their awareness of the transcendent by means of myths and stories. Their perceptions come to be enshrined in systems of beliefs, perhaps in creeds and doctrinal formulations. Usually they accept a certain authority, whether in the form of sacred writings, an historical tradition or an ancestral leader. Rituals and forms of worship are developed and shared; religious education, in matters of faith, history and values, proceeds in both formal and informal settings.

Courses in religious studies, at least in the Australasian setting, tend to be the province of university departments of religion. The study of theology, on the other hand, normally belongs to a seminary or theological college. The student of religion engages in the task of description and analysis, cultivating the sort of impartiality expected within academia. The theologian may also relate responsibly to the academy but, usually, he or she has appropriated and publicly represents a certain religious tradition - some form of Judaism, a Christian denomination, an Islamic school or some other faith community - and is likely to play a key role in preparing candidates for ministry within that tradition.

Theology is an orderly reflection on the content of faith. Its task is to interpret the ultimate life-and-death concerns which find expression in the myths, faith-symbols, rites and practices of a specific religion. Particular attention is paid to whatever claims are made for a special revelation - the covenant of the Jews, the teachings of the Buddha, the coming of the Christ, the sacred book of Islam.

The theologian works with a diverse and often critical company. Scriptural scholars explore the documentary sources of faith, the processes of their being written, handed down and transposed for apologetic purposes. Historians illumine crucial periods, exegete confessional documents and help account for cultural shifts such as from doctrinaire positivism to new forms of religious consciousness. Philosophers serve to keep theology answerable to reason. In the quest for religious meaning, Jerusalem, to invoke Tertullian's rhetoric, had better have something to do with Athens. Meanwhile, the caregivers, sensitive to the voices of hunger, grief and fear calling for redress, question theological formulations which fail to acknowledge the imperatives of freedom and justice. Just so does the discipline of theology require teamwork, at once scholarly and humane.

Currently, theology is also challenged by those who fly the flag of disbelief, who regard the claims of traditional religions as untenable, indeed harmful. Within this context, we shall be noting resources which define heresy, atheism, agnosticism and other forms of heterodoxy, and which posit the decline of religious belief.

The complexity and diversity of religions and their strong emotional content have caused deep divisions throughout history and throughout the world. Absolute claims may still be made for a particular faith; models of exclusivism can hold sway. The mass media constantly report the tragic consequences of religious bigotry and discrimination. But hope derives from a departure from parochialism. The last half-century has seen a new theological style which has been nurtured and nourished by conversations between the major religions and between their subdivisions. These conversations, multi-faith and inter-denominational, are exploring the view that recognises the plurality and diversity of religious traditions. With a new openness, dialogical attempts are being made to find a basis from which to respond to the timeless questions about the meaning of life and how it may be lived.

This guide reflects the multi-dimensional nature of religion and of the theological enterprise - historical, phenomenological, social, dialogical - an enormous territory. Its emphasis on recent material suggests a reliance on a new generation of scholars and on fresh methodologies. Many of the items are characterised by flexibility and pluralism. Be that as it may, an impressive array of resources is available for those engaged in interpreting and evaluating the history, meaning and cultural significance of religious experiences.

Acknowledgements

I acknowledge with appreciation the help of numerous colleagues. Particularly, I am indebted to the staff of the Joint Theological Library in Parkville, Victoria and to the resources of its very fine Reference Collection. I should like to thank the Librarian, Stephen Connelly and also Hal Cain, Helen Cain, Jane Colebrook, Philip Harvey, Ria McMahon and Shanelle Redwood. Their hospitality and helpfulness were very much appreciated. Other librarians have helped with advice and information and these include Judith Bright of Auckland, Kim Robinson of Sydney and Trevor Zweck of Adelaide. Special thanks go to Pam Carswell for reading the introductory material and commenting, as only Pam can. And to Pamela McIntosh for reading much of the manuscript, offering criticisms and suggestions and for being so supportive throughout the many months of this project. Through it all a beloved collegue, Trevor Zweck of Adelaide, who died this September was, characteristically, interested and most encouraging.

John Mills of the Centre for Information Studies, who gave me a good hearing when we discussed the initial plan of the book, Stuart Ferguson of the Centre, who carefully and expeditiously proof-read the work and coordinated its progress from manuscript to printed form, and Andrew Jacobs of Alive Graphics, who prepared it for printing. To all, my sincere thanks.

The *Guide* is better for these collegial contributions; of course I am responsible for the blemishes that remain.

Certain titles scattered throughout the *Guide* were reviewed in an annual feature entitled, 'Major reference resources', which I contributed to the *Australian and New Zealand Theological Library Association newsletter*. I am grateful for permission to reuse some material from this source.

As soon as a tool such as this *Guide* is published, it calls for some form of supplementation. The Australian and New Zealand Theological Library Association, that worthy company to which this present work is dedicated, may well think of ways to augment and improve upon it.

Lawrence McIntosh
September 1996

Introduction

A GUIDE TO THE *GUIDE*

Purpose

The purpose of this *Guide* is to introduce students, teachers and librarians to current reference works in the fields of religion and theology. The items selected are with a view to scholarly research. Students, confronted by a bewildering array of resources, should be helped by a work that organises and describes the key reference works in their subject areas. Members of teaching faculties could find it useful as an advisory aid. In libraries it may assist with reference work and function also as a current check-list for the development of reference and periodical collections.

The *Guide* should help keep scholars reasonably up to date with the mass of reference material being published in these subject fields. Specifically, it updates and augments a number of published guides to religious and theological literature. Unlike some of those earlier guides, the present work is highly selective. It concentrates on items designed to assist with serious study and which have been published since the early 1980s. Some older titles, exceptions to the rule, are included simply because they have been neither superseded nor surpassed.

The standard bibliographic guides to religious reference books have generally ignored items published in Australia and New Zealand. This *Guide* attempts to redress this situation by paying special attention to resources bearing on the study of religion and theology in these countries. Given this particular emphasis the *Guide* could also assist overseas librarians who are finding it difficult to identify religious titles published in or about Australia and New Zealand.

Reference works

Reference works may be defined as publications which are consulted in order to obtain authoritative information. They are distinguished from monographs in that they are not normally read through. Rather they are used piecemeal to retrieve factual information, introductions to subjects or bibliographic access to further sources of information. They include bibliographies and surveys of the literature of a subject, encyclopedias, dictionaries, atlases, directories, biographical sources and indexing and abstracting systems.

Modern information technologies are producing new formats, and traditional print items may either be reproduced in or replaced by online databases or CD-ROM resources. With all this heady technology, however, reference books continue to be published; for some time, at least, students will need them to satisfy their search for quality answers.

Where there is a dearth of current material, the *Guide* may cite a work which is not strictly speaking a reference item but which, because of its bibliographic awareness or indexing apparatus, has reference potential.

Selection criteria

Choosing what to include and what to leave out is never easy. As a librarian I have been guided by the sort of items I have used in reference work and which I have introduced to a generation or more of teachers and students. Almost all the resources cited in this volume have been either used in this way or at least examined. Scholarly book reviews have sometimes helped in distinguishing the definitive from the also-ran.

Usually, inclusions on a particular subject are limited to items that are deemed to be the best available. For certain types of resources, particularly dictionaries and commentaries, the best advice is to consult more than one source.

In this matter of selection it is difficult to pretend to 'objectivity'. We bring to our choices a particular angle of vision whether it be conservative, liberal, pietistic or sceptical. Notwithstanding, the major criteria for selection have been the authority and recency of an item.

More specifically, the following factors have determined selection:

- preference has been given to works which can be regarded as authoritative. This authority derives from the scholarly qualifications of the author, editor or contributors, the reputation of the publisher and the accuracy and currency of the work

- the emphasis is on recency. Most of the items included were published between 1980 and 1995, with a few works published in 1996 also included. As noted earlier, an older work may be cited when that work has assumed the status of a classic in the field or, for some other reason, has retained its usefulness

- with regard to subject bibliographies, usually only extensive works, published within the last decade or so, have been included. No attempt has been made to provide full bibliographic coverage for a particular topic

- there is an emphasis on resources dealing with the nature, history and status of religions in Australia and New Zealand.

The works chosen are likely to be available either in the larger theological libraries in Australia and New Zealand or in other major libraries which support teaching interests in religion and theology.

Languages

Reference materials published in the English language predominate. Publications in languages other than English have been limited mainly to certain works in French and German which, for some reason, are outstanding or unique in their usefulness for religious research. This applies particularly to a number of subject encyclopedias.

A matter of balance

This *Guide* is necessarily incomplete. Items published during the last fifteen years or so do not yield anything like a comprehensive coverage of all subjects. Some areas are not covered at all. The bibliographic gaps have to be filled by means of the earlier guides to reference materials described in Part 1.

Nor does the guide pretend to be a balanced unified list. The bulk of material relates to the major religions of the world, especially to Christianity and, within that religion, to the mainline churches. The imbalance is due to the fact that religious publishing, at least in English-speaking countries, is largely concerned with the Christian majorities. A host of items reflect the history of the churches, their teachings and the multiform expressions of Christian experience. The ways in which the people of the other great religions, the non-Christian majority of the human race, understand their faiths are not nearly as well documented.

It may be noted that certain chapters are much longer than others. Some subject areas have developed numerous subfields, some are supported by an extensive bibliographic apparatus. The discipline of biblical studies, with its mixture of historical, geographical, textual, exegetical and theological material, furnishes a ready example of extensiveness combined with complexity.

Where gaps remain in the subject coverage - for example there is little here on certain Asian churches - it means that no substantial resource on this topic, published during the last decade or so, could be identified. (It is always possible, of course, that such an item eluded the compiler or was overlooked.)

And a matter of labelling

For good reasons librarians avoid labelling like the plague where labelling means the assigning of some category which may serve to censor a work. That is not intended here. Designations, such as 'Catholic' and 'Protestant' are used to categorise certain works which claim to be descriptive of denominational positions. Where a work is avowedly 'conservative evangelical', to name but one option, that designation is recorded, without prejudice.

Arrangement

Any attempt to classify the multi-faceted disciplines of religion and theology is to some extent arbitrary. The ordering of subjects in this *Guide* is not meant to reflect a preference either for religious or theological studies and nothing in the classified arrangement should suggest that a value judgment has been made about the importance of a particular subject.

The work is divided into two parts and into fourteen chapters. Each part and chapter begins with an introductory note and a synopsis of contents. Subdivisions and subheadings are used to divide the items that follow.

Part 1: General reference resources. Comprises one chapter and includes general works of two kinds:

1. general works covering the many areas of human knowledge, including religion and theology, for example the *Dictionary of the history of ideas,* and

2. works providing general coverage of religion and/ or theology, for example the *Encyclopedia of religion* and the *Dictionary of fundamental theology.*

The arrangement throughout Part 1 is by *type* of reference work - bibliographies, directories of libraries and archives, encyclopedias, biographical resources, and so on.

Part 2: Subject reference resources. Chapters 2-13 are on specific subjects in religion and theology. Each subject is divided into divisions and subdivisions, using a traditional or, at least, some convenient heading.

Thus the arrangement in this second part is by *subject* and the subjects are divided by types of material.

Within each subdivision, items are usually arranged alphabetically unless a chronological arrangement makes more sense.

Chapter 14 comprises a list of religious and theological periodicals.

Citations

The bibliographical details as presented should ensure the easy identification of each item. The citations are constructed according to the note-bibliography system of referencing as described in my *Style manual for the presentation of papers and theses in religion and theology* (Wagga Wagga, NSW: Centre for Information Studies, 1994, 1995).

In preparing the citations, the following conventions were adopted:

the main entry

Each item is identified according to what librarians know as its 'main entry'. This entry point is either the name(s) of the author(s) or, in the case of an edited work, the title.

the title

Each title is given in full.

series

Titles published within a numbered series are so identified. The name of the series and the number of the item within that series is enclosed in round brackets.

the publishing details

The place of publication, the name of the publisher and the year of publication are given, in that order.

Certain books are published by more than one publisher, sometimes with a change of title. This is particularly true of a number of works published in both Great Britain and the United States. Preference has been given to the place of origin when this can be established but, in some cases, the names of two publishers are given. This does not necessarily mean, however, that all editions of a work are listed.

the International Standard Book Number (ISBN)

The ISBN is a ten-digit number allocated to each book or edition of that book, which identifies that work as a unique item. Where the same title is published in hard cover and in paperback, the two formats are identified by different ISBNs.

Similarly, an International Standard Serial Number (ISSN) is allocated to each serial title, once again identifying that particular serial as a unique item.

Annotations

The annotations are designed to indicate the scope, methodology and intrinsic usefulness of an item and to highlight any special reference features. They are descriptive rather than evaluative and do not labour the fact that the item merits inclusion.

Periodical literature

Chapter 14 contains a classified list of English-language periodicals which are among the most important for the study of religion and theology. Those published in Australia or New Zealand are so designated.

Cross-references

Where a work is pertinent to more than one area, a cross-reference is made.

Abbreviations

A list of abbreviations used in the text or in citations follows the *Introduction*.

Indexes

Three indexes provide access by author, editor or compiler, by title, and by subject. In all probability the subject index will be the most useful.

Abbreviations

A list of symbols, abbreviations and other shortened forms used in this book.

GENERAL

*	asterisk. In Chapter 14, an asterisk is used to identify periodicals which are edited either in Australia or New Zealand.
3/yr	three times a year, or however numbered
AD	(Lat.) anno domini - in the year of our Lord
ann.	annual, published annually
Aufl.	(Ger.) Auflage - edition
BC	before Christ; BCE is preferred in this work
BCE	before the Common (or Christian) Era
bearb.	(Ger.) bearbeitet - compiled
CE	Common (or Christian) Era
chap.	chapter
corr.	corrected
ed.	editor, edited
edn	edition
enl.	enlarged
erarb.	(Ger.) erarbeiten - achieved by
erw.	(Ger.) erweiterte - enlarged
et al.	(Lat.) et alii - and others
f./ff.	following
Ger.	German
hc	hard cover
hrsg.	(Ger.) herausgegeben - edited
ISBN	International Standard Book Number
ISSN	International Standard Serial Number
Lat.	Latin
m.	monthly
n.	note
neubearb.	(Ger.) neubearbeitet - revised
no.	Italian numero - number
NT	New Testament
p., pp.	page, pages
pbk	paperback
q.	quarterly

repr.	reprinted
rev.	revised
semi-ann.	semi annual
trans.	translated
u.	(Ger.) und - and
v.	(Ger.) von - by, from
vol., vols.	volume, volumes

TEXTS AND VERSIONS OF THE BIBLE

Item numbers are added for versions cited or noted.

KJV	King James Version (378n)
LXX	Septuagint (439, 440)
NAB	New American Bible (373, 374)
NIV	The Holy Bible: New International Version (377)
NJB	New Jerusalem Bible (376)
NRSV	New Revised Standard Version (369)
REB	Revised English Bible (371)
RSV	Revised Standard Version (369n)

ORGANISATIONS

ABS	Australian Bureau of Statistics
ANZATS	Australian and New Zealand Association of Theological Schools
ANZTLA	Australia and New Zealand Theological Library Association
ATESEA	Association for Theological Education in South East Asia
ATLA	American Theological Library Association
CRA	Christian Research Association
NZATS	New Zealand Association of Theological Schools
SBL	Society of Biblical Literature

STATES AND TERRITORIES

Australia

ACT	Australian Capital Territory
NSW	New South Wales
NT	Northern Territory
Qld	Queensland

SA	South Australia
Tas.	Tasmania
Vic.	Victoria
WA	Western Australia

United States of America

Two-letter abbreviations are used for the United States of America States and Territories. Frequent mention is made of the following:

CA	California
CO	Colorado
CT	Connecticut
DC	District of Columbia
GA	Georgia
IL	Illinois
KY	Kentucky
LA	Louisiana
MA	Massachusetts
MD	Maryland
MI	Michigan
MN	Minnesota
NJ	New Jersey
NY	New York
PA	Pennsylvania
TN	Tennessee
TX	Texas

(A more complete list is in the author's, *A style manual for the presentation of papers and theses in religion and theology*, pp.113-114. [Item 84].)

PART

General reference resources

In thinking about the sort of coverage provided by reference resources, it is possible to distinguish three groups

- the first is a general resource which attempts to cover all subjects, for example a general encyclopedia such as the *Encyclopaedia Britannica*

- the second is a resource which covers a broad subject area generally and comprehensively, for example an encyclopedia of religion

- the third is a resource concerned with a *specific* subject, for example an encyclopedia of preaching.

Part 1 includes the first two groups: general reference works which cover all subjects, including religion, and reference works which provide general or comprehensive coverage of religion and/or theology.

These general resources, and religious works of a general nature, are gathered together because there is a good deal of overlapping. As an instance, the *Encyclopaedia Britannica* and the *Encyclopedia of religion* both contain major articles on the several great religions, so they are located in the same section with *EB* listed under the heading, 'General' and the more specialised *ER* under the heading 'Religious'.

It is important also to recognise the principal types of reference resources - bibliographies, encyclopedias, atlases, biographical sources, indexes and so on. Items in Part 1 are arranged by type and not by subject. Where appropriate, under each type-heading, the general items are listed first. These are followed by items which cover religion and theology comprehensively, this latter group being subdivided as required.

Part 2 will deal with specific subject resources.

General reference resources

Bibliographies   **6**

Guides to reference books   6
   General   6
      Australian
      The humanities
   Religious and theological   7
      Comprehensive
      Catholic emphasis
      Protestant emphasis

National bibliographies   8
   Australia   9
      Current
      Retrospective
   New Zealand   9
      Current
      Retrospective

Trade bibliographies, books in print   10
   General   10
   Religious   11
      Retrospective

Dissertations   12
   General   12
      International
      British
   Religious   13
      Australian

Periodical literature   13
   Directories   13
      General
      Religious
   Union lists. Australasian   14
   Periodicals, Bibliographies in   14
   Abbreviations   14

Indexing and abstracting services   15
   General
      Australian
   Religious periodicals   15
      United States / International
      Australasian
   Multi-author works, Festschriften   17
Book reviews   17
   Published reviews   17
   Indexes to book reviews   18
      Australasian

Libraries and archives - Australia and New Zealand   18
General   18
Religious and theological   19

Encyclopedias, subject dictionaries, handbooks   19
General   20
   Australian
   New Zealand
Religious   21
   General coverage
   Deities
   Unbelief
   Religion in politics
   Mythology
   New Age movements

Biographical sources   24
Great Britain   24
Australia   25
   Secularists   25
New Zealand   25

Quotation sources   26
General   26
   Ancient quotations
   Modern quotations
Religious   27

Language dictionaries   27
Historical dictionaries   27
Current usage   28
   Australian
   New Zealand
Theological German   29

Style manuals   **29**
    General   29
        Australian and New Zealand
    Religious and theological   30
  Inclusive language   30
    Comprehensive   30
    Gender and language   31
        General usage
        Religious usage

Copyright   **32**

Statistics   **32**
    Australian   32

BIBLIOGRAPHIES

GUIDES TO REFERENCE BOOKS

General

1.   *Guide to reference books.* 10th edn. Edited by Eugene P. Sheehy.
      Chicago: American Library Association, 1986. 0-8389-0390-8.

2.   *Guide to reference books: covering materials from 1985-1990.*
      Supplement to the tenth edition. Edited by Robert Balay.
      Chicago: American Library Association, 1992. 0-8389-0588-9.

The great American resource which lists and annotates reference works is
arranged by subject. There are five major divisions: 'General reference',
'Humanities', 'Social sciences', 'History and area studies', 'Pure and applied sciences'. International in coverage, but tending to favour American titles and
English language material. In the 1986 volume, some one hundred columns are
given to religion, which section is divided into categories with subdivisions, while
the Supplement adds a further twenty eight. Annotations are descriptive.

3.   *Walford's guide to reference material.* 6th edn. Edited by A. J. Walford
      et al. 3 volumes. London: Library Association, 1993-1994.
      Volume 2: 'Social and historical sciences, philosophy and religion'
      was issued in 1994. 1-85604-044-5 (vol. 2).

Another highly-respected guide which, with its British flavour, broader international coverage and extensive annotations, can be regarded as a worthy complement to the *Guide to reference books* [1, 2]. Arrangement of items is by the
Universal Decimal Classification system. There are author/title and subject indexes in each volume.

Australian

4.   Mills, John J. *Information resources and services in Australia.* 2nd edn.
      (Topics in Australasian library and information studies, 4). Wagga
      Wagga, NSW: Centre for Information Studies, 1992. 0-949060-
      15-1. Reprint, 1994.

Designed for information professionals, librarians and students, this revised and
expanded edition of a work first published in 1990, has two purposes: first to
describe the methodology of research in detail and, second, to identify and assess
a range of Australian information resources available in print, online and on CD-
ROM. There are indexes to authors, titles and databases, and subjects. The discussions of research strategies and the presentation of general and subject-specific
reference resources, for example on 'History' and 'Religion', could prove helpful
for students engaged in religion studies.

The humanities

5.   Blazek, Ron and Elizabeth Aversa. *The humanities: a selective guide to information sources.* 4th edn. Englewood, CO: Libraries Unlimited, 1994. 1-56308-167-9 (hc); 0-56308-168-7 (pbk).

This title has passed through three editions (1974, 1979, 1988), the first two authored by A. Robert Rogers and the third by the present authors. The work begins with an introduction to the Humanities and to general sources, then proceeds to subject areas with chapters on 'accessing information' and 'principal sources' in philosophy, religion, the visual arts, the performing arts, and finally, language and literature. The introductions to subject areas and the extensive annotating of items make this a valuable library tool.

6.   *The Reader's adviser.* 14th edn. Volume 4: The Best in philosophy and religion. Edited by Marion Sader. New Providence, NJ: R. R. Bowker, 1994. 0-8352-3324-3.

A venerable tool which, under various guises, dates back to 1921.

Volume 4 (of the six-volume edition) surveys the literature of philosophy and religion from pre-Socratic philosophers to modern day thinkers, from pre-historic religions to religious movements of the late-twentieth century. Chapter 1, 'Philosophy and religion: general reference' by Mark Stover concentrates on reference resources while the remaining chapters combine reference books with general works. Well-known scholars write perceptive introductions to these subject chapters and then provide annotated bibliographies. For example, Jacob Neusner and Alan J. Avery-Peck contribute the chapter on 'Judaism', while James J. Buckley is responsible for 'Contemporary issues in religious thought'. A good introduction to the classics in the field as well as to new material.

Religious and theological

Comprehensive

7.   Gorman, G. E. and Lyn Gorman. *Theological and religious reference materials.* Westport, CT: Greenwood, 1984- (in progress). Vol. 1: General resources and Biblical studies (1984); vol. 2: Systematic theology and Church history (1985); vol. 3: Practical theology (1986). ISSN 0742-6836.

Construing 'reference materials' very broadly, these wide-ranging volumes list and annotate a vast quantity of titles on many subjects and in numerous languages. While the classification schema is somewhat unwieldy, there are excellent author, title and subject indexes. This is the best guide to historical reference works in these areas and invaluable for identifying and assessing older items.

8.   Melton, J. Gordon and Michael A. Köszegi. *Religious information sources: a worldwide guide.* (Garland reference library of the humanities, 1593; Religious information systems, 2). New York: Garland Publishing, 1992. 0-8153-0859-0.

Material about information resources of all kinds is broken down into sections beginning with religion and the religions of the world which are treated regionally. Christianity is separated and divided into 'issues', church history and denominations. Modern religious movements and a variety of aberrations receive attention. The work furnishes a guide, not only to print materials, but to databases, research facilities, archives and other depositories. While worldwide coverage is attempted there is an emphasis on North American and English-language items. Detailed indexes are to titles, authors, organisations and subjects. Although understandably uneven, this is a most comprehensive directory and particularly valuable for its inclusion of subjects remote and esoteric.

9. Starkey, Edward D. *Judaism and Christianity: a guide to the reference literature*. Englewood, CO: Libraries Unlimited, 1991. 0-87287-533-4.

Identifies, describes, evaluates and compares reference works having to do with the Judeo-Christian tradition from its beginnings to modern times. Special attention is paid to the Bibles of these two traditions, published in English through 1988. The arrangement is by type of resource (e.g. encyclopedias, directories, atlases) rather than by subject. The annotations are thoughtful and often extensive. There are author/title and subject indexes. Especially useful for acquisition and reference librarians.

10. Krentz, Edgar. 'Reference works'. In *Encyclopedia of religion*. Edited by Mircea Eliade. Vol. 12, 231-234.

This article in a major encyclopedia [51], provides a succinct listing of dictionaries, encyclopedias, atlases, catalogues and bibliographies which are supportive of religious studies. Entries are briefly annotated.

Catholic emphasis

11. McCabe, James Patrick. *Critical guide to Catholic reference books*. 3rd edn. Englewood, CO: Libraries Unlimited, 1989. 0-87287-621-7.

'A critical introduction to over fifteen hundred of the most important reference books in English and foreign languages whose contents or point of view relate in some way to Catholicism' (Introduction). Annotations are both critical and comparative. There is an author/title/subject index. An essential guide for research on Catholic history and theology.

Protestant emphasis

12. Kepple, Robert J and John R. Muether. *Reference works for theological research: an annotated selective bibliographical guide*. 3rd edn. Lanham, MD: University Press of America, 1992. 0-8191-8564-7.

An annotated guide to both supportive general reference works and those directly associated with the theological task. The work features retrospective and current Christian sources and, in acknowledging McCabe's *Critical guide to Catholic reference books* [11], includes only major Catholic titles. Given the extensive coverage (some 800 titles), this is a major resource.

NATIONAL BIBLIOGRAPHIES

A national bibliography is a bibliography of books and other type materials produced in a certain country. It may also include works about that country published abroad or works by members of that country who are living abroad. A national bibliography is likely to be the most complete record of a country's publications and therefore a critical resource for identifying and locating titles.

Australia

Current

13. *Australian national bibliography*, 1961- . Canberra: National Library of Australia, 1961- . Frequency varies. ISSN 0004-9816.

The *Copyright Act 1968* requires all Australian publishers to deposit with the National Library a copy of all material published in Australia. This material forms the basis of *ANB*.

The summary of inclusions reads, 'Lists books, pamphlets, serials, printed music and microforms either published in Australia, or of Australian association, within the current or preceding two years' (Preface). Government publications, excepting individual Acts, bills and ordinances, are included. *ANB* comprises four parts: the classified sequence, the author, title and series index, a periodicals listing and, finally, a subject index.

Currently *ANB* is issued monthly in print format. Cumulations are published on microfiche for the periods January-April, January-August and January-December. Certain Australian libraries contribute cataloguing through the Australian Bibliographic Network (ABN) and this data is now made available to *ANB*.

Retrospective

14. Ferguson, John Alexander. *Bibliography of Australia*. 7 vols. Sydney: Angus and Robertson, 1941-1969. Facsimile edition published Canberra: National Library of Australia, 1975-1977.

    _____. *Bibliography of Australia: Addenda 1784-1850*. 4 vols. Canberra: National Library of Australia, 1986. 0-642-99307-6.

The lawyer, Sir John Ferguson (1881-1969), was an eminent book collector and bibliographer of material relating to Australia, New Zealand and the Pacific. His *Bibliography* lists every book, pamphlet, leaflet or record he could find, from 1784 to 1850, and then selectively to 1900. The *Addenda*, published by the National Library, includes additions and corrections to Ferguson's work. The scope of the work is described in the introduction to the first volume. This outstanding work remains of great value for identifying Australiana having to do with religion and theology published during the period, and for locating copies of the titles.

To help fill what has become known as the 'Ferguson gap' the National Library published the following:

15. *Australian national bibliography*, 1901-1950. 4 vols. Canberra: National Library of Australia, 1988. 0-642-210445-X.

Includes some 49,500 entries published during this period. Volume 3 is an author/title/series index; volume 4 a subject index.

New Zealand

Current

16. *New Zealand national bibliography (NZNB)*, Feb. 1967- . Wellington: National Library of New Zealand, 1967- . ISSN 0028-8497.

A selected list of New Zealand and Tokelau books, serials, newspapers, music maps, videos, sound recordings and kits published within the last five years. The selection is made from items deposited at the Legal Deposit Office under copyright provisions, and includes works published in New Zealand, overseas with New Zealand content, of New Zealand authorship, or with a New Zealand setting. (Includes the Tokelau Islands, a territory of New Zealand.)

Since 1983 *NZNB* has been produced monthly on microfiche (January excepted). Each issue is a cumulation of the previous month's issue for that year; the December issue being the complete listing. There are four sections - Register; Author/title; Subjects; Non-books, and addresses.

NZNB is also available online through the New Zealand Bibliographic Network (NZBN).

Retrospective

17. *New Zealand national bibliography to the year 1960*. Edited by Austin Graham Bagnall. 5 vols. Wellington: Government Printer, 1969-1985.

This work lists books and pamphlets published in New Zealand, those published elsewhere with significant New Zealand content, and those by New Zealand authors. Many items are annotated. Periodicals are omitted. Volume 1 covers material to 1889; volumes 2-4 material from 1890-1960. Volume 5 completes the set with an addenda and corrigenda to the earlier volumes and an index to volumes 2-4 (volume 1 having its own index). A further 2,500 items were added in this final volume. The whole work contains about 32,000 entries.

TRADE BIBLIOGRAPHIES, BOOKS IN PRINT

The following resources - Australian, American, British and New Zealand, indicate whether a particular book is in print. Each includes sufficient information to help identify a work and to acquire it either by purchase or loan. The final item comprises a major retrospective bibliography of religious titles.

General

18. *Australian books in print, 1956-* . Port Melbourne: D. W. Thorpe, 1956- (Title varies.). ISSN 0067-172-X.

Now published annually, but with monthly updates on microfiche and along with the *New Zealand books in print*, on THORPE ROM.

The 34th edition was published in 1996 and celebrates Thorpe's 75 years' service in the book trade. General policy is to include a book published in Australia, a book by an Australian published overseas and a book with significant Australian content.

Lists books by authors and by titles. Also provides the titles of series, lists local agents for overseas publishers, and Australian publishers and distributors.

19. *Books in print, 1948-* . New Providence, NJ: Bowker, 1948- . (Title and place of publication vary.) Now (1994-1995) in 10 vols. ISSN 0068-0214.

Books in print is also available on CD-ROM, microfiche, on-line and via tape leasing.

Contents of the 1994-1995 set: Vols. 1-4, Authors; vols. 5-8, Titles; vol. 9, Books declared out of print or out of stock indefinitely; vol. 10, Publishers.

Provides coverage of the full range of English-language books currently published or distributed in the United States with complete bibliographic and ordering information for each title. The final volume contains valuable listings of publishers and distributors.

20. *Subject guide to Books in print, 1957- .* New Providence, NJ: Bowker, 1957- . (Place of publication varies). Now (1994-1995) in 5 vols. ISSN 0000-0159.

Using Library of Congress subject headings, this set provides access by subject to the non-fiction titles covered in *Books in print*. Includes a subject thesaurus and publisher information.

21. *New Zealand books in print, 1957- .* Wellington: D. W. Thorpe, 1957- . (Title and publisher vary.) ISSN 0157-7662.

Available, along with the *Australian books in print*, on THORPE ROM.

Now published annually, but with monthly updates on Thorpe-ROM. The 24th edition was published in 1996. Complete bibliographic information on all in-print New Zealand books, plus books and serials from Pacific Island states. Lists publishers, agents of overseas publishers and also members of the Booksellers Association and the Christian Booksellers Association.

22. *Whitaker's books in print: the reference catalogue of current literature, 1988- .* London: Whitaker & Sons, 1988- . Annual. The 1995 set is in five volumes. ISSN 0953-0398.

Formerly *British books in print* (1874-1987). Uses one alphabetical sequence to list authors and titles published in the United Kingdom and titles published elsewhere provided they are available through an agent based in the UK. The final volume concludes with the names of series and their publishers, ISBNs with publisher prefixes in numerical order, and the names of UK publishers and their addresses.

Note. Trade bibliographies, such as those listed above, are published in many countries. For information about national and trade bibliographies see that section in the tenth edition of the *Guide to reference books*, edited by Eugene P. Sheehy, and the *Supplement* edited by Robert Balay [1,2].

Religious

23. *Religious books in print, 1995: A reference catalogue .* London: J. Whitaker & Sons, 1995. (Now published annually.) ISSN 0305-960X.

The 1995 annual records over 30,000 titles in the Whitaker database which were available in the United Kingdom at January 1995. In addition to British publications, it includes works in English published by overseas firms having branches or agencies in the UK. There are two separate listings: a classified arrangement of titles is followed by an author, title and key-word sequence. There is also a directory of 2,500 religious publishers, with addresses and ISBN prefixes A most valuable resource, particularly for its general and subject access to current titles.

Retrospective

An extensive bibliography of monographs in the fields of religion and theology is:

24. *Religious books, 1876-1982.* 4 volumes. New York: R. R. Bowker, 1983. 0-8352-1602-0 (set).

Volumes 1-3: Subject-arranged listing of complete entries; volume 4: Author and title index. The database for this work of some 130,000 items was assembled from 'one hundred years of Library of Congress cataloging on religious titles published or distributed in the United States' (Preface). While the classification and cataloguing information supplied can be helpful to librarians, this set is also valuable for general research purposes. It functions well as a verification tool and, of course, is a veritable mine of subject bibliographies.

DISSERTATIONS

Dissertations or theses, submitted to a university or college, pose special problems as far as identification and location are concerned. If a dissertation is not available through University Microfilms International (see below), one may assume that the examining institution would either retain a copy or lodge same in a certain library. As a last resort, a request to read a thesis must needs be addressed to its author.

General

International

25. *Dissertation abstracts international.* Ann Arbor, MI: University Microfilms International, 1938- . (Title varies.)
    UMI is represented in Australasia by Information Publications International

DAI is available in print format, through online access and on compact disc. Over one million author-prepared abstracts of doctoral dissertations lodged with University Microfilms by certain universities around the world. Divided into sections - A: Humanities and the Social sciences; B: Sciences and Engineering; C: Worldwide (initially titled, European abstracts in 1976, this section has subsequently been expanded). Entries are listed under subject and the abstracts amount to some 300 words. Indexes are to keywords and to authors.

Printed copies of the dissertations may be obtained from University Microfilms, either in paper copy or on microfilm. This publishing company compiles catalogues from its doctoral dissertations database, including one titled *Religion and theology.* These catalogues are made available, upon request and free of charge, to libraries.

British

Note. Doctoral theses accepted at British universities since 1971 and collected by the British Library are made available, in paper and microform formats, through the British Theses Service (BRITS), which is represented in Australasia by the Information Publications International. Since 1988 dissertations from Great

Britain have been included on the *DAI* database. BRITS distributes subject catalogues including one titled, *Religion and philosophy*.

Religious

Australian

The number of theses presented to Australian universities and to the several Colleges of Divinity or Theology continues to be on the increase. Only a small proportion of these are published commercially and therefore it is difficult to access information about them. To date only one attempt has been made to correct this information gap.

26. *Australian religious studies: a bibliography of post-graduate theses: 1922-1986.* Edited by Peter Bentley. Leichhardt, NSW: National Catholic Research Council, 1988. 0-949347-02-7.

Completed theses, either at Masters or Doctoral level or for the post- graduate Bachelor of Letters are included. These are listed under classified headings with each entry consisting of the author's name, thesis-title, the degree awarded, the date and the name of the institution. There is an author index. For selection, 'the thesis must contain an aspect of religion with an Australian component or orientation' (Introduction). A valuable resource but in constant need of up-dating.

PERIODICAL LITERATURE

The importance of periodical articles, for scholarly purposes, is that they are likely to reflect recent research or do some ground-breaking in particular subject areas. They may also augment the current bibliography of a particular subject.

The major tools for exploiting periodical literature include directories which verify periodical titles and publishing data, union lists which indicate where particular titles may be located, and indexes to the contents of periodicals. Indexes and abstracts will be dealt with in the next section of this chapter.

A list of periodicals which may be regarded as a core collection appears in Chapter 14.

Directories

General

27. *Ulrich's international periodicals directory.* New York: Bowker, 1932- . ISSN 0000-0175.

[The 1993-1994 set was published in five volumes with supplemental updates.]

A classified list of serials and newspapers from around the world. Serial titles are gathered under general headings which are subdivided, for example, 'Religions and theology - Eastern Orthodox'. Entries usually include the title, frequency of publication, ISSN, publisher address, Dewey Decimal Classification number. There are many routes to be explored in this resource but it will prove particularly valuable for its several indexes and for providing information about where a particular serial is indexed or abstracted.

Religious

28. Cornish, Graham P. *Religious periodicals directory.* Santa Barbara, CA: ABC-Clio, 1986. 0-87436-365-9.

Provides full citations and contents-notes for more than 1,700 periodicals in religion, theology and related fields. Gives details of inclusion in indexing and abstracting services. International in coverage and arranged alphabetically by title within six geographic regions. Title and subject/area indexes.

Union lists. Australasian

A union list records the holdings of a certain type of material in a given group of libraries. In this case the holdings are of serials or other type publications which are issued periodically. (It is important not to confuse 'serials' with 'series'.)

29. *Australasian union list of serials in theological collections.* Compiled by Hans Arns. Rev. edn. Manly, NSW: Catholic Institute of Sydney with the Australian and New Zealand Theological Library Association, 1990. 0-908224-18-4.

Features periodical holdings, deemed important for religious/theological research, in some 85 libraries in Australia and New Zealand. Arrangement is by periodical title under which libraries, with holdings, are indicated by State, Territory or country (NZ) initials and particular library symbols. The essential tool for identifying periodical titles and their locations and hence a major resource for inter-library loan purposes.

Periodicals, Bibliographies in

Periodicals are not only of value for presenting recent research, they may also contain bibliographical information. The following resource comments on a number of periodicals which either index or abstract articles, or which regularly contain bibliographies.

30. Walsh, M. J. *Religious bibliographies in serial literature: a guide.* London: Mansell, 1981. 0-7201-1593-0. (Published in USA , CT: Greenwood Press, 1981.)

Describes some 178 bibliographical resources which are either periodical indexes or periodicals. Walsh expertly analyses each resource in detail and indicates its importance for the bibliographic search.

Abbreviations

The major resource for abbreviations of periodical titles is:

31 Schwertner, Siegfried. *Internationales Abkürzungsverzeichnis für Theologie und Grenzgebiete: Zeitschriften, Serien, Lexika, Quellenwerke mit bibliographischen Angaben (IATG 2)/ International glossary of abbreviations for theology and related subjects: periodicals, series, encyclopedias, sources with bibliographical notes.* 2. Aufl. Berlin: de Gruyter 1992. 3-11-011117-9.

The first edition of *IATG* was published in 1974. An expanded version appeared in 1976 as *Theologische Realenzyklopädie: Abkürzungsverzeichnis* (Berlin: de Gruyter). It added some 800 titles and included sections on abbreviations of biblical books, sources and versions of the Bible, deutero-canonical books and Rabbinic texts. The present second edition of 1992 repeats these sections and increases the total to about 14,000 titles. Schwertner provides two directories - the first, from abbreviation to title and the second, from title to abbreviation. Students find it an easy tool to use, the introductory material being in English, French and German, with Italian and Spanish being added to the new edition.

Note: For abbreviations of Australian and New Zealand periodical titles, consult the *Australasian religion index* (1989-) [37], where the abbreviations are constructed according to the Schwertner system.

Note: Those writing in biblical and related fields may be required to consult the guide to style matters, including abbreviations, prepared by the Society of Biblical Literature in the US. The most recent version of this guide appears in the *Journal of biblical literature* 107 (1988): 579-596.

Indexing and Abstracting Services

An index tells where material by an author or on a particular topic may be found in periodical literature or in multi-author works. Indexes themselves do not contain information about the substance of the article. On the other hand, an abstracting service provides a citation for the article or essay and also a summary or abstract of its contents. By reading the abstract, one may intuit whether the article is germane to the research in hand.

Note that indexes or abstracts related to the literature in special subject areas, for example *New Testament* abstracts, are cited in the relevant subject chapters.

General

Australian

32. *APAIS: Australian public affairs information service: a subject index to current literature.* No. 1, July 1945- . Canberra: National Library of Australia, 1945- . ISSN 0727-8926. Monthly, except December; cumulated annually.

The major Australian subject guide to scholarly literature in the social sciences and humanities. *APAIS* comprehensively indexes some 230 Australian scholarly journals and scans other periodicals received in the National Library. Also newspapers for feature articles, certain chapters of books, pamphlets and conference proceedings. Selected overseas publications are checked for material within the subject scope of *APAIS*. An important source for material on religions and religious issues in Australia.

The following thesaurus has been designed to serve the *APAIS* indexers but also as an aid to users.

33. *APAIS thesaurus: a list of subject terms used in Australian Public Affairs Information Service.* 5th edn. Canberra: National Library of Australia, 1994. 0-642-10613-4.

Lists the subject headings used in the index, so describing the access points for searching.

Religious periodicals

The following indexing systems, published in the United states, include periodicals from other countries and issued in various languages.

United States/international

34. *The Catholic periodical and literature index, 1930- .* Haverford, PA: Catholic Library Association, 1939- (Title and subtitle and composition vary). Quarterly with annual cumulation. ISSN 0008-8285.

CPLI currently indexes more than 160 Catholic edited periodicals and also provides a selective list of new books on and about the Catholic faith. It is international in scope. Provides essential citations to papal documents and church promulgations. Annual printed volumes of *CPLI* include separate subject, author/editor, book title and book review indexes. An essential resource for research on all Catholic topics.

In an important development, The Catholic Library Association as publisher and the American Theological Library Association as producer and distributor announced that, as from November 1995 *CPLI* is available on CD-ROM as *CPLI on CD-ROM*. The first issue contains indexing from 1981 to 1994. The subscription includes a user's manual and reference guide.

35. *Religion index one: periodicals, 1949- .* Chicago: American Theological Library Association, 1953- . ISSN 0149-8428.

Paper copy semi-annually, now with annual cumulation.
Also available online and on CD-ROM (see note below).

RIO presently indexes the contents of more than 300 periodicals by subject, author/editor and scriptural passages. Historically *RIO* concentrated on Protestantism but of recent years it has added key Jewish and Catholic journals and is now regarded as an ecumenical undertaking. *RIO* is the most comprehensive periodical indexing resource available in this subject area.

Note: Book reviews were included in *RIO* up to volume 17 (1985). Subsequently they were published separately in *Index to book reviews in religion* [40].

Note. The American Theological Library Association (ATLA) database is available through Dialog Information Services. It can be searched on compact disc on the *ATLA religion database on CD-ROM* and on *Religion indexes: RIO/RIT/IBRR 1975- on CD-ROM*.

Further, the Religion Indexes division of ATLA has published *Religion indexes: thesaurus*. 6th edn. (Evanston, IL: American Theological Library Association, 1994. 0-9604960-8-4.) This thesaurus is to aid searchers of the ATLA religion database on CD-ROM but also the users of the printed indexes - *RIO, RIT, RIM (Research in ministry)*.

Another ATLA index, *Ethics index on CD-ROM*, is described in Chapter 13 [649].

The following item not only indexes periodical material but also provides abstracts of the articles.

36. *Religious and theological abstracts, 1958- .* Myerstown, PA: Religious and Theological Abstracts, 1958- . Quarterly. ISSN 0034-4044. Also available on CD-ROM as *R &TA on CD-ROM*.

The 300 journals cited and abstracted include Christian, Jewish and Muslim publications. The work has five divisions: biblical, theological, historical, practical and sociological. Abstracts, in English, usually signed, average some 100 words. There are author, subject and biblical indexes in each annual volume. Well respected as a non-sectarian abstracting service.

Australasian periodicals

37. *Australasian religion index, 1989- .* Wagga Wagga, NSW: Australian and New Zealand Theological Library Association and Centre for Information Studies, Charles Sturt University - Riverina, 1989- . ISSN 1033-2626. Semi-annual with annual cumulation.

ARI indexes articles and book reviews in over seventy serials published in Australia or New Zealand. Most are religious and theological serials but there is also selective coverage of other scholarly journals which, from time to time, publish articles with religious content. In order, there is an author, subject, scripture passage index, an index to book reviews and to new serial titles. This is the key indexing service for periodical material relating to religious interests in Australasia.

Multi-author works; Festschriften

It has been comparatively difficult to access the contents of books which include essays or chapters by several authors. The most usual example of this sort of compilation is the Festschrift which, in German, means a publication which celebrates an event or, more usually, honours a person. Typically, Festschriften include learned essays contributed by a number of scholars as a tribute to a colleague.

The venerable American tool, *Essay and general literature index, 1900 - ,* New York: H. W. Wilson, 1934- , is an author and subject index to essays and articles in selected collections and anthologies. *EGLI* covers all fields of knowledge but is particularly strong on literature. The specialist tool for religious and theological studies is the following ATLA product:

38. *Religion index two: multi-author works. 1976- .* Chicago: American Theological Library Association, 1978- . ISSN 0149-8436.

Also available online and on CD-ROM (see note under *Religion index one* [35]).

RIT indexes the contents of anthologies, Festschriften and other types of compilations having several contributors, by author and subject. The scope includes all aspects of religion and theology.

BOOK REVIEWS

The publications cited in this section are either compilations of book reviews (the first item cited) or indexes which tell where particular reviews may be found.

Published reviews

39. *Critical review of books in religion, 1988- .* Atlanta, GA: Scholars Press, 1988- . ISSN 0894-8860.

Sponsored by the publishers of the *Journal of the American Academy of Religion* and the *Journal of biblical literature.* Each annual volume begins with lead articles reviewing either major publications or a group of titles in a given subject area. Then there are shorter reviews of books on all aspects of religion and theology. A section lists translations, new editions and reference works. Indexes are to authors, reviewers and publishers. A most important, critical reviewing medium.

Indexes to book reviews

Note that the following resources are indexing resources only. They present citations for reviews but not reviews themselves.

40. *Index to book reviews in religion* . [Feb. 1986]- . Evanston, IL: American Theological Library Association, 1986- (place varies). Quarterly with annual [December] cumulation. Also available online and on CD-ROM.

See note on the ATLA database [35n].

IBRR supersedes the book review index section of *Religion index one* which last appeared in volume 17 (1985). Indexing includes author/editor, title, reviewer, series and an annual classified index arranged under selected subject headings. Because *IBRR* indexes in excess of 500 periodicals of interest to the field of religion, it is the first place to go for review citations.

A retrospective project provides a three-volume series which revises and augments book review citations originally indexed in the *ATLA's Index to religious periodical literature* from 1949 to 1974. These three volumes are:

Index to book reviews in religion, 1949-1959. Evanston, IL: ATLA, 1990.

Index to book reviews in religion, 1960-1968. Evanston, IL: ATLA, 1992.

Index to book reviews in religion, 1969-1974. Evanston, IL: ATLA, 1993.

Australasian

For the indexing of book reviews appearing in Australian and New Zealand religious periodical literature, see the *Australasian religion index [37]*.

LIBRARIES AND ARCHIVES - AUSTRALIA AND NEW ZEALAND

The purpose here is simply to note guides to libraries and archives in the two countries. The first is an indispensable directory of Australian and certain overseas libraries, including those in New Zealand and other neighbouring countries. The second is a comprehensive guide to religious and theological collections. Finally there are tools which assist with the tracing of elusive archival material.

General

41. *Australian interlibrary resource sharing directory*. 2nd edn. Edited by Lee Kirwan. Canberra: National Library of Australia, 1992. 0-642-0575-8.

The most accessible directory of Australian libraries. Gives name, address and contact information for each institution and also notes its interlibrary loan policy. Each library or other-type institution is identified by the National Union

Catalogue (NUC) symbol. The 'Y' coding distinguishes 'overseas' libraries and includes major New Zealand institutions (the YNZ sequence). The arrangement is alphabetical by symbol and an index sequence lists the libraries and other organisations by name. *The Australian Interlending Code* is printed near the front of the volume. An essential library resource.

Religious and theological

42. Jenkin, Coralie. *Collections of religion and theology in Australia and New Zealand*. Adelaide: Auslib Press, 1992. 1-875145-11-7.

A valiant attempt to list Australian and New Zealand libraries and other collections holding religious and theological material. All types of libraries are included, for example, university, public, theological, those belonging to religious orders and private collections. An entry is likely to include name, religious affiliation, address, foundation date, staff details, hours of opening, collection size, subject strengths, the classification system used and a note about access. This is the most extensive guide to religious and theological collections in Australasia.

43. *Register of church archives*. Edited by Leo J. Ansell. 2nd edn. Toowoomba, Qld.: Church Archivists' Society, 1985. 0-959314-58-X.

Earlier edition, 1982. This is a preliminary listing of Australian depositories for Christian and some Jewish materials, compiled by an experienced church archivist. The work is divided by Australian Territories and States and for each collection it provides details of contact persons, addresses, hours of opening, accessibility, holdings and services available. The questionnaire upon which the *Register* was constructed is given as an appendix. There is an agency index.

44. Vine Hall, Nick. *Parish registers in Australia: a list of originals, transcripts, microforms, and indexes of Australian parish registers*. 2nd edn. Albert Park, Vic.: Vine Hall (Nick) 1990. 0-9597208-4-7.

Lists 5524 Australian church registers at 153 different record centres throughout the country. The work is divided by State and Territory and then, alphabetically, by cities and towns. The codes and symbols used in the entries are spelled out and there is a further chapter of notes and an extensive bibliography. The entries reflect records created by these bodies in connection with baptisms, marriages and burials. Note that, while the title refers to '*parish* registers', the volume encompasses the major church denominations. Indeed there is mention of other faiths including Buddhist, Jewish and Islamic. This is an important reference resource for social historians and genealogists.

ENCYCLOPEDIAS, SUBJECT DICTIONARIES, HANDBOOKS

A dictionary is a work which lists selected words, usually in alphabetical order and, minimally, gives their meanings. There are language dictionaries but also dictionaries about particular subjects, for example, the *Dictionary of spirituality*.

A general encyclopedia, such as the *Encyclopaedia Britannica*, attempts to include entries on every branch of human knowledge, while a subject encyclopedia for example, the

Encyclopedia of unbelief, limits coverage to a specific subject area. An entry in an encyclopedia may define a word or concept but, usually, its interest and coverage is more comprehensive than a dictionary entry.

It should be noted, however, that to distinguish dictionaries and encyclopedias in this way has its frustrations. Increasingly the designations 'dictionary' and 'encyclopedia' are being used interchangeably to describe resources which provide access to definitions and information about particular subjects.

General

45.   *The new Encyclopaedia Britannica.* 15th edn. 32 vols. Chicago: Encyclopaedia Britannica. 0-85229-493-X (1989).

Since 1985 the contents are: Propaedia (Outline of knowledge), one volume, un-numbered; Micropaedia (Ready reference), vols. 1-12; Macropaedia (Knowledge in depth), vols. 13-29; Index, 2 vols. un-numbered.

Remains a great scholarly resource which includes substantial articles on all religions. The reinstatement of the index (in the 1985 revision) to volumes 1 to 29, in two additional volumes, was a major improvement. This index is usually the place to begin a search of the *EB.*

46.   *Britannica book of the year, 1938-* . Chicago: Encyclopaedia Britannica, 1938- . ISSN 0068-1156.

Designed to keep the *EB* current with major events of the year, updates of key articles and of statistics. The 1995 issue provides a complete 10-year Book of the Year cross-reference. Note that the date in the title always refers to the year of publication; the material relates to the previous year.

Australian

47.   *The Australian encyclopaedia.* 5th edn. 9 vols. Terrey Hills, NSW: Australian Geographic for the Australian Geographic Society, 1988. 1-86276-000-4 (standard set).

The present edition presents revisions of the earlier editions (which go back to 1925-1927) and much new material. Illustrations and maps continue as a feature. Volume 9 comprises appendixes with lists and statistics and also an index to the whole work. Highly regarded for its comprehensiveness and accuracy.

Note that the substantial, second edition of *The Australian encyclopaedia,* edited by Alec H. Chisholm (Sydney: Angus & Robertson, 1958, 10 vols), remains valuable for historical work.

48.   *Australians: a historical library.* 11 vols. Broadway, NSW: Fairfax, Syme & Weldon , 1987. 0-949288-09-8 (set).

Five volumes cover Australian history in 50-year intervals beginning with 1788. These are followed by six reference volumes - *Historical atlas, Events and places, Historical dictionary, Guide to sources, Historical statistics,* and, finally, a guide and index volume. Together these six volumes provide the most extensive reference library ever produced in Australia. In particular, the volume, *Australians: a guide to sources,* edited by D. H. Borchardt and Victor Crittenden, has sections on reference works and statistics, and a chapter on 'Religion' (pp. 344-355), authored by Lawrence McIntosh.

New Zealand

49. *The Illustrated encyclopedia of New Zealand.* Edited by Gordon McLauchlan. 4th edn. Auckland: David Bateman, 1992. 0-908610-21-1.

An update of the *Bateman New Zealand encyclopedia* (1984), this is a popular yet reliable work. Now includes a general index.

An older work, *An Encyclopedia of New Zealand*, edited by A. H. McLintock. 3 vols. (Wellington: Government Printer, 1966), is a more substantial work and still of value.

Religious

A fine line divides certain general religious encyclopedias from theological encyclopedias. In this section are listed works which treat religion and religions comprehensively. Works devoted to certain major religions are to be found in Chapter 2, while those relating specifically to Judaism are in Chapter 3, and to Christianity in Chapters 4 and 5.

General coverage

50. *The Encyclopaedia of religion and ethics.* Edited by James Hastings. 13 vols. New York: Charles Scribner's Sons; Edinburgh: T and T Clark, 1908-1928.

This work is of classic proportions and, although showing its age, it remains a most valuable resource for its comprehensive and detailed coverage of matters relating to religions and to ethical systems. The indexing in the final volume is invaluable.

Much of *ERE* is updated, but not superseded by the following set:

51. *The Encyclopedia of religion.* Edited by Mircea Eliade. 16 vols. New York: Macmillan, 1986. 0-02-897135-3.

Now the standard reference work in the field, offering an unrivalled range of information about the history, beliefs, and practices of religions great and small. Its stated intention is to 'introduce educated, non-specialist readers to important ideas, practices and persons in the religious experience of humankind from the Paleolithic past to our day' (Foreword). Articles are signed and there are numerous composite entries which present several aspects of a topic. Particularly useful for its coverage of non-Western religions, including the religions of the Australian Aboriginal peoples and of the Maori. Volume 16 provides an alphabetical list of all entries, a synoptic outline of contents and an extensive and intensive general index. This outstanding resource, with all its sophistication, is surprisingly accessible to students.

Three valuable one-volume resources are:

52. *Chambers dictionary of beliefs and religions.* Edited by Rosemary Goring. Edinburgh: W. & R. Chambers, 1992. 0-550-15000-5.

Some 2,900 entries by numerous contributors, define all aspects of major faiths and ideologies, both historical and current. Biographies are included. Appendixes include a calendar of major religious festivals throughout the world, and the population distribution of the major religions. Note that an index of entries by subject is at the front of the volume (pp. viii-xxxii). This is an accurate, introductory resource and of particular use for work on the multi-faith dialogue.

53   *The HarperCollins dictionary of religion*. Edited by Jonathan Z. Smith et al. New York: HarperCollins, 1995. 0-06-067515-2.

A team of 327 scholars, drawn from the American Academy of Religion, provide more than 3,200 entries, including several feature-length articles. The volume covers the people, places, concepts, practices and sacred writings of the religions of the world. Timelines, graphs, photos and illustrations make this an attractive and easy-to-use guide, while the prestigious sponsoring body ensures its authority.

54.   Macgregor, Geddes. *Dictionary of religion and philosophy*. New York: Paragon House, 1989. 1-55778-019-6.
      Also published in the United Kingdom as *The Everyman dictionary of religion and philosophy*. London: Dent, 1990. 0-460-87020-3.

The primary focus of this dictionary, with its some 3000 entries, is on religious studies. Those entries with philosophical content usually have a direct bearing on religious discourse or concerns. A wide spectrum of religions receives attention although there is a concentration on the Judeo-Christian traditions. The work is cross-referenced and there is a bibliography. The remarkably comprehensive and accurate coverage makes this a most useful ready-reference.

Deities

55.   Jordan, Michael. *Encyclopedia of gods: over 2,500 deities of the world*. London: Kyle Cathie, 1992. 1-85626-038-0.

From 'A-a', the sun goddess of Mesopotamia, to 'Zurvan', the Persian god of fate, more than 2,500 names of gods of all times and places are listed and described. Each entry provides details of the relevant culture, the role of the god or goddess and particular characteristics. In some cases representations in art and literature are noted, as are festival days. There is a chronology of principal religions and cultures and the work concludes with a bibliography. A possible resource for researchers in the fields of religions, anthropology, history and archaeology.

Unbelief

56.   *The Encyclopedia of unbelief*. Edited by Gordon Stein. 2 vols. Buffalo, NY: Prometheus Books, 1985. 0-87975-307-2 (set).

Serves by filling a gap in existing reference works. Signed articles include definitions of terms, biographies of unbelievers, histories of unbelief from ancient times and in all areas of the world. Appendices include a bibliography and details about institutions and their literature. The whole is well indexed.

Religion in politics

57.   *Religion in politics: a world guide*. Edited by Stuart Mews. Harlow, Essex: Longman, 1989. 0-582-05058-8. Published also by St James Press, Chicago, 1989. 1-55862-051-6.

Fills a real gap by providing a review of the religious-political situation in every country of the world, taking special account of developments since 1987. For example, the article, 'Australia', by Ian Breward, describes religious patterns, constitutional issues, religion in politics, the participation of the churches and the claims of the Aboriginal people. The article, 'New Zealand' is by Ron O'Grady. Although in need of constant updating, this resource is important for providing contextual background material for the study of religious developments in particular countries.

Mythology

A myth can be defined as a story or epic which tells of the exploits of divine or super-human figures or of divine-initiated events and institutions. The creation myths of the Book of Genesis, the myths of the gods of Greece and Rome, or the expressions of the Dreamtime of the Australian Aborigines, all point to mythology having to do with a people's intuitions of the transcendent.

58. *A dictionary of world mythology*. Rev. edn. Edited by Arthur Cotterell. Oxford University Press, 1986. 0-19-217747-8.

Originally published in 1980. The emphasis is on 'world' as this resource covers all parts of the globe including Oceania. The work is in fact divided geographically with analyses of mythological developments in each area. Each division includes entries on gods, names associated with myths and places, arranged alphabetically. This edition includes maps, illustrations and a bibliography.

59. *Funk & Wagnall's standard dictionary of folklore, mythology, and legend*. Edited by Maria Leach and Jerome Fried. New York: Funk and Wagnalls, 1972. Reprinted, San Francisco: Harper & Row, 1984. 0-06-250511-4.

A reprint of a work, originally published in 1949-1950, but with added keys to countries, regions, cultures and peoples described in the text. Long survey articles on major subjects and shorter articles on gods, heroes, myths, beliefs, customs, songs, dances and a host of other interests. Long regarded as a quality reference work.

60. *Leach, Marjorie. Guide to the gods*. Santa Barbara, CA: ABC-Clio, 1992. 0-87436-591-0.

A large work describing more than 20,000 mythological gods acknowledged in all parts of the world. This assemblage is arranged under major divisions: cosmogonical, celestial, atmospheric, terrestrial, life-death cycle, economic associations, sociocultural concepts, and religion. Each god is identified by name, country, place or culture. An index to names and an extensive bibliography. A most comprehensive array.

Note. In the *Encyclopedia of religion* [51], edited by Mircea Eliade, the section headed 'Myth' includes an overview by Eliade himself, and an article, 'Myth and history' by Paul Ricoeur (volume 10, pp. 261-273; 273-282).

New Age movements

It has been difficult to find a term which describes and comprehends the new religious movements which began to emerge in the 1960s and which, for many people, are replacing traditional religions and religious attitudes. These alternative movements may differ considerably one from the other. Some organisations are public, others secretive. They may affirm health and healing or embrace forms of mysticism, the occult, parapsychology and the channelling of messages from the spirit world or some combination of any of these.

61. *New Age encyclopedia: a guide to beliefs, concepts, terms, people, and organizations.* Edited by J. Gordon Melton et al. Detroit, MI: Gale Research, 1990. 0-8103-7159-6.

Melton has produced several valuable reference works on religion in American life and in this volume he defines the New Age movement as 'the new global movement toward spiritual development, health and healing, [and] higher consciousness'. Following an introduction, which attempts to explain the nature of the belief system, there are entries that cover the areas described in the subtitle. The work is descriptive and remains thoroughly objective. There are bibliographies, a chronology and an index to the whole. In a field which has attracted works lacking all credibility, this encyclopedia functions as a most helpful guide.

BIOGRAPHICAL SOURCES

Biographies will be found in reference resources such as encyclopedias and subject dictionaries. In this section are listed titles which are devoted exclusively to biographical information. The coverage is general and national, with the exception of one specialist work on freethinkers which is included here. Note that national biographies have been published for a number of countries (see *Guide to reference books*, edited by Sheehy [1], pp. 279-313; Balay [2], pp. 72-81)

Biographical sources covering people associated with particular periods of history, professions or denominations are cited in the respective subject chapters. The saints are gathered in Chapter 4.

GREAT BRITAIN

62. *Dictionary of national biography.* Edited by Leslie Stephen and Sidney Lee. 63 volumes, including Supplement. London: Smith, Elder, 1855-1901. Reissued in 22 volumes, 1908-1909. Several supplements update the work to 1960.

DNB is the definitive biographical resource for tracing noteworthy persons from Great Britain, Ireland and the British colonies. The basic set contained over 29,000 articles from a page length to some fifty pages. Entries include primary and secondary bibliographies. No living person was included. This is a major source of information about those who were important to English church history, including those whose sense of mission took them to the colonies. Invaluable for historical studies.

63. *The Concise dictionary of national biography.* 3 volumes. Oxford University Press, 1992. 0-19-865305-0.

Revises and augments earlier editions of the *Concise DNB*, which appeared first in 1903 and again in 1953. This new edition contains summaries of all the biographies appearing in the main work of the *DNB* and its supplements, thus covering lives from the earlier times to 1985.

Students may find that some libraries will only have this concise version of *DNB*. It does, however, serve several purposes. It provides an index to the main work and also abstracts of its entries, each about one fourteenth of the length of the original. The aim of these epitomes is to present the essential facts of a life for quick reference. With this information one may gauge the usefulness of going in quest of the *DNB* itself.

AUSTRALIA

64. *Australian dictionary of biography*. Editors vary. Carlton, Vic.: Melbourne University Press, 1966- . 0-522-84236-4 (set).

This multi-volume work, which is still proceeding, provides concise, informative descriptions of prominent people who contributed their vision and energies to a growing nation.

Volumes 1-2 cover the years 1788-1850; volumes 3-6 span 1851-1890; volumes 7-12 deal with the period 1891-1939. Volume 13 begins the next period to be covered which is from 1940 to 1980. The *Index* to *ADB*'s first twelve volumes (1788-1939) was published in 1991.

The *Index* volume is a valuable research tool in itself, listing the names of major and minor subjects as well as their occupations and places of birth. Archbishops, bishops, chaplains, clergy, preachers, theologians are among the occupations gathered here.

Secularists

65. Dahlitz, Ray. *Secular who's who: a biographical directory of freethinkers, secularists, rationalists, humanists and others involved in Australia's secular movement from 1850 onwards . . .* Balwyn, Victoria: R. Dahlitz, 1994. 0-646-17950-0.

'This is the first directory of Australian and New Zealand secular, freethinking individuals and the organisations they created' (Introduction, p. vi). The work is divided into three parts, each spanning fifty years: 1850-1900, The secular beginning; 1900-1950, The rationalist age; 1950-2000, The humanist challenge. Each part has a brief introductory essay and a chronological chart showing the sequence of the major organisations formed during the period and then follow the biographical entries. Although the emphasis is on Australian representation, New Zealand entries draw attention to the cross-linkage and interaction between the two countries. The work begins to fill a serious gap in their religious and non-religious histories.

NEW ZEALAND

66. *Dictionary of New Zealand biography*. Edited by W. H. Oliver and Claudia Orange. Wellington: Allen & Unwin / Department of Internal Affairs. Volume 1- , 1990- . 0-04-641052-X (vol. 1) Volume 2 was published by Bridget William Books /Department of Internal Affairs. 0-908912-49-8 (vol. 2).

Projected in five volumes. Volume 1 (1990) covers the period 1769-1869; volume 2 (1993) covers 1870-1900; and volume 3 will cover 1901-1920.

While the *Dictionary* gives due place to pre-eminent figures, it also includes people who did not achieve national standing, but whose importance was in a specific regional, tribal, ethnic or social context. Major religious leaders are, of course, included. Note that biographies of Maori people are published in both Maori and English and that the whole set will be available also in five Maori-language volumes. [The compiler is indebted to a 'General Information' sheet on the *Dictionary*, prepared by the Department, for much of the data in this annotation.]

67. *The Book of New Zealand women.* Edited by Charlotte Macdonald et al. Wellington: Bridget Williams Books, 1991. 0-908912-04-8.

Biographical portraits of more than 300 women, who have left their mark on New Zealand's culture, include those who have informed the religious scene. The focus is not on famous achievers although they are there. Rather the accent is on less prominent women who have assumed particularly creative roles, so the work can be regarded as complementing *DNZB* [66]. Essays include bibliographic sources, primary and secondary as available. The work is well illustrated. There are indexes to biographees, fields of activity and to contributing authors. This venture in feminist scholarship provides a valuable resource for historians.

QUOTATION SOURCES

Books of quotations are used to trace or verify a particular quotation or to suggest a quote for a given occasion. It is important to establish how the book of quotations you are using is arranged - alphabetically by author, chronologically by the author's dates or by the date of the quotation, or by topic - and what sort of indexing systems are employed.

General

68. Bartlett, John. *Familiar quotations: a collection of passages, phrases, and proverbs traced to their sources in ancient and modern literature.* 16th edn. Edited by Justin Kaplan. Boston: Little, Brown, 1992. 0-316-08277-5.

The classic American collection, published first in 1855. Recent editions have added new quotations but also omitted some previously included. Bartlett is arranged chronologically by author. Note that there are separate sections for anonymous works, the Bible, the Book of Common Prayer and the Koran. There is a wonderfully detailed index to keywords.

69. *The Oxford dictionary of quotations.* Edited by Angela Partington. 4th edn. Oxford University Press, 1992. 0-19-866185-1

The *ODQ* was first published in 1941 and that and the further editions of 1953 and 1979 are still very useful. The present edition contains 7,500 quotations from 2,500 authors and, incidentally, retrieves hymns and songs which were dropped from the 1979 edition. Quotations are arranged alphabetically by author; non-English quotations are accompanied by translations. A keyword index is detailed enough to enable the identification of a quotation when only a word or two is known.

Ancient quotations

70. *Ancient quotes and anecdotes: from crib to crypt.* Edited by Vernon K. Robbins. Sonoma, CA: Polebridge Press, 1989. 0-944344-02-X (hc); 0-944344-03-8 (pbk).

Designed to capture the wit and wisdom of the ancient world, this is an anthology of sayings and deeds culled from Jewish, Greek, Roman, Islamic and Christian sources. Stories and sayings are from orators, statesmen, military and religious leaders and others. Entries are grouped around the stages of life and are complemented by indexes and explanatory notes. The editor is a prominent New

Testament scholar and this resource is important partly for its illuminating the nature of 'pronouncement stories'.

Modern quotations

71. *The Oxford dictionary of modern quotations.* Edited by Tony Augarde. Oxford University Press, 1991. 0-19-283086-4 (pbk).

Quotations are from the twentieth century or from contributors who lived past the year 1900. Arrangement is the same as *ODQ* (above) and, once again, non-English quotations appear with a translation. According to the cover, the reviewer in the *Church Times* wrote, 'I can heartily recommend total immersion.'

72. *The Penguin dictionary of twentieth-century quotations.* Edited by J. M. Cohen and M. J. Cohen. London: Penguin Books, 1993. 0-670-82165-9.

A much revised and expanded third edition of a work first published by Penguin in 1971 and now extended into the 1990s. The arrangement is alphabetical by author's name and the author's dates are given. The index is by keyword. The selection tends to be more popular than the Oxford dictionary (above) with many quotations being drawn from songs, the screen and advertisements. Politicians are well represented but Chesterton does as well as Churchill while God, religion and the churches also poll well, whether for better or for worse.

Religious

73. Parrinder, Geoffrey. *A dictionary of religious and spiritual quotations.* London: Routledge, 1990. 0-415-04128-7.

Designed by a well-known scholar of world religions, this work provides a wide range of ancient and modern quotations from representatives of all faiths. The work is arranged by topic and therefore has a text/author index and also a subject index.

74. *Dictionary of religious quotations.* Edited by Margaret Pepper. London: André Deutsch, 1989. 0-233-98373-2. Also published as *The Harper religious & inspirational quotation companion.* New York: Harper & Row, 1989. 0-06-016179-5.

What began as a personal anthology of favourite quotations has been turned into a useful resource. Quotations spring from all the major religions and span the centuries from classical times to the present. The arrangement is by topic, 'abandonment' to 'zeal', and there are indexes to subjects, authors and major works.

LANGUAGE DICTIONARIES

HISTORICAL DICTIONARIES

A dictionary 'based on historical principles' provides a historical review of the origin and the development of the meaning of a word, with definitions and illustrative quotations, arranged chronologically, for each usage. In this way it is possible to discern changes in meaning over time. This facility may well prove important in exegeting a historical document or in intuiting a correct nuance.

The famous work in this field is:

75.   *The Oxford English dictionary*. 2nd edn. Edited by J. A. Simpson and E. S. C. Weiner. 20 volumes. Oxford University Press, 1989; reprinted 1991. 0-19-861186-2.
Available on CD-ROM as *OED2 on CD-ROM* (1991).

The predecessor was the *New English dictionary on historical principles (NED)*, edited by James A. H. Murray in 10 volumes (1879-1928), with supplement (1933).

The *OED*, with its enormous store of information, is without parallel in the English language for vocabulary entries, definitions, etymologies and citations covering the history and development of words.

Note: a work, based on the *OED*, is *A Dictionary of American English on historical principles*, edited by William A. Craigie and James R. Hulbert. 4 volumes. Chicago: University of Chicago Press, 1938-1944. This work traces the origins and development of English words in the American colonies and the United States. It is a valuable source for American religious history.

CURRENT USAGE

It is usual to distinguish two types of dictionaries. A 'prescriptive' dictionary is one in which the editors affirm that their spellings and usages are *correct*, and so are prescribed. A 'descriptive' dictionary records or describes the language as it is now being used and is likely to add variant spellings.

The best advice on dictionaries is to choose an appropriate one and stay with it. Consistent usage is critical. The style manuals, published by the Australian Government Publishing Service and the New Zealand Government Printing Office respectively, state their preferences with regard to spelling:

Australian

The spellings recommended by the *Style manual for authors, editors and printers* (5th edn., 1994) [82] 'are currently those given in the latest edition of the *Macquarie Dictionary*, published in 1991' (p. 39). Here is a citation for this edition:

76.   *The Macquarie dictionary: the national dictionary*. Ed. A. Delbridge et al. 2nd edn. McMahons Point, NSW: Macquarie Library, 1991. 0-949757-63-2.

New Zealand

The *New Zealand style book* (1992) [81] states, 'With only a few exceptions, the *Concise Oxford Dictionary* has been adopted by most New Zealand publishers as the guide to the spelling of words (not including compound words)' (p. 50). Here is a citation for a recent edition of this dictionary:

77.   *Concise Oxford dictionary of current English*. Ed. R. E. Allen. 8th edn. Oxford: Clarendon Press, 1990. 0-19-861200-1 (plain).

THEOLOGICAL GERMAN

78. Ziefle, Helmut W. *Dictionary of theological German*. Grand Rapids, MI: Baker Book House, 1982. 0-8010-9929-3.

Contains approximately ten thousand entries of basic theological vocabulary to assist in reading the German Bible and theological texts. Each word is accompanied by the general meaning in English and there are scriptural references to Luther's Bible. An appendix lists the principal parts of eighty-six irregular and semi-irregular verbs. Finally there is a listing of the books of the Bible, including the Apocrypha, with their names given in full and in abbreviation. Those beginning German, for theological purposes, have found this work of real assistance.

A valuable supportive work is Helmut Ziefle's, *Theological German: a reader* (Grand Rapids, MI: Baker Book House, 1986, 0-8010-9931-5), which is designed to help English-speaking students read and translate the German Bible and the works of German theologians.

STYLE MANUALS

General

79. Butcher, Judith. *Copy-editing: the Cambridge handbook*. 3rd edn. Cambridge University Press, 1992. 0-521-40074-0.

Clear, up-to-date information for authors, copy-editors and also those involved in preparing typescript for publication. Covers all aspects of the editorial processes involved in converting text or disc to the printed page. Some of the advice on style reflects the author's British point of view.

80. *The Chicago manual of style, for authors, editors and copywriters*. 14th edn. Chicago, IL: Chicago University Press, 1993. 0-226-10389-7.

This great compendium remains the standard American reference resource for scholarly and formal writing with many US publishers regarding it as being prescriptive. The new edition adopts a more flexible approach than previously and includes more examples.

Australian and New Zealand

The two government style manuals are:

81. *The New Zealand style book for New Zealand writers, editors, journalists, and students*. Rev. edn. Edited by Peter Devereux et al. Wellington: GP Publications, 1992. 0-477-00056-X.

First issued in 1958, this manual, prepared for writers, editors, journalists, students, companies and government departments, has become the standard guide for those preparing manuscripts for publication in New Zealand.

82. *Style manual for authors, editors and printers*. 5th edn. Canberra: Australian Government Publishing Service, 1994. 0-644-29770-0 (hc); 0-644-29771-9 (pbk).

Aims to set standards for Commonwealth government publishing. Its influence has been more extensive and it is regarded as the standard reference work for writers in Australia. Very good sections on non-discriminatory language and the influence of desktop production technology on copy preparation.

Another important style guide which acknowledges the intrinsic character of Australian English is:

83.   Peters, Pam. *The Cambridge Australian style guide*. Cambridge University Press, 1995. 0-521-43401-7.

'The alphabetical list contains two kinds of entries: those which deal with general topics of language, editing and writing, and those dealing with particular words, word sets or parts of words' (Overview). A wise, refreshing work, generally descriptive rather than prescriptive.

Religious and theological

84.   McIntosh, Lawrence D. *A style manual for the presentation of papers and theses in religion and theology*. Wagga Wagga, NSW: Centre for Information Studies, in association with Australian and New Zealand Theological Library Association and Australian and New Zealand Association of Theological Schools, 1994. Reprinted with corrections, 1995. 0-949060-27-5.

This manual, designed for students and institutions, describes and illustrates style practices for those writing papers and theses in the areas of religion and theology. Topics covered include physical presentation, liaising with one's supervisor, spelling, capitalisation, abbreviations, quotations, numbers and dates, biblical references and inclusive language. A major section on the documentation of sources presents the note-bibliography method of citation and the author-date method as optional systems.

INCLUSIVE LANGUAGE

Inclusive language is an attempt to redesign language in order to do away with traditional forms which discriminate, stereotype or otherwise trivialise people because of their race, colour, class, religion, age, disability or sex.

Note. For an extensive discussion of issues and solutions see the *Style manual for authors, editors and printers* [82], Chapter 8, 'Non-discriminatory language'.

Also, McIntosh, *A style manual for the presentation of papers and theses in religion and theology* [84], chapter 8, 'Inclusive language', for a presentation of issues involved in the field of religion.

Comprehensive

85.   Schwartz, Marilyn. *Guidelines for bias-free writing*. Bloomington, IN: Indiana University Press, 1995. 0-253-35102-2 (hc); 0-253-20941-2 (pbk).

This volume was prepared as part of the work of the Task Force on Bias-Free Language of the Association of American University Presses. Its concise chapters reflect the Association's guidelines for gender-neutral and bias-free language, particularly in relation to gender, race, ethnicity, citizenship and nationality, religion, disabilities, sexual orientation and age.

Gender and language

The debate on 'inclusive language' has focussed primarily on the analysis and correction of sexist language.

General usage

86. Frank, Francine Harriet Wattman and Paula A. Teichler. *Language, gender, and professional writing: theoretical approaches and guidelines for nonsexist usage.* New York: Modern Language Association, 1989. 0-87352-178-1 (hc); 0-87352-179-X (pbk).

Supported by the highly-respected Modern Language Association, two experienced linguists present scholarly, most comprehensive guidelines for non-discriminatory usage. Contains an extensive bibliography.

87. Miller, Casey and Kate Swift. *The handbook of nonsexist writing.* 2nd edn. New York: Harper & Row, 1988. 0-06-181602-7 (hc).

Originally published in 1980, this has been deemed a standard work because of its sensible recommendations on the avoidance of sexist language and its proposals for alternative wordings. Includes a thesaurus of gender-free terms.

Religious usage

88. Hardesty, Nancy A. *Inclusive language in the church.* Atlanta, GA: John Knox Press, 1987. 0-8042-1686-X.

A church historian articulates ways in which inclusive language is appropriate for the doing of theology and for worship.

89. *An Inclusive-language lectionary: readings for year A.* Rev. edn. Published for the Cooperative Publication Association by John Knox Press, Atlanta, GA; The Pilgrim Press, New York; Westminster Press, Philadephia, 1986 (this volume).

The introduction and appendix describe ways in which this lectionary series has recast language about God. This introductory material is reprinted in the separate volumes for Year B (1987) and Year C (1985). The readings themselves follow the pattern of a three-year cycle, beginning with the first Sunday in Advent.

90. Queensland Catholic Education Commission. *Guidelines on the use of inclusive language and non-discriminatory language: presentation and practice in Catholic educational institutions.* n.pl.: Queensland Catholic Education Commission, 1990. No ISBN printed.

Formulated to help school communities discern 'sensitive and appropriate ways to put new or emerging understandings of language into practice' (Introduction). A succinct and most useful guide.

COPYRIGHT

The *Style manual for authors, editors and printers* (5th edn, 1994) [82], provides a brief outline of copyright law within the Commonwealth in Chapter 12, 'The Law relating to Publication', pp. 208-211. Another helpful summary, covering the questions most often asked about literary copyright is in Nicholas Hudson, *Modern Australian usage* (Oxford University Press, 1993), 91-96. Anyone in Australia, requiring advice on the use of copyright material may contact the Australian Copyright Council, Suite 3, 245 Chalmers Street, Redfern, NSW, 2016. The Council prints and keeps up-to-date numbered bulletins dealing with different aspects of copyright. Among the bulletin topics of relevance to libraries, students and religious organisations are the following:

No. 47 Copyright and writers
52 Libraries and copyright
59 Journalists and copyright
62 Historians and copyright
67 A teacher's guide to copyright
70 Music and copyright
77 Copyright and book publishers.

A full list is available from the Council.

STATISTICS

Australian

The Australian Bureau of Statistics (ABS) is the country's official statistical authority. ABS publishes *Year book Australia*, State yearbooks, and numerous studies and summaries of statistics on Australia's social and economic conditions. ABS also maintains a consultancy service, a National Dial-a-Statistic line, electronic data services, and makes its information available via the Internet. With its main office in Canberra, the Bureau operates State offices in each of the other capital cities.

For ABS titles in print consult the *ABS annual Catalogue of publications and products* (No. 1101.0) and its monthly updates. (Each published title is identified by a catalogue number.)

In every national census, now conducted at five-yearly intervals, a voluntary question is asked on religious affiliation. *Year book Australia* has a section, 'Religion' which provides major religious affiliations at each census since 1911 along with a brief commentary on trends and shows the breakdown of religious groupings by number and percentage of affiliates. Among the numerous products and services related to the 1991 Census the following titles make reference to religious affiliation:

1991 *Census - Census characteristics of Australia.* (Sets of tables include 'Religion by age'.) (No. 2710.0)

1991 *Census - Ethnicity package.* (Includes a religious profile of characteristics of all persons with a selected religion.) (No. 2803.0)

1991 *Census - Australia in profile.* (Key findings on a range of social issues, including religion.) (No. 2821.0)

PART

Subject reference resources

Part 2 includes reference works which are devoted to the particular subject areas of religion and theology.

In certain areas the subject material is preceded by items of a more general nature, where these are deemed to be particularly supportive of religious studies. For example, the chapter on church history begins with some general resources designed for historical research, while the chapter on pastoral care, acknowledging the practitioner's need for definitional tools, begins with dictionaries of psychology.

It is always possible that, in a given subject area, there may be a dearth of current resources. Where this is the case, material from general reference works, cited in Part 1, may be invoked to help fill gaps in the literature.

Chapter 14 departs somewhat from the main purpose of this volume. It lists a number of periodical titles of which students of religion and theology should be aware. The list may also suggest a core collection for libraries supporting teaching programs in these areas.

2

Religions in the world

This chapter is divided into two sections. The first is devoted to the major religions, considered separately, concentrating on Buddhism, Hinduism and Islam. Where specific resources are lacking, the reader will find that all religions, ancient and modern, major and lesser-known, are well covered in the encyclopedias and dictionaries of religions cited in Part 1, and particularly in the historical and descriptive articles in *The Encyclopedia of religion*, edited by Mircea Eliade [51].

The second section is given to recent resources on the presence of religions in various countries. It should be noted that material relating more specifically to Judaism and Christianity is to be found in Chapters 3, 4 and 5.

The major religions   **37**

  Buddhism   37
    Buddhism in Australia   37
  Hinduism   37
    Hinduism in Australia   37
  Islam   38
    Koran   39
      Text
      Concordances
      Dictionaries
    Islam in Australia   39

Religions in various countries   **39**

  The Americas   39
  Asia   40
  Australia   40
    Guides
    Bibliographies
    Yearbooks
    Indexes
    Series
    Australian Aboriginal religions   42
      Encyclopedias
      Bibliographies
      Surveys

China   43
Great Britain   44
New Zealand   44
        Bibliographies
                Women and religion
        Histories
        Surveys
        Indexes
Oceania   45
        Bibliographies
Russia and the Soviet Union   46

THE MAJOR RELIGIONS

BUDDHISM

91. Prebish, Charles S. *Historical dictionary of Buddhism.* (Historical dictionaries of religions, philosophies, and movements, no.1).
Metuchen, NJ: Scarecrow Press, 1993. 0-8108-2698-4.

Introductory material includes a pronunciation guide, an overview of the Buddhist Scriptures, a chronology of history and a valuable introduction which traces the origin of Buddhism in India, its spread to other parts of Asia and its influence upon the West. The dictionary section has entries on 'significant persons, places, events, texts, doctrines, practices, institutions and movements' (Foreword). The work concludes with an extensive bibliography. A most authoritative work.

Buddhism in Australia

92. Croucher, Paul. *History of Buddhism in Australia, 1848-1988.*
Randwick, NSW: University of New South Wales Press, 1989.
0-86840-195-1.

There are now some 80,000 Buddhists in Australia. This work represents the first attempt to chronicle the history of Buddhism and its influence upon poetry, art and religious life in this country. A feature is the author's sensitivity to the variety of Buddhist traditions which are catered to by a diverse array of approximately one hundred Buddhist organisations. The reference potential is enhanced by well-developed notes, a list of sources, a glossary of terms and a comprehensive index.

HINDUISM

93. Werner, Karel. *A popular dictionary of Hinduism.* Richmond, Surrey: Curzon Press, 1994. 0-7007-0279-2.

A dictionary of terms and other references covering the complex phenomenon of Hinduism. Contains explanations of Sanskrit and vernacular terms and concepts important to the understanding of Hindu rituals and spiritual practices as well as Hindu religious and philosophical teachings.

Hinduism in Australia

94. Bilimoria, Purusottama. *Hinduism in Australia: Mandala for the gods.*
Melbourne: Spectrum Publications, 1989. 0-86786-201-7.

The author, a university teacher, has an Indian background and is a long-time resident of Australia. The work begins with a short introduction to the Hindu tradition, then traces the arrival of Hindu-Indians from the early nineteenth to twentieth centuries, along with the emergence of Hindu-influenced spiritualists, sects, cults, gurus and yoga groups in Australia. The end-notes are extensive and there is a detailed index.

ISLAM

Islam is the second largest of the world's religions. The following resources, tracing its history and development, include an encyclopedia of classic proportions and a recent Oxford set devoted to contemporary Islam. The first item is unsurpassed in size, authority and learning.

95. *Encyclopaedia of Islam.* New edn. Prepared by a number of leading orientalists under the patronage of the International Union of Academics. Leiden: Brill, 1954 - . (In progress, eight bound volumes plus fascicles have been issued to date.)

The first edition was published in four volumes with supplement (1913-1938).

The new edition, issued in volume or fascicle format, was begun in 1954 (some of the earlier volumes in the set have been reprinted) and continues with Volume 8, 'Ned-Sam', scheduled to be published in 1995. Several indexes to volumes 1-7 and to Supplement fascicles should help simplify the huge amount of information contained in the *Encyclopaedia.* These comprise an index to proper names (1993), to subjects (1994), and a glossary and index of technical terms due in 1995. Simply the greatest work in the field and essential to all engaged in Islamic studies.

Note: The one-volume *Shorter encyclopaedia of Islam*, edited by H. A. R. Gibb and J. H. Kramers (Leiden: Brill, 1953, 4th impression, 1995) is an abridgment of material, mainly related to law and religion and taken from the first edition of the *Encyclopaedia.* Bibliographies, however, have been up-dated.

Yet another Brill by-product of the *Encyclopaedia* is the following:

96. *Islamic desk reference: compiled from the Encyclopaedia of Islam* . By E. van Donzel. Leiden: Brill, 1994. 90-04-09738-4.

A condensation of the multi-volumed *Encyclopaedia of Islam*, this attractive volume presents concise and factual information about the history and culture of Islam. A quick reference tool presenting the religion, the believers and the countries of the Islamic world.

97. Glasse, Cyril. *The concise encyclopedia of Islam.* San Francisco: Harper & Row, 1989. 0-06-063123-6.

A highly-regarded reference work on all aspects of Islamic culture, religion and law written by a practising American Muslim and scholar. Well illustrated, with maps, charts, and sections of photographs. Chronology and bibliography.

98. *The Oxford encyclopedia of the modern Islamic world.* Edited by John L. Esposito. 4 vols. New York: Oxford University Press, 1995. 0-19-506613-8 (set).

A major work providing 'access to current scholarship on the presence and influence of Islam on a global scale' (Preface, vol. 1, p.ix). The concentration is not on classical texts or on classical and medieval history, but on ways in which Muslims have expressed themselves in the modern period through political and social action. Lengthy articles by scholars conclude with annotated bibliographies. Note also that the entry, 'Reference books' (vol. 3:415-420) comprises a comprehensive bibliographic essay. A subject index to the whole set is in the final volume. A timely, essential resource for the better understanding of the faith and practice of Islam.

Koran

Text

99. *Koran. al-Qur'an: a contemporary translation*. Translated by Ahmed Ali. 2nd rev. corr. edn. Princeton, NJ: Princeton University Press, 1988. 0-691-07329-5 (hc); 0-691-02046-9 (pbk).

The first edition was published in Karachi in 1984. The Arabic text and contemporary English translation are in parallel columns. This edition contains explanatory notes and there are indexes to subjects and to the names of prophets with both Arabic and English names being given. A highly-regarded translation.

Concordances

100. Kassis, Hanna E. *A concordance of the Qur'an*. Berkeley, CA: University of California Press, 1983. 0-520-04327-8 (hc); 0-520-04409-6 (pbk).

Uses the English text of A. J. Arberry's well-known, *The Koran interpreted* (Oxford University Press and Macmillan, 1964, and frequently reprinted). The concordance arrangement is alphabetical by the transliterated form of the Arabic term. An index to the English words is in two parts, the first devoted to the name of Allah and the second to the remaining vocabulary.

Dictionaries

101. Mir, Mustansir. *Dictionary of Qur'anic terms and concepts*. (Garland reference library of the humanities, 693). New York: Garland, 1987. 0-8240-8546-9.

Brief entries, arranged alphabetically by the English translation of the Arabic word or phrase, cover definitions and the subjects of the Qur'an. A basic tool for introductory work.

Islam in Australia

102. Bouma, Gary D. *Mosques and Muslim settlement in Australia*. Canberra: Australian Government Publishing Service, 1994. 0-644-35329-5.

Using demographic data and in-depth interviews, the author presents a picture of what it is like to be a Muslim in Australia. Covers 'the historical background to Australia's changing religious profile, the patterns of Muslim settlement and the role of religion and mosques in this' (Foreword). Bibliography. An important resource for understanding Australia's transition to a multicultural society.

RELIGIONS IN VARIOUS COUNTRIES

THE AMERICAS

103. *The encyclopedia of American religions*. 4th edn. Edited by J. Gordon Melton. Detroit: Gale, 1993. 0-8103-6904-4. *Supplement,* 1994. 0-8103-8818-9.

This work has been constantly revised since the earlier editions of 1978, 1987 and 1989. It covers approximately 1,600 religious groups in North America, whether prominent or obscure. Two distinct sections describe the historical development of religious families in the US and Canada, and give factual information about each religious group. Justly deserves its reputation for comprehensiveness and accuracy. The several indexes include educational and religious organisations and institutions.

The following is an important companion volume:

104. *The encyclopedia of American religions: religious creeds: a compilation of more than 450 creeds, confessions, statements of faith, and summaries of doctrine of religious and spiritual groups in the United States and Canada.* 2nd edn. Edited by J. Gordon Melton. Detroit: Gale, 1993. 0-8103-5491-8.

Includes credal statements from Christian, Jewish and other faiths, including native American religions. Foreign language creeds are translated. There is an index of creed/organisation names and also a keyword index.

105. *Encyclopedia of the American religious experience: studies of traditions and movements.* Edited by Charles H. Lippey and Peter W. Williams. 3 vols. New York: Scribner's, 1988. 0-684-18062-6 (set).

Long essays on all aspects of religious history and life in North America, with particular reference to the United States. Coverage includes history, sociology, religion, theology and philosophy. Cross-references abound and there is an extensive index in the final volume. A most comprehensive and authoritative work.

106. Mead, Frank S. *Handbook of denominations in the United States.* New 9th edn. revised by Samuel S. Hill. Nashville, TN: Abingdon Press, 1990. 0-687-16572-5.

Objectively describes the history, doctrines and organisation of some 220 religious denominations including Christian and Jewish groups. There are useful appendixes, a glossary of terms, both general and denominational bibliographies and an index. Highly regarded over many years.

ASIA

107. Smart, Ninian. *Religions of Asia.* Englewood, NJ: Prentice Hall, 1993. 0-13-772427-6.

The well-known author of several books on comparative religion presents an experienced and lucid survey of the major religions of Asia. A good place to start.

AUSTRALIA

Guides

108. Hughes, Philip J. *Religion: a view from the Australian census.* Kew, Vic.: Christian Research Association, 1993. 1-875223-10- X.

Detailed information about the fifteen major religious groups in Australia based on personal responses to the question, 'What is your religion?' in the 1991 national census. Statistics and valuable commentary cover growth and decline since 1911, size of groups in State and city, church attendance, age, ethnicity and other factors. A basic reference work for understanding Australian society and the place of religion within it.

Note. The Christian Research Association, which was formed in 1985, has as its charter to provide reliable information about religious beliefs and practices in Australia. It has published a *Yearbook for Australian churches* which, for 1996 has been re-titled *Yearbook of Australian religious organisations* [113]. Its small journal, *Pointers: quarterly bulletin of the Christian Research Association* reports on research relevant to the Australian religious scene and on new publications. From time to time the CRA also publishes its own research papers and reports. For information about the CRA, the address is Locked Bag 23, Kew, Victoria, 3101.

109. Humphreys, Robert and Roland Ward. *Religious bodies in Australia: a comprehensive guide*. 3rd edn. Wantirna, Vic.: New Melbourne Press, 1995. 0-646-24552-X.

A fully revised and greatly expanded version of the earlier editions published in 1986 and 1988, this guide to the diversity of belief in Australia now includes over 300 religious groups. A feature is the amount of attention paid to non-Christian religions. The work begins with definitional, statistical and other general material on the Australian religious scene. Then religions are arranged according to the following classification: Trinitarian-Christian, non-Trinitarian, other world monotheistic religions, mental, psychic and other religions, nature and traditional religions and finally, Buddhism. Bibliographic sources and contact addresses are supplied. There is an index to religious groups and principal subjects. Certainly the most comprehensive Australian resource of its kind.

110. *Many faiths, one nation: a guide to major faiths and denominations in Australia*. Edited by Ian Gillman. Sydney: William Collins, 1988. 0-7322-2406-3.

A directory to the diversity of faith groups in Australia. Following an introductory essay, 'Religion in Australian life - an exploration', Gillman, with information gathered from representatives of forty-six faiths and denominations, outlines the history, beliefs, forms of worship, membership and governmental structures of each particular group. These range from Aboriginal religions to Baha'i. The major non-Christian religions are included in this well-crafted, objective guide.

Bibliographies

111. *Religion in Australian life: a bibliography of social research*. Edited by Michael Mason; compiled by Georgina Fitzpatrick. Bedford Park, SA: National Catholic Research Council and the Australian Association for the Study of Religions, 1982. 0-908083-09-2.

Concentrates on materials reflecting research published here and overseas from 1945 to 1977. A supplement adds selected items to 1981. Sections cover world views and values in Australian culture, religious culture, religious groups including the major religions, and religion and society. Still a most important resource for work in history and sociology

112. Thompson, Roger C. 'Bibliography'. In his *Religion in Australia: a history*. Melbourne: Oxford University Press, 1994. 0-19-553516-2. Pages 149-158.

Although the main emphasis of this monograph is on Christianity, Aboriginal spirituality, Judaism, Islam and other religions are also treated and represented in the bibliography.

Yearbooks

113. *A Yearbook of Australian religious organisations, 1996- .* Edited by Peter Bentley, 'Tricia Blombery and Philip Hughes. Kew, Vic.: Christian Research Association, 1995. ISSN 1035-8137.

Formerly titled *A Yearbook for Australian churches, 1991-1995* [see 339] which, in spite of its title, included reference material on other religious groups. This is an important directory of Christian churches, ecumenical organisations and other religious bodies in Australia with short histories, statistics and contact addresses. Each volume features a special theme; in this volume for 1996 it is 'Youth ministry'. There is a selected bibliography of religious books published during the past year or so, an ecumenical calendar and lectionary and a diary of future events. A most accessible and useful guide.

Indexes

The key index to periodical literature for the study of religion in Australia is the *Australasian religion index* [37], which is cited in Part 1.

Series

The Australian Government Publishing Service intends a series of monographs entitled, 'Religious community profiles', which will cover the five major religions in Australia and the eight largest Christian denominations. Through descriptions of religious identification and involvement this series will provide information that is pertinent to an understanding of Australian society and culture. The first item in the series, *Judaism in Australia*, by W. D. Rubinstein, was published in 1995 [163].

Australian Aboriginal religions

Encyclopedias

114. *The Encyclopaedia of Aboriginal Australia.* Edited by David Horton. 2 vols. Canberra: Aboriginal Studies Press for the Australian Institute of Aboriginal and Torres Strait Islander Studies, 1994. 0-85575-234-3 (set).

A comprehensive reference on all aspects of Australian Aboriginal and Torres Strait Islander history, society and culture. The second volume concludes with an extensive bibliography and appendixes providing social, legal, linguistic and statistical information. There is a list of Christian missions among Aboriginal and TSI peoples (pp. 1301-1303). The work concludes with several entry-guide indexes.

Bibliographies

The major on-going bibliography in the field is:

115. *The Annual bibliography of the Australian Institute of Aboriginal and Torres Strait Islander Studies, 1977- .* Canberra: The Institute, 1977- . ISSN 1320-1158.

Includes entries for books, chapters, periodical articles, conference papers, manuscripts, theses, sound recordings and photographs. Arranged by main entry, usually the author or contributor, and is indexed by title and broad subject categories. Note that 'Religion' is among those categories.

116. Swain, Tony. *Aboriginal religions in Australia: a bibliographical survey.* (Bibliographies and indexes in religious studies, 18). New York: Greenwood Press, 1991. 0-313-26044-3.

The compiler's aim was to list every published work that includes 'a substantial section on Aboriginal religion and which intends to be an accurate documentation' (Preface). The volume begins with three interpretative surveys of scholarship to date on the history of the study of Aboriginal religions, major religious themes and their regional distinctions. The classified bibliography which follows contains some 1064 entries with annotations which can be both descriptive and evaluative. Indexes are to authors, titles, tribes, places and general subjects. A most comprehensive resource.

Note the extensive bibliography in the following monograph:

117. Harris, John. *One blood: two hundred years of Aboriginal encounter with Christianity.* 2nd edn. Sutherland, NSW: Albatross Books, 1994. 0-86760-095-0 (hc). Also published in the UK by Lion Publishing, Oxford, 0-7459-1496-9 (Lion).

The items for this bibliography (pp. 913-966) are culled from government documents, biographical indexes, theses, books and periodicals.

Surveys

Note Swain's chapter, 'The history of the study of Australian Aboriginal religions', in the work cited above.

See also the four articles, under the general heading, 'Australian religions', in *The Encyclopedia of religion*, edited by Mircea Eliade [51], noting the annotated bibliographies for each article. The authors and titles of the articles are,

> Berndt, Ronald M. 'Australian religions: an overview'. Vol. 1: 529-547.
> Berndt, Catherine H. 'Mythic themes'. Vol. 1: 547-562.
> Wild, Stephen A. 'Modern movements'. Vol. 1:562-566.
> Maddock, Kenneth. 'History of study'. Vol. 1: 566-570.

See also the section on Aboriginal art in Chapter 11.

CHINA

118. MacInnis, Donald E. *Religion in China today: policy and practice.* Maryknoll, NY: Orbis Books, 1989. 0-89344-594-8 (hc); 0-88344-645-6 (pbk).

The author, formerly director of the China Program of the National Council of Churches of Christ, provides more than 130 documents, articles, press reports and first-hand interviews describing China's official policies on religion since 1979. There are sections on the major religions in China - Buddhism, Taoism, Islam, Christianity, Catholic and Protestant, Judaism and Confucianism - with an introduction to each section. The volume is indexed. MacInnis is an experienced guide to these policy formulations and has produced an essential tool for specialists and students alike.

GREAT BRITAIN

119. *Religions in the UK: a multi-faith directory.* Edited by Paul Weller. Mickleover, Derby: University of Derby in association with the Inter-faith Network for the United Kingdom (London), 1993. 0-901437-06-9.

Designed to encourage inter-religious contacts and dialogue in the U.K. Describes a range of religious traditions and communities, including Buddhist, Christian, Hindu, Jain, Jewish, Muslim, Sikh and Zoroastrian and provides comprehensive data about them. A mine of hard-to-find information.

NEW ZEALAND

Bibliographies

120. Lineham, Peter J. and Anthony R. Grigg. *Religious history of New Zealand: a bibliography.* 4th edn. Palmerston North: Department of History, Massey University, 1993. 0-908665-79-2.

First published in 1984, with succeeding editions in 1987 and 1989, this is the most extensive bibliography on religions in New Zealand. It covers Maori religion and missions, regional and denominational histories, other non-Christian religions, social issues and movements, non-denominational organisations and, finally, theology, theologians and religious studies. Includes books, periodical articles, essays and theses; many entries being annotated. Items are arranged alphabetically by author and then gathered in a detailed classified index. This is a key bibliographic resource covering all aspects of religion in New Zealand.

Note: on the front cover of the copy consulted the subtitle is incorrectly printed as 'a biography' rather than 'a bibliography'. The title page is correct.

121. Gilling, Bryan D. 'New Zealand religious history'. *Stimulus 1, 1* (Feb 1993): 36-39.

This annotated bibliography, published in a New Zealand periodical, covers reference items, generalia, missionaries, denominations, revivalism, Maori religion and particular topics.

Women and religion

122. Simpson, Jane. 'Women, religion and society in New Zealand: a literature review'. *Journal of religious history 18, 2* (Dec 1994), 198-218.

This discerning bibliographic essay concentrates on writing from the late 1950s, and notes some of the major influences on the historiography of these related topics. Ranges widely over matters concerning both Maori and Pakeha.

Histories

The following general history is of value for contextual work:

123. *Oxford history of New Zealand.* Edited by Geoffrey Rice. 2nd edn. Auckland: Oxford University Press, 1992. 0-19-558257-8.

First edition, 1981. A comprehensive historical account is provided by means of an integrated set of essays compiled by some twenty-two scholars. There are chapters on Maori and on social history, a glossary of Maori terms and extensive chapter bibliographies (pp. 665-735).

Surveys

124. *Beliefs and practices in New Zealand: a directory*. Edited by Peter Donovan et al. 2nd edn, rev. and enl. Palmerston North: Department of History, Massey University, 1985.

Data for this work were obtained from representatives of churches, religious movements and other groups in New Zealand who had completed a questionnaire about their beliefs and practices. With each new edition entries have been brought up to date. The self-reporting may include statements about history, faith, symbolism, purposes, festival days, membership requirements and publications.

125. *Religions of New Zealanders*. Edited by Peter Donovan. Palmerston North: Dunmore Press, 1990. 0-86469-125-4.

A set of descriptive essays about the religious beliefs and practices current in New Zealand. Major religions - Maori, Baha'i, Buddhism, Christianity (seven of the eighteen essays are on the various Christian traditions), Hinduism, Islam, Judaism, Sikhism are represented along with 'esoteric religions', humanism and the women's spirituality movement. Charts, illustrations, bibliographic notes and a general index enhance the reference potential of this volume. It is a major resource for understanding the roles played by religions in New Zealand culture.

Indexes

The key index to periodical literature for the study of religion in New Zealand is the *Australasian religion index* [37].

OCEANIA

All definitions agree that the countries of Oceania include the islands of the Pacific, including Micronesia, Melanesia and Polynesia. By some, however, it is taken to embrace all land masses lying between Asia and America and south to Australia and New Zealand.

Bibliographies

126. Turner, Harold W. *Bibliography of new religious movements in primal societies*. Volume 3: Oceania. Boston, MA: G. K. Hall, 1990. 0-8161-8984-6 (Volume 3).

This is the third volume of a six-volume set: Volume 1. Black Africa; 2. North America; 3. Oceania; 4. Europe and Asia; 5. Latin America; 6. Caribbean.

The series is concerned with religious movements 'which arise in the interaction of a primal society with another society where there is great disparity of power and sophistication' (Introduction to Volume 1). Volume 3 is devoted to Oceania which, in this case, means Australia, Melanesia, Micronesia, Polynesia (New Zealand is in this section) and 'particular movements' which include Ratana and

Ringatu of the Maori. Australia attracts some 56 entries while the main body of material on New Zealand amounts to a substantial 459 entries. Many entries are briefly annotated. There are indexes to authors and sources.

See also the entries under, 'Oceania' in Chapter 5.

RUSSIA AND THE SOVIET UNION

The following items are concerned with all the major religions in Russia.

127. *The Modern encyclopedia of religions in Russia and the Soviet Union.* Edited by Paul D. Steeves. Gulf Breeze, FL: Academic International Press, 1988- . Volume 1- 'Aaron' - 'Annunciation'. (In progress; number of volumes not yet announced.) 0-87569-106-4 (set).

Volume 5: 'Burials' 'Council of 1589, Orthodox Church' was published in 1993.

This multi-volume work is intended to provide detailed information on the religious culture of the peoples of the Soviet Union. The rich diversity of faiths, past and present, ranges from Russian Orthodoxy and the Armenian Church to Judaism, Buddhism, Islam, Shamanism and many indigenous sects. Experts contribute entries, some of essay length, in such fields as music, literature, history, theology, art and architecture. The bibliographic coverage, within each volume, is a feature. The work, projected over some fifteen years, promises to be an objective, scholarly and much-needed resource in this comparatively barren reference area.

128. *Religion in the Soviet Republics: a guide to Christianity, Judaism, Islam, Buddhism and other religions.* Edited by Igor Troyanovsky. New York: HarperSanFrancisco, 1991. 0-06-250875-X.

Translated from the Russian. Authentic documents and expert analyses portray the Soviet religious situation in both its positive and negative aspects. The volume begins with the once-secret letters of Trotsky and Lenin on their plans for dealing with religion in the Soviet state. Then there are the texts of recent legislation on freedom of conscience and religious organisations. Material on religion and culture includes religious radio and television programming, the reopening of churches and the rehabilitation of religious leaders. The bulk of the work is given to overviews of every major religious group in the Republics. There is a directory of organisations and finally an index to the whole. A most thorough, one-volume resource on Soviet religious life.

3

Judaism

The Jewish people understand themselves as being part of a covenant relationship with the One God, a covenant as old as Abraham and confirmed by the children of Israel's having received the Scriptures, the Law and the Land. In spite of suffering and exile, and of dispersion throughout the world, this covenant continues to provide the varying modern Judaisms with an identity and consciousness.

That the holy and secular histories of the Jews are so inextricably entangled helps explain the comprehensiveness of the numerous reference resources available. Remarkably fine works deal with their history, religion, theology and ethics, their contributions to world culture, their endurance of the Holocaust and the issues they confront today.

Recent times have witnessed an important dialogue between Jews and Christians. Conversations and collaborative scholarly work are fostering mutual respect and a sympathetic awareness of the other's faith. Resources for understanding this dialogue, including important Australian contributions, are included in the final section.

General   **49**
       Bibliographies
       Dictionaries and encyclopedias

Jewish history, culture and literature   **50**
       Encyclopedias
       Atlases
  Jerusalem   51
       Bibliographies

Ancient period   **51**
       Histories
  Philo Judaeus   52
       Bibliographies
  Josephus, Flavius   52
       Surveys
       Bibliographies
       Concordances
       Text

Rabbinic literature   **53**
       Introductions
  The Mishnah   54

The Talmud 54
  Palestinian 54
  Babylonian 55
    Commentary
Midrash 55

The Samaritans **56**
    Guides
    Bibliographies

Modern period **56**
General 56
    Bibliographies
The Holocaust 57
    Bibliographies
    Encyclopedias
Judaism in Australia 57

The Jewish-Christian dialogue **57**
    Bibliographies
    Dictionaries
    Guidelines

GENERAL

Bibliographies

129. *The Book of Jewish books: a reader's guide to Judaism.* Edited by Ruth S. Frank and William Wollheim. San Francisco: Harper & Row, 1986. 0-06-063008-6 (hc); 0-06-063009-4 (pbk).

Intended for the general reader, this work contains reviews of all types of Jewish literature and so introduces all aspects of Jewish history and culture. Each subject chapter is introduced by an authority and the wide-ranging resource includes analyses of works on philosophy and history, prayer books and also children's books. There is a glossary of Jewish words and an index to names and titles cited. Most useful for its well-written introductions to the forms and subject matter of Jewish literature.

130. Griffiths, David B. *A critical bibliography of writings on Judaism.* 2 vols. (Jewish studies, 2). Lewiston, NY: E. Mellen Press, 1988. 0-88946-252-2 (vol. 1); 0-88946-257-7 (vol. 2).

Part 1 covers reference works, Judaism in antiquity, medieval to early modern times, thought and culture.
Part 2: modern history, the Holocaust, Zionist thought and history, modernity and modern thought.

Annotated entries, arranged in classified order cover books and periodical literature. It is essential to consult the tables of contents, there being no index.

See also, Edward Starkey, *Judaism and Christianity: a guide to reference literature* [9].

Dictionaries and encyclopedias

The following great work remains authoritative for all topics concerning Jews and Judaism:

131. *Encyclopaedia Judaica.* Edited by Cecil Roth et al. 16 vols. Jerusalem: Encyclopedia Judaica (Keter), 1971-1972; New York: Macmillan, 1972.

Particularly strong on biographies. Note that the extensive index is in volume 1. The main set is supplemented by the following volumes:

Decennial book, 1973-1982: events of 1972-1981. Jerusalem, 1982.
Yearbook, 1973- . Jerusalem, 1973- . ISSN 0303-7819.

Three valuable one-volume works are:

132. Cohn-Sherbok, Dan. *The Blackwell dictionary of Judaica.* Oxford: Blackwell Reference, 1992. 0-631-16615-7.

More than 7,000 concise entries on every aspect of Jewish history, civilisation and religion. Accessible, up-to-date, and easy to use. A useful partner to the *Blackwell companion to Jewish culture* [135].

133. *The Encyclopedia of Judaism.* Edited by Geoffrey Wigoder. New York: Macmillan, 1989. 0-02-628410-3.

A well-produced, beautifully illustrated volume with articles by authorities covering the vast spectrum of Jewish life and thought. The volume reflects the denominational diversity of contemporary Judaism. Richly informative, this is the major one-volume reference work in this field.

134. *The Jewish religion: a companion.* Edited by Louis Jacobs. Oxford University Press, 1995. 0-19-826463-1 (hc).

The concentration here is on Jewish belief and practices from the earliest times to the present. Entries present religious perspectives on biblical matters, traditions, customs and social behaviour, and define attitudes to theological issues. The work, supervised by a well-known Rabbi, is a mine of information on Judaism and contemporary Jewish thought.

JEWISH HISTORY, CULTURE AND LITERATURE

Encyclopedias

135. *The Blackwell companion to Jewish culture: from the eighteenth century to the present.* Edited by Glenda Abramson et al. Oxford: Basil Blackwell, 1989. 0-631-15111-7.

Experts survey the Jewish contribution to modern civilisation, starting around the period of the Enlightenment, and assess Jewish elements in much of Western culture. Contains biographical articles on influential figures and thematic essays on such topics as philosophy, art, music, education and humour. Entries are signed, there are bibliographies and the work is well-indexed.

136. *Encyclopedia of Jewish history: events and eras of the Jewish people.* Edited by Ilana Shamir and Shlomo Shavit et al. New York: Facts on File, 1986. 0-8160-1220-2.

Israeli scholars offer concise information about events, eras and key figures in the annals of the Jewish people from the dawn of their history. The text is lavishly illustrated. The volume closes with a detailed glossary, an extensive synchronic chart of key events and an index. A most readable, well-documented reference work.

Atlases

137. *A historical atlas of the Jewish people: from the time of the patriarchs to the present.* Edited by Eli Barnavi. New edn. London: Kuperad, 1994. 1-85733-139-7. (First edition, 1992).

More than a thousand maps along with photographs and drawings are used to track some 4000 years of Jewish history. The work is organised by theme as well as by period; the authoritative text being accompanied by illustrations, including reproductions of paintings, timelines and chronologies. Every aspect of the Jewish experience, including the recent history of the State of Israel receives detailed attention. There is a glossary of terms and an extensive index. In all a splendidly produced and highly informative resource.

138. De Lange, Nicholas. *Atlas of the Jewish world.* New York: Facts on File, 1984. 0-87196-043-5.

> An instance of an atlas becoming an encyclopedia. This volume covers Jewish history and culture from earliest times to the present. Fifty nine maps are accompanied by text and an excellent selection of illustrations. Includes a gazetteer and index.

JERUSALEM

Bibliographies

139. Purvis, James D. *Jerusalem, the Holy City: a bibliography.* (American Theological Library Association bibliography series, 20). Metuchen, NJ: American Theological Library Association and Scarecrow Press, 1988. 0-8108-1999-6.

_____. *Jerusalem, the Holy City: a bibliography.* Volume 2. (American Theological Library Association bibliography series, 20). Metuchen, NJ: American Theological Library Association and Scarecrow Press, 1991. 0-8108-2506-6.

> The first volume lists some 5,800 research items on Jerusalem, with an emphasis on its being a *holy* city. These have been culled from books and articles in numerous languages. The classified arrangement in forty chapters, employing chronological divisions, covers the city from biblical to modern times. There is an index to authors and subjects.

> The supplemental volume adds a further 5000 entries and the earlier divisions are expanded. There is cross-referencing to the first volume and additional indexes. This two-volume work is an essential resource for those engaged in any aspect of research on the Holy City - ancient, medieval or modern.

ANCIENT PERIOD

Histories

140. *The Cambridge history of Judaism,* edited by W. D. Davies and Louis Finkelstein. Cambridge University Press, 1984- , vol. 1- (in progress, projected in four volumes).

> When completed this set will present a scholarly history of the Jews from 586 BCE to the codification of the Mishnah in 250 CE. Volume 1 (1984) presents an introduction to the geography of Palestine and the Levant and to numismatics, calendars and chronology. It goes on to cover the 'Persian period'. Volume 2 (1989) is titled, 'The Hellenistic age'. Succeeding volumes will cover the Roman period to CE 70, and from CE 70 to 235. The work incorporates 'new data provided by archaeology, new knowledge of the Apocryphal, Pseudepigraphic, Qumranic and Gnostic writings, and recent critical work on the Rabbinic sources' (Preface). Contributors from numerous countries and with various backgrounds ensure that these volumes are as ecumenical as they are international. Chapter bibliographies, at the end of the volume, are most valuable.

141. Schürer, Emil. *The history of the Jewish people in the age of Jesus Christ (175BC - AD135)*. New English version. Edited by Geza Vermes et al. 3 vols. in 4. Edinburgh: T & T Clark, 1973-1987. 0-567-02242-0; 0-567-02243-9; 0-567-02244-7; 0-567-09373-5.

Thoroughly updates the earlier English edition (1885-1891). In covering Jewish history, institutions and literature, it is an indispensable resource for work on the intertestamental period. The bibliographic coverage is a feature. Volume 3, part 2 is completed by a detailed index to the whole work.

Two highly-influential writers of the first century CE were the Jewish philosopher and theologian in Alexandria, Philo (c.20 BCE-c.40 CE) and the Jewish historian, Josephus (c.37 - c.100). Their writings continue to attract much scholarly interest, partly as they inform our understanding of the intertestamental period.

PHILO JUDAEUS

Bibliographies

142. Radice, Roberto and David T. Runia. *Philo of Alexandria: an annotated bibliography , 1937-1986*. (Supplements to *Vigiliae Christianae*, 8). Leiden: Brill, 1988. 90-04-08986-1. Reprint of this edition published in 1992.

An essential resource for all working in the areas of Philonic and related studies. The work is divided into two parts. The first deals with existing bibliographies, editions, commentaries and other research aids; the second is an annotated bibliography of critical studies published from 1937 to 1986. The arrangement here is chronological. There are indexes to authors, reviewers, biblical passages, Philonic passages, subjects and, finally, Greek terms. Note the short survey, 'Brief observations on fifty years of Philonic scholarship' (Introduction, pp.xxiii-xxix).

JOSEPHUS, FLAVIUS

Surveys

For an authoritative bibliographic essay describing recent research on Josephus see:

143. Attridge, H. W. 'Josephus and his works'. In *Jewish writings of the Second Temple period*. Edited by Michael E. Stone. (Compendium Rerum Judaicarum ad Novum Testamentum, 2/2). Philadelphia, PA: Fortress Press, 1984. pp. 185-232.

Bibliographies

144. Feldman, Louis H. *Josephus and modern scholarship (1937-1980)*. Berlin: de Gruyter, 1984. 3-11-008138-5.

_____. *Josephus: a supplementary bibliography*. (Garland reference library of the humanities, 645). New York: Garland, 1986. 0-8240-8792-5.

This massive work includes coverage of the texts, translations, the life of Josephus, his biblical-exegetical methods, interpretation of history, his sources, views on

Jewish religion and law, the religious movements of his time, including the Samaritan, Essenes and early Christians, and his influence until the twentieth century. Subject indexes cover all areas and there are indexes to Greek, Latin, Hebrew and Aramaic words and those in other languages. Also an author index. The Supplement, which allows Feldman to revise and augment Schreckenberg's earlier bibliographic work on Josephus, has its own classification system.

Concordances

145. *A Complete concordance to Flavius Josephus*. Edited by K. H. Rengstorf et al. 4 vols. Leiden: E. J. Brill, 1973-1983.

The result of many years work, this concordance to the writings of Josephus is a vital resource. A separate volume edited by A. Schalit, *Namenwörterbuch zu Flavius Josephus*, published by Brill in 1968, provides a concordance to proper names. Perhaps librarians should be warned to check the price of this set.

Text

Josephus' first work, *The War of the Jews*, which has become a basic source of Jewish history from the Maccabean revolt (167-164 BCE) to the fall of Jerusalem and the aftermath, has been released in the following new edition:

146. Josephus, Flavius. *Josephus, the Jewish war*. Edited by Gaalya Cornfeld et al. Grand Rapids, MI: Zondervan, 1982. 0-310-39210-1.

A new translation of the text is accompanied by an extensive commentary with archaeological-background illustrations (including thirty-two pages in full colour). Explanations of historical, geographical and cultural points adds to the understanding of the events of the time.

RABBINIC LITERATURE

The Rabbinic period is usually dated from 70 CE to the seventh century. The first century or so of this period witnessed the rise of rabbinical patriarchs both in Israel and in Babylonia. They were recognised as the supreme Jewish teachers and, with their successors, were responsible for the editing of the body of oral law known as the Mishnah, the Talmud which was to become a most formative influence on Jewish life and the Midrash which reflects the Rabbinic interpretation of the Scriptures and contains a wealth of moral teachings. For a succinct summary of the Rabbinic period and its literature, see Frederick Danker, *Multipurpose tools for Bible study* [354], pp. 215-219. For more extensive introductions, see the first two items cited below.

Introductions

147. Strack, H. L. and Stemberger, Günter. *Introduction to the Talmud and Midrash*. Minneapolis, MN: Fortress Press, 1992. 0-8006-2542-2. Also Edinburgh: T & T Clark, 1992. 0-567-09509-6 (hc); 0-567-29509-5 (pbk).

Hermann Strack (1848-1922) published his original *Einleitung* in 1887. This is the English translation of the seventh edition of 1982. It provides literary and historical introductions to the Mishnah, Tosefta, Palestinian and Babylonian Talmuds and the major Midrashic works of the Talmudic period. A highly regarded, comprehensive and up-to-date bibliographical study of Rabbinic literature.

148. Neusner, Jacob. *Introduction to Rabbinic literature.* (The Anchor Bible reference library). New York: Doubleday, 1994. 0-385-47093-2.

The author is a pre-eminent authority on Judaism in the first centuries of the Christian era. He explores the formative age of Rabbinic literature, describes the documents and their location and advises on their interpretation. The Mishnah, the Tosefta, the Talmuds of the Land of Israel and of Babylonia, the Midrash compilations are all covered. Attention is paid to the literature of the rabbis as it pertains to the Hebrew Scriptures and to Christianity. A definitive guide.

The Mishnah

A six-part collection of oral Rabbinic laws and learning which were codified in the first decades of the third century CE. The Mishnah (learning with regard to the law) and the Gemara (discussion or commentary) provided the structure and rabbinical commentary for the Talmud (see below). The standard English translation is:

149. Danby, H. *The Mishnah: translated from the Hebrew with introduction and brief explanatory notes.* Oxford University Press, 1933 (often reprinted). 0-19-815402-X.

A widely-used, reliable translation in fluent English. Contains explanatory notes. A recent and more literal translation is:

150. Neusner, Jacob. *The Mishnah: a new translation.* New Haven, CT: Yale University Press, 1988. 0-300-03065-7.

As close to a 'literal rendition of the Hebrew as possible in American English' (Preface). There is a glossary of terms and a detailed subject index.

The Talmud

The Talmud comprises the Mishnah and the Gemara, oral law and commentary, and so furnishes the most influential body of Jewish teaching, tradition and interpretation.

There are two quite dissimilar versions of the Talmud. The Talmud of the Land of Israel (c. 400 CE), known also as the Palestinian Talmud (or in Hebrew, Yerushalmi-Jerusalemite) was left unfinished. The much longer Talmud of Babylonia (or in Hebrew, Bavli) (c. 600 CE) is regarded as the authoritative document. After the Hebrew Scriptures, the Talmud is regarded as the most formative influence on Jewish life and devotion.

Palestinian

151. *Talmud of the Land of Israel: a preliminary translation and explanation.* Edited by Jacob Neusner et al. 35 vols. Chicago: University of Chicago Press, 1984-1993.

To date the only complete translation into any European language of the Palestinian Talmud. Translations are by various scholars who view their work as 'preliminary', given that the state of scholarship on *Talmud Yerushalmi* texts is regarded as still being at an early stage.

Babylonian

152. *The Babylonian Talmud: translated into English with notes.* Edited by Isidor Epstein. 35 vols. London: Soncino, 1935-1952. (Republished in 18 volumes in 1948.)

The first translation of the complete Talmud into English. Another translation, based on the principles of form analysis, is:

153. *The Talmud of Babylonia: an American translation.* Translated by Jacob Neusner. 75 vols. (Brown Judaic studies). Missoula, Chico, then Atlanta, GA: Scholars Press, 1984-1993.

Commentary

154. *The Talmud: the Steinsaltz edition.* Commentary by Adin Steinsaltz. Vol. 1: *Tractate Bava Metzia*, part 1- . New York: Random House, 1989- .

Each volume in the series offers a double translation of the Babylonian Talmud, a literal and an expanded translation, with commentary, notes and accounts of legal decisions reached by the Rabbis. The commentary of Rashi, which accompanies all editions of the Talmud, is printed but not translated. A beautifully produced work. Those engaged in Talmudic studies will need to consult this edition. Note the following companion volume:

155. Steinsaltz, Adin. *The Talmud: the Steinsaltz edition: a reference guide.* New York: Random House, 1989. 0-394-57665-9.

Designed as a companion to the Steinsaltz edition of the Babylonian Talmud (see above), this volume provides essential guidelines for its use and understanding. It covers the historical background, structure, language, meaning and logic of the text. There is a glossary of terms, a key to abbreviations and a general index. Perspectives conform generally to those held in certain sections of current Orthodox Judaism.

MIDRASH

The Hebrew root means 'to inquire' and refers to the interpretation or study of Scripture. The large body of midrashic material reflects the hermeneutical positions taken by the ancient and medieval Rabbinic schools. There are numerous translations of Midrash-compilations but the following first complete English translation of the popular *Midrash Rabbah* (fifth century) remains useful.

156. *Midrash Rabbah.* Edited by Harry Freedman and Maurice Simon. 10 volumes. London: Soncino, 1939.

The first nine volumes contain a translation of the Great Midrash on the Pentateuch and on Lamentations, Ruth and Ecclesiastes, Esther and Song of Songs. The final volume contains a glossary, a general index and indexes to Scriptural and Talmudic references.

157. Neusner, Jacob. *The Midrash reader.* Minneapolis, MN: Fortress Press, 1990. 0-8006-2433-5.

There are two introductory essays on reasons for studying Midrash and the creation of this literature. Then follow 'the principal documents that comprise Midrash-exegesis and show how Midrash works in philosophy, theology, and morality' (Prologue, P. 1). The author supplies introductions and commentary on the selected texts. There is a bibliography, general index and an index of biblical and Talmudic references. An accessible and authoritative tool for those beginning studies in this area.

Neusner has written several works on the Midrash. A general introduction to the subject is his, *What is Midrash* (Minneapolis, MN: Fortress Press, 1987. 0-8006-0472-5).

THE SAMARITANS

The animosity between the Jews and the Samaritans is proverbial. In recent years, however, there has been a revival of interest in this religious community, its history, faith and external relationships, for example with Islam. Contemporary research on the Samaritans has been informed considerably by the contributions of Alan D. Crown who edited the massive volume, *The Samaritans* (Tübingen: Mohr, 1989). Crown is also responsible for the following two reference works.

Guides

158. *A Companion to Samaritan studies.* Edited by Alan D. Crown et al. Tübingen: Mohr, 1993. 3-16-145666-1.

An encyclopedic dictionary with entries by leading authorities. Arranged alphabetically, the entries, many with bibliographies, cover the history, practices, beliefs, law, art and culture of the Samaritans. The work complements *The Samaritans* (1989) (see above), but also stands in its own right as a guide to contemporary scholarship.

Bibliographies

159. Crown, Alan David. *A bibliography of the Samaritans.* 2nd. edn. (ATLA bibliography series, 32). Metuchen, NJ: American Theological Library Association and The Scarecrow Press, 1993. 0-8108-2646-1.

Revises and updates the version published in 1984 and makes more extensive reference to the connections between New Testament scholarship and Samaritan studies. A single sequence, arranged alphabetically by author, covers all aspects of the subject. The subject index, however, has its own key (pp. 301-307), and there is a short-title index.

MODERN PERIOD

GENERAL

Bibliographies

160. Edelheit, Abraham J. and Hershel Edelheit. *The Jewish world in modern times: a selected, annotated bibliography.* Boulder, CO: Westview Press, 1988. 0-8133-0572-1. Also London: Mansell, 1988. 0-7201-1988-X.

Entries in Part 1 deal with the Jewish world as a whole. In Part 2 the focus is upon individual Jewish communities and this section is organised by geographical regions which include Australia (16 entries) and New Zealand (1 entry). Annotations are both descriptive and critical. There is a glossary and three indexes - author, title and subject. The editors are authorities on the literature of the Holocaust which comprises a major chapter of this work. They also compiled *Bibliography on Holocaust literature* (Boulder CO: Westview Press, 1986).

THE HOLOCAUST

Bibliographies

161. Cargas, Harry J. *The Holocaust: an annotated bibliography*. 2nd edn. Chicago: American Library Association, 1985. 0-8389-0433-5.

Divided into sections which detail the history of the Jews from the rise of Nazism and reflect descriptions of the Holocaust in the arts and literature. The 500 entries are annotated both descriptively and critically. There are indexes to regions, concentration camps, and an author-title index.

See also Edelheit, Abraham J. *The Jewish world in modern times: a selected annotated bibliography* [160].

Encyclopedias

162. *Encyclopedia of the Holocaust*. Edited by Israel Gutman. 4 volumes. New York: Macmillan, 1990. 0-02-896090-4.

Entries describe the history, impact and implications of the Jewish Holocaust from 1933 to 1945. Articles are followed by bibliographies and there is also a glossary, and chronology. Appendixes include a history of Jewish organisations in Germany from 1893 to 1943, the trials of war criminals and estimated Jewish deaths, by country. The work is illustrated and there are maps. Clearly a major resource.

JUDAISM IN AUSTRALIA

A recent work, by a well-known authority, could function as a reference resource:

163. Rubinstein, W. D. *Judaism in Australia*. (Religious community profiles). Canberra: Australian Government Publishing Service, 1995. 0-644-35789-4.

The author describes the beliefs and history of the Jewish people and then examines the contemporary Jewish community in Australia in the light of data in the 1991 Census and other recent research. The work covers relevant social and religious issues. There are tables and figures, a glossary of terms and an annotated bibliography. A succinct but authoritative survey.

THE JEWISH-CHRISTIAN DIALOGUE

The Jews look back on some 4000 years of history and know only too well that, for half of that time, they have been accompanied by Christians. Only in recent years has there been reasonable dialogue between the two communities of faith. Dan Cohn-Sherbok, in his preface to *A dictionary of Judaism and Christianity* [167], suggests two reasons. The first is the collaborative work on the background to the New Testament which has 'broadened the Jewish and Christian understanding of their own religious inheritance'. The second relates to the friendships which have developed among scholars on a personal and associational basis.

Bibliographies

164. Shermis, Michael. *Jewish-Christian relations: an annotated bibliography and resource guide*. Bloomington, IN: Indiana University Press, 1988. 0-253-33153-6.

An introductory essay on 'educational aspects' of the dialogue is followed by an annotated bibliography covering all periods and issues and including all types of materials. Syllabi from various American universities and seminaries are presented as possible resources for those teaching in this field. Well indexed.

165. *In our time: the flowering of Jewish-Catholic dialogue*. Edited by Eugene J. Fisher and Leon Klenicki. New York: Paulist Press, 1990. 0-8091-3196-X.

Note the extensive bibliographic essay, Section 5: 'A new maturity in Christian-Jewish dialogue.', pp. 107-161. Includes works published between 1975 and 1989.

166. Anderson, Robert. 'Jewish-Christian relations: an annotated bibliography.' In *Pathways to understanding: a handbook on Christian-Jewish relations*. Edited by Marianne Dacy. Melbourne: Victorian Council of Churches, 1994. 0-85821-132-7. Pages 149-161.

This bibliography covers collections of church statements, general introductions, historical studies, Jewish approaches, New Testament studies and the historical Jesus, Christology, antisemitism, the Holocaust and the Land of Israel. Items are graded as introductory, of use to preachers and teachers, and more specialist. The annotations are most informative.

Robert Anderson has also contributed an annotated bibliography in *Rightly dividing the Word of Truth* [170].

Note: the above item, *Pathways to understanding*, is a set of essays contributed by Australian scholars - Jewish, Catholic and Protestant. It is published by the Victorian Council of Churches Working Group on Christian-Jewish Relations.

The address of the Victorian Council of Churches is Causeway House (4th Floor), 306 Little Collins Street, Melbourne, Victoria 3000.

Dictionaries

167. Cohn-Sherbok, Dan. *A Dictionary of Judaism and Christianity*. London: SPCK, 1991. 0-281-04538-0.

A Rabbi explains and compares the key concepts, beliefs and practices of Judaism and Christianity. Designed for the general reader, it is an objective and accurate work providing students with vital information about the differences and parallels between the two religious traditions. An invaluable, introductory resource.

168. *A Dictionary of the Jewish-Christian dialogue*. Edited by Leon Klenicki and Geoffrey Wigoder. New York: Paulist Press, 1984. 0-8091-2590-0.

Jewish and Christian scholars collaborated to produce this book of paired essays on major religious and theological topics ranging from 'Afterlife' and 'Antisemitism' to 'Tradition' and 'Universalism'. Index to Hebrew terms and meanings and to subjects. Most helpful for pointing up agreements and decisive differences between the two faiths.

The important German reference work in this area is:

169. Petuchowski, Jakob J. and Clemens Thoma. *Lexikon der Jüdisch-Christlichen Begegnung*. Freiburg: Herder, 1989. 3-451-21245-5.

Two internationally-known scholars who teach in the areas of Jewish-Christian relations, biblical studies and Judaism contribute long entries which deal with concepts from 'Abendmahl/Seder' to 'Zionism'. Where applicable, varying perspectives are detailed, or the Jewish contextuality for certain Christian teaching, for example on the incarnation, is described. There is an interesting listing of those persons, throughout history, who are relevant to the dialogue. The work is well supported bibliographically and is comprehensively indexed.

Guidelines

170. *Rightly dividing the Word of truth: guidelines for Christian clergy and teachers in their use of the New testament with reference to the New Testament's presentation of Jews and Judaism*. Kew, Vic.: Council of Christian and Jews (Victoria) Inc., 1995.

In this document, a committee of the Council has sought to identify and interpret passages in the New Testament which 'are capable of provoking feelings of hostility towards Jews' (Introduction). Passages include those on the trial and death of Jesus, the 'new' and the 'old', the depiction of the Pharisees, the expression 'the Jews' in the Fourth Gospel, and Jesus, Judaism and the Torah. An appendix describes what happened to Judaism in the first and second century and there is an annotated bibliography. The whole of this brief work reflects careful research and understanding.

The address of the Council is 'Shalom' Centre, 179 Cotham Road, Kew, Victoria 3101.

4

Christianity: Church history

Information sources on Christianity are divided into two chapters. This chapter covers the long history of Christianity from its beginnings to modern times and includes material on its missionary enterprises and the ecumenical movement. Chapter 5 focuses on the Christian denominations and on the churches in various countries.

Historians must needs be familiar with a range of general resources which assist with the retrieval of historical information. For example, the encyclopedic and biographical sources, described in Part 1, are likely to form part of their equipment. The present chapter, however, begins with tools designed specifically for historical studies. Church historians must be aware of the types of resources available as well as particular titles.

Resources for historical research   **64**

    Guides, bibliographies
    Oral history
    Historiography
    Chronologies, tables
    Perpetual calendars

History of Christianity   **66**

    Bibliographies
    Guides
    Research methodology
    Dictionaries and encyclopedias
    Documents
    Atlases
Creeds and councils   68
Saints and saints' days   69
Feminism and the role of women in the churches   70
    Bibliographies
    Dictionaries
Heresies   71
    Encyclopedias

Patristic period   **71**

    Bibliographies, guides and indexes
    Surveys
    Dictionaries and encyclopedias

Atlases

Patrology   74
Guides
Early texts
Collections of sources
Databases

Augustine   78
Bibliographies
Lexicon

Medieval and Renaissance   78
Guides
Dictionaries and encyclopedias
Atlases
Biographies

Religious orders   80
Learning and literature   80
Thomas Aquinas   80
Bibliographies
Thomas More   81
Guides

The Church and its Reformation   81
Guides and bibliographies
Encyclopedias

The Reformation in England   83
Bibliographies
Documents

Reformers   84
Bibliographies in series
Luther and Lutheranism   84
Bibliographies
Indexes
Concordances

Calvin   85
Bibliographies

The Enlightenment and modern periods   85
Surveys
Dictionaries and encyclopedias

Evangelicalism   86
Biographies

Missions   86
Bibliographies
Dictionaries
Directories and histories
Biographies

The Oxford Movement   88
Bibliographies

The ecumenical movement   89
        Guides and bibliographies
        Dictionaries
        Biographies
World Council of Churches   90
        Yearbooks
        Documents
        Indexes
Ecumenism in Australia   91
        Histories
        Documents

RESOURCES FOR HISTORICAL RESEARCH

Guides, bibliographies

171. *The American Historical Association's guide to historical literature.* 3rd edn. Edited by Mary Beth Norton and Pamela Gerardi. 2 vols. New York: Oxford University Press, 1995. 0-19-505727-9 (2-vol. set).

The Association's purpose is that which informed the earlier editions of 1931 and 1961, namely 'the selection and listing, with appropriate commentary, of the finest and most useful books and articles available in every field of historical scholarship' (Introduction, p. xi). The classified arrangement begins with a section on theory and practice in historical study and then proceeds along regional, national and chronological lines. Each field is introduced and then follow the citations which include descriptive/critical annotations. The Melbourne historian, Stuart Macintyre, is responsible for the section, 'Australasia and Oceania' (pp. 1526-1546) which includes some 383 entries. Although there are no specific sections on religious or church-history, the subject index indicates reasonable coverage. No other single work offers such an inventory of recent historical scholarship.

172. Fritze, Ronald H. et al. *Reference sources in history: an introductory guide.* Santa Barbara, CA: ABC-CLIO, 1990. 0-87436-164-8 (hc); 0-87436-679-8 (pbk).

Organises, describes and evaluates the major reference works for all periods of history and for all geographical areas. Arranged by types of resources (guides, bibliographies, indexes, encyclopedias) which are then subdivided geographically. The interests of biblical and church history are well served.

173. Slavens, Thomas P. *Sources of information for historical research.* New York: Neal-Schuman, 1994. 1-55570-093-4.

Well-annotated entries cover general history and then the history of all continents. There are also sections on the holdings of archives, on chronologies and other auxiliaries such as heraldry, genealogy and biography. Although somewhat limited and outdated on Oceania, this tool is generally useful in pointing up resources for the study of particular countries. Entries are arranged by Library of Congress classification with both a subject and an author/title index.

174. *Teaching bibliographic skills in history: a sourcebook for historians and librarians.* Edited by Charles A. D'Aniello. Westport, CT: Greenwood Press, 1993. 0-313-25266-1.

Chapters on the study of history, bibliographic instruction, special topics and an annotated bibliography on the methods and materials of historical research. Although the space given to philosophy and religion is limited, the cumulative value of this resource for historical studies is high indeed.

An important annual bibliographic survey is:

175. *Annual bulletin of historical literature.* Oxford: Basil Blackwell for the Historical Association of London, 1910- .

Provides selective and critical analysis of historical books, journals and articles. Covers historical periods and countries. There is a separate section for 'The Middle

East, Asia, Australia, New Zealand, and the Pacific Islands'. Chapters are subdivided by types of material, historiographical interests and types of history including 'Religious history'.

Oral history

Oral history is a spoken account of happenings by a person who has witnessed or somehow been involved in those events. The importance of this form of recording is that it may provide the only opportunity for a person to add to the historical record, indeed to provide unique information. It is a method which one could use, for example, in collecting data for the history of a local church.

176. Bolton, Alexander. *Interviewing for oral history at the National Library of Australia.* Canberra: National Library of Australia, 1994. 0-313-25266-1.

   This brief guide to the recording of oral history at the National Library of Australia will assist others working in this field of documentation. Bolton's identification of the key steps and techniques involved in the construction and conduct of interviews reveals his awareness of the need for sensitivity and discretion. A splendid, how-to resource for history students.

Historiography

177. *The Blackwell dictionary of historians.* Edited by John Cannon et al. New York: Blackwell Reference, 1988. 0-631-14708-X.

   Includes some 450 biographical entries (Eusebius, Bede and Migne are there), but also essays on various types of history (oral history, social history), articles on terms (historicism, positivism), historiography of particular countries (Australian, New Zealand) and of institutions and movements (feminist historiography). Very helpful for definitions and contextual work. The index is essential for pointing to numerous references for the study of 'ecclesiastical historiography'.

Chronologies, tables

178. Steinberg, S. H. *Historical tables, 58 BC-AD 1990.* 12th edn., updated by John Paxton. London: Macmillan, 1991. 0-333-56661-0.

   A listing of events and their dates in columns which allows comparisons and contextual conclusions. Ecclesiastical history, for example, is featured from the beginning of the ninth century until the middle of the seventeenth and can be correlated with constitutional and economic history and cultural life. This edition has an index to major events.

Perpetual calendars

   Perpetual calendars for the Julian and Gregorian systems correlate the date and day of the week in a given year. They help answer the following sort of question, 'On what day of the week did 1 April fall in 1928?' Such calendars can be found in a number of sources, particularly in almanacs such as *Whitaker's almanack* (London: Whitaker) and *The World almanac and book of facts* (New York: Funk & Wagnalls) or encyclopedias, for example under ' Perpetual calendar' in *Encyclopedia Britannica* (*Micropedia*).

HISTORY OF CHRISTIANITY

Bibliographies

The bibliographies and guides to the literature of religion cited in Part 1 contain a mass of material on the history of Christianity. The most extensive and intensive resource is G. E. and Lyn Gorman, *Theological and religious reference materials. Volume 2: Systematic theology and Church history* [7].

See also 'Bibliography: selected aids to the study of church history and historical theology'. In James E. Bradley and Richard A. Muller, *Church history* [182], pp. 167-214.

Another useful annotated guide to reading in church history is in *The Oxford illustrated history of Christianity* [180], pp. 667-685.

179. *Revue d'histoire ecclésiastique.* 'Bibliographie.' Louvain: Université Catholique de Louvain, 1900 - . 3/yr.

Now issued as an independently paged section of the *Revue*. The most comprehensive bibliography of church history from New Testament times to the present. *RHE* indexes journals, books and other sources. Coverage is international; emphasis, however, is on European history and the Catholic church.

Note: There is no other indexing service devoted to church history in particular. For indexes to periodical literature on historical topics, see *Religion index one* [35], *Religion index two* [38], and the *Catholic periodical and literature index* [34], all cited in Part 1.

Guides

180. *The Oxford illustrated history of Christianity.* Edited by John McManners. Oxford University Press, 1990. 0-19-822928-3. Also issued in paperback, without illustrations, as *The Oxford history of Christianity.* Oxford University Press, 1993.0-19-285291-4.

Essays by a team of eminent scholars span 2000 years and reflect recent research. The work is divided into three sections: 'From the origins to 1800', 'Christianity since 1800', and 'Christianity today and tomorrow'. The text, illustrations, bibliography, chronology, maps and index combine to make this a most authoritative reference resource.

181. Chadwick, Owen. *A history of Christianity.* London: Weidenfeld & Nicolson, 1995. 0-297-81577-6.

This recent work by an eminent church historian explores the history of Christian faith from the perspective of a people's religion - 'how the presentation of the gospel affected ordinary men and women, a majority of whom were illiterate; and in affecting them, whether the axioms about the world which they already took for granted could affect the nature of their faith' (Introduction, p. 9). With this selective historiography the work covers the whole span of church history. It is lucidly written and lavishly illustrated.

Research methodology

182. Bradley, James E. and Richard A. Muller. *Church history: an introduction to research, reference works and methods.* Grand Rapids, MI: Eerdmans, 1995. 0-8028-0826-3 (pbk).

A lucid introduction to research methodologies in the fields of church history and historical theology. There are chapters on research and the proper use of primary sources, text databases and materials in microform, and on the craft of writing history. Concludes with an extensive, briefly annotated bibliography of resources for the task. An important appendix, devoted to computer applications, lists and annotates relevant network databases, online public access catalogues and projects and databases on CD-ROM. There is also a section on materials in microform. This experienced guide to theory and practice is directed to the advanced history student. It could also prove of value to the professional church historian.

Dictionaries and encyclopedias

183. *Dictionnaire d'histoire et de géographie ecclésiastiques.* Paris: Letouzey & Ané, 1912- .

A most comprehensive, scholarly resource on church history covers the Roman Catholic Church from its beginnings and other churches as they relate to the Catholic Church. After some eighty-two years and twenty-four volumes the project has reached the letter 'I' in 1995; surely an indication of its intensity.

184. *The Oxford dictionary of the Christian church.* Edited by E. A. Livingstone and F. L. Cross. 2nd rev. edn. Oxford University Press, 1983. 0-19-211545-6.

For many years the standard English language reference work for church history. Particular emphasis is on Western Europe, especially Great Britain, and on Anglican and Catholic churches. Valuable for bibliographic coverage of both primary and secondary sources.

Thematic

The following specialised dictionary provides a guide to Christian themes which have inspired artists, musicians and writers.

185. Metford, J. C. J. *Dictionary of Christian lore and legend.* New edn. London: Thames and Hudson, 1986. 0-500-27373-1.

In over 1700 entries the author details Christian lore (the learning and background knowledge which underpins Christian culture) and legend (the historical, traditional or symbolic content of Christianity) which have informed artistic endeavour across the years. Historical events, traditions, biblical figures, saints, sacred vessels, liturgical terms, symbols, 'animals, vegetables and minerals' are all here. The work is well illustrated. Its comprehensive coverage of the unusual makes it a valuable resource.

Documents

186. *Documents of the Christian church.* Edited by Henry Bettenson. 2nd rev. edn. Oxford University Press, 1967. 0-19-283006-6 (pbk).

First published 1943. Introductory collection of primary sources covering the whole history of the church. 'In general it has been thought of more value to give a few documents at some length rather than a multitude of scraps . . .' (Prefatory note). Name and subject index.

Atlases

187. *Atlas of the Christian church.* Edited by Henry Chadwick and G. R. Evans. London: Macmillan, 1987. 0-333-44157-5.

Exceptional quality with detailed maps, well-chosen illustrations and an authoritative commentary.

188. *Atlas zur Kirchengeschichte: die christlichen Kirchen in Geschichte und Gegenwart.* Edited by Hubert Jedin et al. 3rd edn. Freiburg: Herder, 1988. 3-451-20869-5.

First published 1970, this outstanding atlas of church history has been extensively revised and expanded. Those with little German should still be able to profit from the maps and charts.

CREEDS AND COUNCILS

189. Schaff, Philip. *The creeds of Christendom: with a history and critical notes.* 3 vols. Grand Rapids, MI: Baker Book House, 1977 (reprint of 1931 edition). Various reprintings and revisions, sometimes with main title: *Bibliotheca symbolica ecclesiae universalis.*

First edition 1877. Contents: Vol. 1, The history of the creeds; vol. 2, the Greek and Latin creeds, with translations; vol. 3, the Evangelical Protestant creeds, with translations.

The commentary sometimes reflects the Protestant perspectives of this well-known nineteenth-century historian, but the set is still useful for its comprehensive collection of documents and translations.

The following source publishes the texts of the twenty-one ecumenical councils as recognised by the Catholic church, beginning with Nicaea I and concluding with Vatican II.

190. *Decrees of the ecumenical councils.* Edited by Norman P. Tanner. 2 vols. London: Sheed & Ward, 1990. 0-7220-3010-X (set); Washington, DC: Georgetown University Press, 1990. 0-87840-490-2 (set).

Contents: Volume 1, Nicaea I to Lateran V; volume 2, Trent to Vatican II.

The text of the decrees of the ecumenical councils of the Catholic Church appears in Latin or Greek with an English translation. There are ten valuable indexes in volume 2: chronological, biblical passages, councils, magisterium, fathers and the early church, canon law, liturgical books, proper names, authors, subjects. This is the best translation of this material available.

SAINTS AND SAINTS' DAYS

Still essential is:

191. Butler, Alban. *Lives of the saints.* Complete edn, edited, revised and
supplemented by Herbert Thurston and Donald Attwater. 4 vols.
New York: P. J. Kenedy, 1956.
Reprinted Westminster, MD: Christian Classics, 1981, 0-87061-
045-7 (set); 0-87061-137-2 (pbk).

Butler's *Lives*, first published 1756-1759, has been thoroughly revised and
expanded. Arrangement is by feast day. Indexes to each volume and a general
index in volume four.

192. *The Book of saints: a dictionary of servants of God canonized by the
Catholic Church.* Compiled by the Benedictine monks of St
Augustine's Abbey, Ramsgate. 6th edn. London: A & C Black,
1989. 0-7136-3006-X.

This edition, which reflects changes in the Roman Calendar promulgated in 1969,
covers over 10,000 saints, including modern ones. The work is noted for its scholarship and accuracy. Illustrated and with a correlated index of emblems. Also a list
of patron saints.

193. Farmer, David Hugh. *The Oxford dictionary of saints.* 2nd edn. Oxford
University Press, 1987. 0-19-869149-1 (hc); 0-19-282038-9
(pbk).

Accounts of 1,100 saints who lived or died or who have been venerated in Great
Britain and Ireland. Includes also a selection of other well-known saints. Succinct
articles contain primary and secondary sources and bibliographies. Appendixes list
unsuccessful English candidates for canonisation, patron saints, iconographical
emblems, associated places and a calendar of feasts. Useful, particularly for the
obscure.

194. Duchet-Suchaux, G. and M. Pastoureau. *The Bible and the saints.* Paris,
New York: Flammarion, 1994. 2-08013-564-3.

An art historian together with a professor at the Sorbonne have produced this
well-illustrated volume which identifies over five hundred Christian saints as well
as certain biblical characters and provides concise definitions of the attributes by
which they are known in Western and Byzantine art. The array of visual material
and extensive cross-referencing make this work as attractive as it is useful.

Dictionaries of saints are likely to have a calendar of the principal feasts of saints,
for example, David Farmer, *The Oxford dictionary of the saints* [193].
A resource which is arranged by saints' days is:

195. Bentley, James. *A calendar of saints: the lives of the principal saints of
the Christian year.* London: Orbis/Macdonald, 1986. 0-85613-
781-2. (Reprinted London: Popular Press/ Macdonald, 1990.
0-356-13781-2.)

A selection of saints and their special days assembled by a well-known English
historian. The work comprises lively biographies, with quotations from the saints,
and lavish illustrations, with more than three hundred paintings, mostly in colour.

The index of saints provides the necessary finding device. A good source for introductory material and particularly for a rich gallery of portraits.

Feminism and The Role of Women in The Churches

Bibliographies

196. Finson, Shelley Davis. *Women and religion: a bibliographic guide to Christian feminist liberation theology.* Toronto: University of Toronto Press, 1991. 0-8020-5881-7.

Bibliographic coverage of women in Christian churches, arranged topically under the following headings - Bible, history, Judaism, languages, Mariology, ministry, pastoral care, religion and the church, spirituality, theology and worship. Entries are from books, articles, dissertations and reports published between 1975 and 1988. An appendix lists several bibliographies and certain journals which focus on women and religion. There is an author index.

197. Kadel, Andrew. *Matrology: a bibliography of writings by Christian women from the first to the fifteenth centuries.* New York: Continuum Publishing Company, 1994. 0-8264-0676-9.

Claims to include every Christian woman who wrote before 1500 and to list all of her writings that have appeared in print, in English or in the original language, since 1800. Manuscripts and 'rare books' are not included. Each person-entry begins with a brief description of the author or authors it contains. Then there is a list of English editions, followed by editions in the original languages and then modern editions in languages other than English. Concludes with a bibliography of secondary sources, an index and a chronological index. An essential tool for women's studies and for work on early and medieval Christianity. PS: do not miss the introduction.

Dictionaries. General

The following general item provides definitional and contextual support for women's studies:

198. Humm, Maggie. *The dictionary of feminist theory.* Columbus, OH: Ohio State University Press, 1990. 0-8142-0506-2 (hc); 0-8142-0507-0 (pbk).

The author's intention is to make accessible 'some of the commonest terms and issues in current English-speaking feminism' (Preface p. ix), and to show how feminist theory both challenges, and is shaped by the academy and society. Where appropriate, entries offer varying definitions and so reveal the process of meaning-making. Concludes with an extensive bibliography. This highly-regarded, comprehensive guide to the terminology and history of feminist theory provides a basic guide for all definitional work in this area of studies.

Specialised

199. *Women's studies encyclopedia.* Volume 3: *History, philosophy, and religion.* Edited by Helen Tierney. New York: Greenwood Press, 1991. 0-313-27358-8 (vol. 3).

Lengthy, signed articles, averaging 1,000 to 1,500 words, most including a bibliography, cover the three disciplines. Although the focus is on the United States and Western society, attention has also been paid to women in eastern and southern Asia. The famous philosophers are well-quoted, area studies, including entries on Australia and New Zealand, deal with historical issues, while religion is represented by numerous approaches. The volume reflects a wide variety of feminist approaches and is useful for definitions and contextual information.

See also, Walker, Barbara G. *The women's dictionary of symbols and sacred objects* [614].

HERESIES

Encyclopedias

200. Clifton, Chas S. *Encyclopedia of heresies and heretics*. Santa Barbara, CA: ABC-CLIO, 1992. 0-87436-600-3.

Describes the battles between Christian orthodoxy and heterodoxy from the earliest times to the Reformation by citing material, judged to be heretical, from a primary source where available, or from a reconstructed text. Both heresies (so-called) and heretics, including such freethinkers as Abelard, receive fair treatment. This unusual source is a mine for historical studies.

201. George, Leonard. *Crimes of perception: an encyclopedia of heresies and heretics*. New York: Paragon House, 1995. 1-55778-519-8.

600 detailed entries provide accounts of the history of heresy and the lives of heretics who range from vilified outsiders to revered leaders, teachers, even saints. Three main currents are identified: Christianity, Judaism and the occult traditions. Appended is a listing of the entries arranged by topic and period and an extensive classified bibliography. This attractive, introductory work is useful for definitions and brief profiles.

PATRISTIC PERIOD

The patristic period is commonly thought of as embracing the history of the church from the end of the first century to the close of the eighth. The study of the writings of the church fathers has been a preoccupation of later historians and theologians because this literature constitutes the major source for understanding not only the events of the time but also the formation of Christian doctrine. No period of Christian history is better served with documentary sources and supportive commentary material than this one.

Bibliographies, guides and indexes

202. *Bibliographia patristica: internationale patristische Bibliographie. 1956- .* Berlin/ New York: de Gruyter, 1959- . ISSN 0523-2252.

The most comprehensive bibliography. Lists studies about the church fathers and related historical and theological subjects. Book reviews are included. However, note the delay in publication (vol. 29 for 1984 appeared in 1989). This means that one needs to turn to general periodical indexes and *RHE* [179] for more recent research on the period.

203. Jacobs, Philip Walker. *A guide to the study of Greco-Roman and Jewish and Christian history and literature.* Lanham, MD: University Press of America, 1994. 0-8191-9517-0.

Describes 'the broad context of social and religious development in the Hellenistic world between 200 BCE and 260 CE' (Preface). There are two main sections - a chronological outline of the history and literature of the period is followed by a bibliography of English translations of that literature. There are indexes to the literary titles and to persons. This most practical tool should help, particularly the beginning student, with basic information about dates, persons, groups, movements, events and, of course, the literary sources.

204. Robinson, Thomas A. et al. *The early church: an annotated bibliography of literature in English.* (ATLA Bibliography series, 33). Metuchen, NJ: American Theological Library Association and The Scarecrow Press, 1993. 0-8108-2763-8.

An exceptionally helpful, extensively annotated survey of literature in English on this period. Includes the citing of book reviews. Introductory chapters are dedicated to reference works. A very fine compilation.

A specialised indexing tool for patristic studies is:

205. *Biblia patristica: index des citations et allusions Bibliques dans la littérature patristique.* Paris: Editions du Centre Nationale de la Recherche Scientifique, 1975- . 6 volumes to date, plus a *Supplement* (1982).

A verse by verse index of biblical texts used in the writings of the fathers from the beginnings. Volume 5 (1991) includes Basil of Caesarea, Gregory of Nazianzus, Gregory of Nyssa and Amphilochius. Volume 6 (1995) includes Hilary of Poitiers, Ambrose of Milan and Ambrosiaster. The *Supplement*, published in 1982, was devoted to Philo of Alexandria.

Surveys

206. *Early Christianity: origins and evolution to AD 600.* Edited by Ian Hazlett. London: SPCK, 1991. 0-281-04476-7.

A gathering of essays by leading patristic scholars results in a comprehensive, authoritative survey of the period. Includes bibliographies, a glossary and a conspectus of the history to AD 600. A most useful, accessible compendium.

Dictionaries and encyclopedias

General

207. *A Dictionary of ancient history.* Edited by Graham Speak. Oxford: Blackwell Publishers, 1995. 0-631-18069-9.

Intended as 'a layman's guide to the history of the ancient Greco-Roman world' (Preface), this work provides coverage from 776BCE to CE476. Concise information is presented on major events, institutions, individuals, periods, places and styles. Cross-referencing, an extensive bibliography, maps and genealogies add to its usefulness. Contributors are experts in their fields and the entries are as authoritative as they are lucid. A useful source for early church history.

208. Grant, Michael. *A guide to the ancient world: a dictionary of classical place names.* New York: H. W. Wilson, 1986. 0-8242-0742-4.

Grant's entries on places usually provide more detail than the encyclopedias. Also includes a useful listing of ancient authors with details of their lives and works.

Specialised

209. *Encyclopedia of early Christianity.* Edited by Everett Ferguson et al. New York: Garland, 1990. 0-8240-5745-7.

An authoritative, reliable work on the church from its foundation to about 600 CE. Contributions by specialists include articles on people, places, doctrines, heresies, schisms, liturgy and art. Note the detailed subject index. This volume should be consulted in conjunction with the following, somewhat more extensive work:

210. *Encyclopedia of the early church.* Edited by Angelo Di Berardino. 2 vols. Cambridge, England: James Clarke, 1992. 0-227-67895-8 (set).

Translated from the Italian, with bibliographies supplemented by references to English-language works. More comprehensive than the *Encyclopedia of early Christianity* [209] and with coverage extending to Bede in the West and John Damascene in the East. Note the lists of abbreviations in volume 1 and the sections of maps and illustrations in volume 2. There is a general index. The whole work, with its 150 contributors from many countries, reflects recent scholarship and is a most important research tool.

The major German reference work in this area is:

211. *Reallexikon für Antike und Christentum: Sachwörterbuch zur Auseinandersetzung des Christentums mit der antiken Welt.* Editors vary. Stuttgart: Anton Hiersemann, 1950- (in progress).

An historical account of the project and indexes to subject headings and authors for the first sixteen volumes was published in 1994 as *Das Reallexikon für Antike und Christentum und das F.J.Dölger-Institut in Bonn: mit Registern der Stichwörter A bis Ianus sowie der Autoren Bände 1-16.* Edited by Ernst Dassmann. Stuttgart: Hiersemann.

Publication began in 1950 and with volume 16 (1994) had reached the letter 'I'. Long, signed articles by authorities deal with the classical world and its relationship to Christianity up to the sixth century AD. Note that indexing for the first sixteen volumes is available, as mentioned in the supplementary title above.

212. *The Coptic encyclopedia.* Edited by Aziz S. Atiya. 8 vols. New York: Macmillan, 1991. 0-02-897025-X (set).

Through to the fourth century the Coptic church was intrinsically bound up with the rest of Christianity and its famed catechetical school at Alexandria functioned as a leading theological centre. Some 2,800 entries describe the history of the Copts, their ancient church in Egypt and their survival. Volume 8 contains maps, an appendix on linguistics and a well-crafted index to the set. Particularly valuable for material on Coptic saints and church leaders, their theological perspectives and accents, their monasteries and councils.

213. *The Oxford dictionary of Byzantium.* Edited by Alexander P. Kazhdan et al. 3 vols. New York: Oxford University Press, 1991. 0-19-504652-8.

Covers all aspects of Byzantine civilisation from the foundations of Constantinople in AD 325 to its capture by the Turks in 1453. Christianity permeated much of the history and culture of this period and so the text reflects religious events, personalities, doctrines and schisms. The Eastern churches are well represented along with their saints, patriarchs, liturgies, councils and several art forms. This set comprises a most accessible resource for information about the churches in the Byzantine empire.

214. Nicol, Donald M. *A biographical dictionary of the Byzantine Empire.* London: Seaby, 1991. 1-85264-048-0.

The author, an authority on the Byzantine world, provides succinct accounts of persons of note and influence in the Empire from 300 to 1453. Along with the secular leaders and teachers of Constantinople are the patriarchs and theologians of the church. A learned, attractive guide.

Atlases

In addition to the sections on the patristic period in the comprehensive atlases, cited earlier in this chapter, the following two works are particularly relevant.

215. Meer, Frederic van der and Christine Mohrmann. *Atlas of the early Christian world.* Edited by Mary F. Hedlund and H. H. Rowley. London: Nelson, 1958.

Not superseded after some forty years. Brilliant mapping, very fine plates illustrating the spread of Christianity from the first to the eighth centuries and a commentary on this history.

216. Cornell, Tim and John Matthews. *Atlas of the Roman world.* New York: Facts on File, 1982. 0-87196-652-2.

Provides a comprehensive view of the Roman world in its physical and cultural setting over some 1300 years. The Christianisation of the Empire after Constantine receives special attention. Brilliant combination of text, maps, photographs and drawings. Well indexed.

PATROLOGY

Patrology is the study of the writings of the church fathers while, in at least one title, the word, 'matrology', has been coined to describe the study of the writings of women.

Guides

In 1986, a fourth and final volume was translated from the Italian (1978) and added to the following well-known patrology:

217. Quasten, Johannes. *Patrology.* 4 vols. Vols 1-3 reprinted Westminster, MD: Christian Classics, 1983. Vol. 4, edited by Angelo Di Berardino, was published 1986.

Vol. 1. Beginnings of patristic literature; vol. 2. Ante-Nicene literature after Irenaeus; vol. 3. Golden age of Greek patristic literature from the Council of

Nicaea to the Council of Chalcedon; vol 4. Golden age of Latin patristic literature from the Council of Nicaea to the Council of Chalcedon.

Remains an essential, scholarly guide to authors, texts and available translations.

218. Ramsey, Boniface. *Beginning to read the fathers.* New York: Paulist Press, 1985. 0-8091-2691-5.

A non-technical introduction to patristic writings and a discussion of particular themes. Note the section, 'A patristic reading program' (pp. 229-237).

Early texts

219. *New documents illustrating early Christianity.* Vol. 1- , 1981- . Editors vary. Ancient History Documentary Research Centre, Macquarie University, NSW, 1981- . Published irregularly. Volume 7 appeared in 1995.

This series reviews and reproduces newly discovered Greek inscriptions and papyri which have been published in recent years. The texts are accompanied by translations, philological notes and commentary. Depending upon the texts included in a volume, there are indexes to Hebrew, Greek and Latin words, to subjects, Greek, Latin and Jewish writers and to the texts in the corpora. There may also be indexes to Hebrew and New Testament literature. An important contribution to knowledge about the historical and social milieu of the early Christians.

Collections of sources

In listing the major source collections of patristic documents it may be useful to include series which have concluded as well as those in progress.

There are certain series which reflect particular themes, for example *Classics of western spirituality* [593], and these are cited within the relevant subject chapters.

Original languages

220. Migne, Jacques Paul. Patrologiae cursus completus . . . Series Graeca (PG). 161 vols. in 166. Paris: Migne, 1857-1866.

Migne, Jacques Paul. Patrologie cursus completus. . . Series Latina (PL). 221 vols. Paris: Migne, 1844-1880.

(Supplemental volumes and indexes were added by later hands.)

Migne is still the most comprehensive collection. PG has texts dating from the earliest Christian writings times to the ninth century; PL from the earliest times to the death of Innocent III in 1216. Texts in PG are in both Latin and Greek, in parallel columns. Criticised for its occasional dependence on uncritical editions and for typographical errors. Both sets, but particularly PL, are well-endowed with subject indexes.

Chadwyck-Healy of Cambridge, England is publishing the full text and apparatus of Patrologia Latina on CD-ROM and also on magnetic tape. Clearly this software will enable scholars to do word-searches, construct concordances, identify elusive phrases, trace biblical references, and all this with speed and accuracy.

The following series is designed to replace Migne by presenting the best critical texts available.

221. Corpus christianorum: Series graeca. Turnout, Brepols, 1977- .
     Corpus christianorum: Series latina. Turnhout, Brepols, 1953- .
     Corpus christianorum: Series apocryphorum. Turnhout, Brepols, 1983- .
     Corpus christianorum: Continuatio Mediaevalis, 1966- .

     Other Brepols' series provide concordances to selected texts and other lexicological resources. The publishers distribute an annual catalogue plus seasonal issues which provide full details of these series and of forthcoming titles.

222. Sources chrétiennes. Paris, Editions du Cerf, 1942- .

     Excellent introductions; the texts are accompanied by translations into French. There are scholarly notes and indexes.

Collections in English

223. Ancient Christian writers series 1946- . Editors vary. Formerly Newman
     Press (Westminster, MD), now being published by Paulist Press
     (New York and Mahwah, NJ).

     Includes more scholarly apparatus than *The fathers of the church* [225]. Introductions, extensive notes and bibliographies.

224. Ante-Nicene Christian library: translations of the fathers down to AD
     325. Edited by Alexander Roberts and James Donaldson. 24 vols.
     Edinburgh: T & T Clark, 1867-1872. The American edition of this
     series is titled, *Ante-Nicene fathers*. Reprinted by Eerdmans
     (Grand Rapids, MI), 1956, and later printings.

     This much-used nineteenth-century set, now betrays a certain datedness. Better texts and translations have emerged but, with its detailed subject indexes to each volume, it is still of value.

225. The Fathers of the church: a new translation. Editors vary. Washington:
     Catholic University of America Press (present publisher), 1947- .

     Translations accompanied by an introduction, scriptural and general index. Not as scholarly a resource as the Ancient Christian writers series (above).

226. Library of Christian classics. Editors vary. 26 vols. London: SCM Press;
     Philadelphia: Westminster Press, 1953-1969.

     Volumes 1-8 cover the patristic period to Augustine, volumes 9-13 the Medieval period and volumes 14-26 the Reformation period. Very good introductions, extensive foot-noting with detailed indexes.

227. Oxford early Christian texts. Edited by Henry Chadwick. Oxford:
     Clarendon Press, 1970- .

     Scholarly introductions reflecting recent research. Provides Greek or Latin text with English translation. Extensive notes on the problems of dating, authorship and editions, as appropriate.

228. A Select library of Nicene and post-Nicene fathers of the Christian
     Church. Edited by Philip Schaff. 1st-2nd series. 28 volumes.
     Oxford: J. H. Parker, 1887-1892 (first series); 1890-1900 (second
     series). Reprinted by Eerdmans (Grand Rapids, MI), 1975, and
     later printings.

First series, 14 vols, is given to the translation of works by Augustine and Chrysostom. Second series, 14 vols, contains various other fathers to Gregory the Great. Comment on the Ante-Nicene Christian library [224] applies.

The following single-volume anthologies, edited by Henry Bettenson, are kept in print and remain most useful.

229. *The Early Christian fathers: selections from the writings of the fathers from St. Clement of Rome to St. Athanasius.* New edn. Oxford University Press, 1969. 0-19-283009-0.

230. *The Later Christian fathers: a selection from the writings of the fathers from St. Cyril of Jerusalem to St. Leo the Great.* New edn. Oxford University Press, 1973. 0-19-283012-0.

The arrangement in both volumes is by subject, which allows one to trace the development of a doctrine.

Recent revisions have been made to the following classic collections:

231. *A New Eusebius: documents illustrating the history of the church to AD337.* 2nd rev. edn. Edited by J. Stevenson. Revised by W. H. C. Frend. London: SPCK, 1987. 0-281-04268-3 (pbk).

232. *Creeds, councils and controversies: documents illustrating the history of the church AD337-461.* Edited by J. Stevenson. Revised, augmented edn. by W. H. C. Frend. London: SPCK, 1989. 0-281-04327-2.

These two volumes of selected documents together illustrate the history of the church from the beginnings to the fifth century. Useful notes, chronologies and indexes.

Databases

The *Thesaurus Linguae Graecae (TLG)* is an ever-expanding computerised databank of Greek literature beginning with Homer in the eighth century BCE. The project, which is centred at the University of California at Irvine, is particularly important to church historians for its coverage of the Greek church fathers and its facility for updating existing patrologies. The following item is a register of the information stored in the *TLG* to 1990.

233. Berkowitz, Luci and Squitier, Karl A. *Thesaurus Linguae Graecae canon of Greek authors and works.* 3rd edn. New York: Oxford University Press, 1990. 0-19-506037-7.

The data is all but complete from Homer to CE 600 and this edition represents also the coverage, to date, of works from 600 to 1453. It comprises the largest bibliography of Greek works available to us. The arrangement is alphabetical by author, or title if anonymous. The entry includes the field of literature, century, location and any cross-referencing. Then follows a list of titles, a citing of the best printed edition, the format, a word count and the item's genre. There are several indexes.

Augustine

Bibliographies

234. Donnelly, Dorothy F. and Mark A. Sherman. *Augustine's De civitate dei: an annotated bibliography of modern criticism, 1960-1990.* New York: Peter Lang, 1991. 0-8204-1607-X.

Includes all studies published in the United States and Canada in monograph, essay, article, introduction and dissertation format. There are sections on earlier works as well as selected foreign studies. The work concludes with a list of the writings by Augustine and a selected general bibliography. In all, a more comprehensive resource than its title suggests.

Lexicon

235. *Augustinus-Lexikon.* Edited by Cornelius Mayer et al. Basel: Schwabe, 1988- . 3-7965-0854-5 (complete work).
Vol. 1: Aaron - Conuersio, issued in fascicles, 1986-1994.

The *Lexikon* provides an extensive and intensive account of Saint Augustine, his world and thought. Introductory material is given in German, English and French and entries are in one of those languages. They cover biblical characters about whom Augustine wrote, major persons associated with him and places of importance. Each of Augustine's works is analysed and related terms defined. Extensive bibliographies. Augustinian scholarship abounds in this major, comprehensive resource.

MEDIEVAL AND RENAISSANCE

We think of the Middle Ages as from roughly 600 to 1500 with the Renaissance overlapping from about 1300. It was a period of great change for the church politically, socially and theologically. The Eastern and Western churches divided, crusades were planned and tried, and the power of the papacy was severely tested. Theology was informed variously by the twelfth-century rediscovery of Aristotelianism, by scholasticism, conciliarism, mysticism, and then by the critical impact of Renaissance humanism.

While there was general allegiance to the church throughout Europe, there were the free spirits who questioned the nature of its authority. The period closes with attempts at reform from within and without the church, so paving the way for the Reformation and for the dramatically different way in which Christianity would present itself to the world.

Guides

236. *The New Cambridge medieval history.* Various editors. Cambridge University Press, 1995- . To be published in seven volumes with Volume 4 being divided into two parts.

The original *Cambridge medieval history* was published between 1911 and 1936, with a new edition of Volume 4 appearing in the 1960s. This replacement set, to be issued from 1995 to 1997, promises a reliable, detailed history from late antiquity to c.1500. The first volume to be published is Volume 2, c. 700- c.900, edited by Rosamond McKitterick (1995)(0-521-36292-X). Doubtless the set will become a standard guide for research on medieval life and thought and, in particular, for studies on church and society.

The following two-volume set is not strictly a reference work but, because of its comprehensiveness, appendixes and indexes, it provides authoritative and accurate information on a host of topics.

237. *Handbook of European history, 1400-1600: Late Middle Ages, Renaissance and Reformation.* Edited by Thomas Brady, Heiko Oberman and James Tracy. 2 vols. Leiden: E. J. Brill, 1994, 1995. 90-04-09762-7 (set).

Vol. 1: Structures and assertions. Vol. 2: Visions, programs and outcomes.

Contributions by forty leading scholars discuss the grand themes, major controversies and recent trajectories in research on this period. Volume 1 deals with the ingredients of everyday life and with the political and ecclesiastical assertions of the time. Volume 2 covers humanism, the Reformation period and the process by which newly established confessional structures began to work their way in the world. The two volumes include maps, tables and figures and are separately indexed.

Dictionaries and encyclopedias

238. *Dictionary of the Middle Ages.* Edited by Joseph R. Strayer. 13 vols. New York: Scribner's, 1982-1989. 0-684-19073-7 (set).

Covers from roughly AD 500 to 1500 and includes lengthy articles as well as short entries on every aspect of medieval life and thought. A superb set and an essential resource for ecclesiastical history.

See also: *The Oxford dictionary of Byzantium* [213], and Nicol, *A biographical dictionary of the Byzantine Empire* [214].

239. *Encyclopedia of the Renaissance.* Edited by Thomas G. Bergin and Jennifer Speake. London: Batsford, 1988. 0-7134-5967-0.

Brief entries on the period from 1300-1620 explore the individuals and movements in all fields of human endeavour. The scope includes the Reformation. There is a bibliography of primary and secondary sources and a chronology.

Atlases

240. *The Atlas of the Crusades.* Edited by Jonathan Riley-Smith. New York: Facts on File; London: Times Books; 1991. 0-7230-0361-0.

Describes, by text and graphics, the crusading movement over some 700 years in Spain, the Baltic, North Africa and within Europe. Maps, plans of cities and other illustrations are accurately and delightfully presented. Includes a detailed chronology, a glossary, bibliography and index.

Biographies

241. *Contemporaries of Erasmus: a biographical register of the Renaissance and Reformation.* Edited by Peter G. Bietenholz. 3 vols. Toronto: University of Toronto Press, 1985-1987. 0-8020-2507-2 (v.1); 0-8020-2571-4 (v.2); 0-8020-2575-7 (v.3).

A companion to the *Collected works of Erasmus* (Toronto University Press, 1974-). Presents whatever biographical information is available for the more than 1900 persons referred to in the *CWE*. Essential, of course, for studies on Erasmus, but also valuable for material about the major and, more especially, the obscure figures of the time.

RELIGIOUS ORDERS

The early medieval period saw the rise of monasticism and the development of religious orders. The following Italian dictionary provides the most comprehensive coverage available.

242. *Dizionario degli istituti de perfezione*. Diretto da Guerrino Pelliccia e da Giancarlo Rocca. Rome: Edizioni Paoline, 1974- (in progress).

Projected in nine volumes; volume 8: 'Saba-Spirituali' was published in 1988.

Entries in this great Italian resource cover religious orders, societies, their founders and leaders, monasticism in all its forms and the nature of the religious life. There are also area studies. Note that while Roman Catholic orders predominate, institutions other than Christian and Catholic, for example Buddhist, are also included. Entries range from paragraphs to essays and many include substantial bibliographies of primary and secondary material. The credentials of the contributors ensure that this the most important resource in this field.

LEARNING AND LITERATURE

243. Kaske, Robert Earl et al. *Medieval Christian literary imagination: a guide to interpretation*. (Toronto medieval bibliographies, 11). Toronto: University of Toronto Press, 1988. 0-8020-2636-2 (hc); 0-8020-6663-1 (pbk).

A sure guide to the allusive density of medieval literature. Kaske analyses the major repositories - biblical exegesis, liturgy, hymns, sermons, pictorial arts, paying special attention to medieval encyclopedias - and shows the extent to which much of the imagery depends upon bodies of Christian learning. An index to subjects, medieval authors and texts and another to modern authors, editors and translators. An important resource for those doing research in this field of literary scholarship.

Thomas Aquinas

Bibliographies

244. Ingardia, Richard. *Thomas Aquinas: international bibliography, 1977-1990*. Bowling Green, OH: Philosophy Documentation Center, 1993. 0-912632-92-5.

Note that the choice of items is quite selective. The focus of the bibliography is Aquinas' philosophy and, while allowing for correlations, strictly theological studies may be omitted. Primary and secondary sources are subdivided by language and there is a section on congresses, special collections and dissertations. Author abstracts of books and articles are included as available. Several indexes conclude this superb resource.

Thomas More

Guides

245. Boswell, Jackson Campbell. *Sir Thomas More in the English Renaissance.* (Medieval & Renaissance texts and studies, 83). Binghamton, NY: Center for Medieval and Early Renaissance Studies, State University of New York at Binghamton, 1994. 0-86698-094-6.

This is a compilation of all references or allusions to Sir Thomas More in *A Short-title catalogue of books printed in England, Scotland, & Ireland and of English books printed abroad 1475-1640* (2nd edn. London, 1976-1991). All works and editions by More are also included. Entries are arranged alphabetically by authors' surnames (of course *STC* would provide additional details), and are cited and annotated with their *STC* numbers. The work would be invaluable to scholars interested in tracing More's reputation and reception, but useful also for those engaged in work on religion and culture in the Renaissance period.

THE CHURCH AND ITS REFORMATION

Among the important directional changes in recent Reformation research has been a focusing on its impact on countries, cities and localities. Comparisons are being drawn between areas where the Reformation was strikingly successful and those where it failed to make an impact. National variants and local peculiarities reveal the many-sided nature of the Reformation as it emerged in varying contexts. The recent 'revisionism' of a number of standard histories stems from this sort of socio-historical examination. The interim conclusion appears to be that there was less of revolution and more of continuity than we had been led to think.

The literature usually divides between the so-called Protestant Reformation and the Catholic Reformation, the latter somewhat misleadingly referred to as the Counter-Reformation. Modern scholarly resources on this complex period reflect a more careful use of sources and offer interpretations less prejudicial to one side or the other, than was once the case.

Guides and bibliographies

The basic annual bibliography for this period continues to be:

246. *Archiv für Reformationsgeschichte. Beihefte: Literaturbericht*, vol. 1- . Gütersloh, G. Mohn, 1972- . Annual.
Added title page: *Archive for Reformation history: an international journal concerned with the history of the Reformation and its significance in world affairs. Supplement: Literature review.*

This supplement volume to the parent journal presents an annual bibliography of books, essays and periodical articles, arranged by subject, with brief annotations in German, English or French. There are indexes to authors, names (e.g., Calvin, Campion, Cromwell) and places. This is the standard up-dating resource.

Titles in the following series, 'Reformation guides to research', are designed to document trends in Reformation studies and set an agenda for future research.

The three volumes, to date, follow the same pattern of bibliographic essays accompanied by extensive bibliographies. They are important both for historiographical analyses and bibliographic coverage.

247. *Reformation Europe: a guide to research.* Edited by Steven Ozment. (Reformation guides to research, 1). St Louis, MO: Center for Reformation Research, 1982. 0-910345-01-5.

Acknowledged authorities contribute essays on a variety of Reformation topics and deal with the present state of research in particular subfields, the key issues, and the availability of research collections. Each essay has a bibliography and there is a comprehensive index of names. Sections of the work are effectively updated by the third title in the series (below).

248. *Catholicism in early modern history: a guide to research.* Edited by John O'Malley. (Reformation guides to research, 2). St Louis, MO: Center for Reformation Research, 1988. 0-910345-02-3.

Concentrating on Catholic reform, this volume covers the religious orders, the Council of Trent, the Inquisition, popular piety, education, preaching, the role of women and the decline or revival of Catholicism in given political or cultural units.

249. *Reformation Europe: a guide to research, II.* Edited by William S. Maltby. (Reformation guides to research, 3). St Louis, MO: Center for Reformation Research, 1992. 0-910345-04-X.

Continues to reflect the intention of the series by surveying the development of literature in numerous areas of Reformation studies. It features the major Protestant reformers, the Reformation in the cities, the status of Jews, women and family, and the nature of reform in several countries, with particular emphasis on Italy.

The following work provides a well-crafted overview of the Reformation period and includes an extensive bibliography:

250. Cameron, Evan. *The European Reformation.* Oxford: Clarendon Press, 1991. 0-19-873094-2 (hc); 0-19-873093-4 (pbk).

See, 'Suggestions for further reading' (pp. 517-536), for a classified listing of books and articles, with preference being given to English language items and to English translations of foreign-language works.

See also *Handbook of European history, 1400–1600* [237] and, in particular, its Volume 2 which covers the Reformation period.

Encyclopedias

251. *Oxford encyclopedia of the Reformation.* Edited by Hans J. Hillerbrand. 4 vols. Oxford University Press, 1995. 0-19-506493-3 (set).

An array of 450 international and ecumenical scholars extend the traditional historical parameters by considering the reform impulses and rich diversity of religious life throughout the sixteenth century. Entries, ranging from essay-length to brief, 300-word accounts, cover not only ecclesiastical and theological changes but also the social, political, economic and demographic repercussions as well as influences in the areas of the arts and literature. Jewish interests and scholarship are also represented. The work is strong on biographies and, intentionally, retrieves the comparatively obscure figures. There is an extensive system of cross-referencing and volume 4 includes an appendix of maps, a directory of contributors, an outline of contents and a superb index to the whole work. This set will be an essential reference resource for studies in the Reformation period for many years to come.

See also the *Encyclopédie du Protestantisme* [309], cited in Chapter 5.

THE REFORMATION IN ENGLAND

Bibliographies

252. Smeeton, Donald Dean. *English religion, 1500-1540: a bibliography.* (NABPR bibliographic series, 2). Macon, GA: Mercer University Press, 1988. 0-86554-325-9.

Lists 'significant primary sources and secondary studies on any aspect of English religion as it was conceived, defined, practised, governed and debated during the first four decades of the sixteenth century' (Introduction, p. 1). Material included was published between 1960 and 1986. An introduction sketches the historiography of the period and then the arrangement of entries is alphabetical by author, with a subject index and an index to authors, editors and translators. A most useful resource.

253. Allison, A. F. and D. M. Rogers. *The contemporary printed literature of the English Counter-Reformation between 1558 and 1640; an annotated catalogue.* 2 vols. Aldershot, England: Scolar Press, 1989, 1994. 1-85928-060-9 (set).

Vol. 1: Works in languages other than English. Vol. 2: Works in English.

A bibliography of Catholic books with annotations, historical, literary and bibliographical, and with locations provided. Volume 1 covers 'religious literature in Latin and other foreign languages published abroad by the English Catholics' (Foreword). Volume 2 provides an extended revision of the compilers' *A Catalogue of Catholic books in English . . .* , 1956 (referred to as *A & R*). There is a concordance linking the old *A & R* numbers with the new numbers in volume 2, and both volumes have indexes to titles, publishers, dates and proper names. A monumental achievement, this is the essential bibliographic guide for the study of Catholicism in this period.

Documents

254. *Documents of the English Reformation.* Edited by Gerald Bray. Cambridge: James Clarke, 1994. 0-2276-7930-X.

A comprehensive collection of documents covering the Reformation in England from 1526 to 1700. The emphasis is on texts of a constitutional nature which represent the development of the church's doctrine and government during the period. Latin texts are given with a translation.
Appendixes include lists of sovereigns, popes, dates of Easter and Moveable Feasts and comparative tables of the different articles and confessions which emerged from the Reformation churches.

REFORMERS

Bibliographies in series

Note that the following series regularly include bibliographies of writings on the reformers:

Sixteenth century bibliographies. St Louis, MO: Center for Reformation Research.

Sixteenth century essays and studies. Kirksville, MO: Sixteenth Century Journal Publishers. This series has included a major, 'Bibliography of the works of Peter Martyr Vermigli' as Volume 13 (1990).

Luther and Lutheranism

Bibliographies

255. *Annotated bibliography of Luther studies, 1984-1989.* Edited by Kenneth Hagen, Franz Posset and Terry Thomas. (Sixteenth century bibliography, 29). Saint Louis, MO: Center for Reformation Research, 1991.

The Center published a similarly titled work covering the years 1977 to 1983 as Volume 24 in the series, which in turn was a sequel to Volume 9 encompassing the years 1967-1976. With the main focus being on theology, this work provides access to material on Luther, written in German and English, produced in all parts of the world and which appeared before the end of May, 1989. A brief introduction reflects upon observed trends in Luther research.

The 'Lutherbibliographie' which appears in the *Lutherjahrbuch: Organ der internationalen Lutherforschung.* (1919-) provides comprehensive annual coverage. With its essays, reports on seminars, book reviews and this classified bibliography, it remains the major up-dating resource for Luther studies.

Indexes

The long-awaited index to the fifty-four volume set of the American edition of Luther's Works was released in 1986 as the final Volume 55 in this series:

256. *Luther's works: index.* Edited by Joel W. Lunden.(*Luther's works*, vol.55). Philadelphia, PA: Fortress Press, 1986. 0-8006-0355-9.

The index is of names, subjects (not words), and pieces of literature (both the titles cited by Luther and his own titles). Also there is an index of scriptural passages discussed or referred to by Luther (excepting passages treated in the course of Luther's general commentaries). An indispensable tool for exploiting the most complete English edition of Luther's writings.

Concordances

The *Book of Concord*, either in entirety or in part, became the doctrinal standard for certain branches of Lutheranism. The following work is a concordance to its contents:

257. *Concordance to 'The Book of Concord'.* Edited by Kenneth E. Larson. Milwaukee, WI: Northwestern Publishing House, 1989. 0-8100-0313-9.

Using the Tappert text of *The Book of Concord* (Fortress Press, 1959), this computer-generated concordance uses a combination of letters and numerals to indicate the location of a word in one of the works included in the English editions of the *Book of Concord* (excluded are the three creeds of the early church). An appendix lists the words not indexed in the *Concordance*; another provides a complete index to every scriptural passage.

Calvin

Bibliographies

258. Greef, W. de. *The writings of John Calvin: an introductory guide.* Grand Rapids, MI: Baker Books, 1993. 0-8010-3021-8.

Translated from the Dutch edition of 1989, this guide provides an overview of Calvin's life, an analysis of his writings in their historical context and then a guide to the vast quantity of secondary literature. There are bibliographies of primary sources and of recent secondary material, a chronological index and a general index. An accessible and most useful tool for Calvin studies.

A recent authoritative listing of Calvin's works, published in the sixteenth century, is:

259. Peter, Rodolphe and Jean-François Gilmont. *Bibliotheca Calviniana: les œuvres de Jean Calvin publiées au XVIe siècle.* 2 volumes. (Travaux d'Humanisme et Renaissance, 255, 281). Geneva: Librairie Droz, 1991, 1994.

   1. Écrits théologiques, littéraires et juridiques, 1532-1554;
   2. Écrits théologiques, littéraires et juridiques, 1555-1564.

It is planned that further volumes will describe editions of Calvin's works to the end of the sixteenth century.

For information on Calvin and the other Protestant leaders of Zurich and Geneva and for the phenomenon of Calvinism, see the *Encyclopedia of the Reformed faith*, edited by Donald McKim [319], which is cited in Chapter 5.

THE ENLIGHTENMENT AND MODERN PERIODS

There are few major reference resources which specifically support studies on the church in the Enlightenment period. However, works on the history of philosophy should assist with the church's concern with the intellectualism of the time, particularly the scientific revolution and the religious scepticism it engendered.

Likewise church history in the modern period, say from 1800, has attracted little in the way of comprehensive resources. The period, however, has been characterised by several new directions. The missionary movement, triumphalist but also heroic, has been comparatively well served by reference resources. The Oxford Movement has received good bibliographic coverage. The ecumenical movement is now well referenced with dictionary and directory-type items providing information about the participating bodies and current dialogues.

Note. Other new directions, including new ways of doing theology and, in particular, the emergence of liberation theology are in Chapter 7, 'Christian theology'.

Surveys

See, particularly *The Oxford illustrated history of Christianity* [180]. Chapter 8, 'Enlightenment: secular and Christian (1600-1800) and chapter 9: 'The expansion of Christianity'. Also chapters 10-15 which treat Christianity in the major areas of the world since 1800. Note the respective bibliographies, pp. 675-683.

Dictionaries and encyclopedias

A reminder that a number of encyclopedias, listed among the general resources in Part 1, cover the history of the modern church. See also *The Blackwell encyclopedia of modern Christian thought*, edited by Alister McGrath [527], which is cited in Chapter 7. General coverage is afforded by:

260. *Blackwell companion to the Enlightenment.* Edited by John W. Yolton. Oxford: Basil Blackwell, 1991. 0-631-15403-5.

Focussing on the years from 1720 to 1780, this work encompasses many disciplines from philosophy to art history, from science to music. It begins with a survey of the period by Lester G. Crocker and then there are substantial signed entries and shorter definitional articles by authorities, with bibliographies. The work features biographies. The text is illustrated with over eighty contemporary paintings and drawings. A scholarly volume which furnishes a context for the study of the fate of religion in the Enlightenment period.

EVANGELICALISM

Biographies

261. *The Blackwell dictionary of evangelical biography, 1730-1860.* Edited by Donald M. Lewis. 2 vols. Oxford: Blackwell Publishers, 1995. 0-631-17384-6 (set).

This work 'seeks to provide biographical treatment and to indicate the sources for study of figures of historical, literary or religious significance who flourished at any time between 1730 and 1860 and were associated with the evangelical movement in the English-speaking world' (Preface, p. xviii). The preface supplies reasons for the periodising and a careful definition of evangelicalism. There are over 3,570 entries contributed by 360 historians worldwide. Entries range from a fraction of a column for a lesser-known person to four columns for a John Wesley and, where possible, sources for further study are included. There is a good representation of figures related to Australia (84 entries) and New Zealand (52). The index is to figures by country of association, by denomination(s), and occupation. So, 'New Zealand. Anglican. Ashwell, B. Y. MISY' (= missionary). The work may add little to knowledge about the famous but will prove an invaluable resource for tracing the more obscure. It fills a real gap in reference literature by presenting, in summary format, recent scholarship on the evangelical movement.

MISSIONS

Bibliographies

The following key resource for studying Catholic missionary developments is neither sufficiently known nor used:

262. Streit, Robert and P. Johannes Dindinger. *Bibliotheca missionum*. 30 vols. Freiberg: Herder, 1916-1974.

The most complete bibliography of Catholic missions. Each volume covers a particular region with entries arranged chronologically. These include histories, diaries, letters, documents of all sorts and other bibliographies.

Volume 21, *Bibliotheca missionum: Missions Literatur von Australien und Ozeanien, 1525-1950* (1955), is devoted to Australia and Oceania and is a key resource for studying Catholic missionary developments in this area.

The following two journals (cited in full in chapter 14) , are devoted to reporting on missionary developments and recent research. They are especially important for their bibliographies.

International review of mission(s) 59 (1970-). Quarterly.

Each issue of this journal features a classified bibliography of books, articles and dissertations, presently titled, 'Bibliography on mission studies'.

International bulletin of missionary research. 5 (1981-). Quarterly.

Regularly includes lists of outstanding books for the year as well as notices of dissertations.

Dictionaries

Although, in many respects, dated, the following work has not been superseded:

263. *Concise dictionary of the Christian world mission.* Edited by Stephen Neil, Gerald Anderson and John Goodwin. London: Lutterworth Press, 1970. 0-7188-1687-0.

Attempts international and ecumenical coverage of all aspects of the expansion of Christianity from 1492. The entries on countries, biographies of leaders and the histories of organisations are necessarily brief but the scholarship and comprehensiveness ensure its continued usefulness.

264. Huiskamp, Harrie. *A genealogy of ecclesiastical jurisdictions: schematic outline, illustrating the development of the Catholic Church in territories assigned to Portugal by Treaty of Tordesillas in 1494.* (Church and theology in context, 23). Kampen: Kok, 1994. 90-390-0502-8.

An intriguing work marking the 500th anniversary of the Treaty which heralded the beginning of new missionary developments. This study outlines the history of Catholic missions, prefectures and vicariates, and dioceses. A schematic survey, using lines, names, dates and maps, is used to describe the development of the various mission territories. Summaries of mission history accompany the schema. Attention is paid to derivative areas and so a section is given to Australasia with Scheme 13 - Australia, and Scheme 14 - New Zealand and the islands of the Pacific. The work concludes with an index of places and a bibliography.

Directories and histories

265. *Mission in the nineteen 90s.* Edited by Gerald Anderson et al. Grand Rapids, MI; Eerdmans, 1991. 0-8028-0542-6.

Essays by international mission leaders, representing the major Christian traditions, assess the record, trends and prospects for mission. Reference use is enhanced by statistics, a selected bibliography of books in English, 1970-1990, and a further listing of 'outstanding books'.

266. Pate, Larry D. *From every people: a handbook of two-thirds world missions with directory/histories/analysis.* Monrovia, CA: MARC, 1989. 0-912552-67-0.

Published by the Mission Advanced Research and Communication Center (MARC), a division of World Vision. The analytical and historical sections are followed by a directory which describes mission agencies from Africa, Asia, Latin America and Oceania. Entries include addresses, personnel and fields of service.

Biographies

267. *Mission legacies: biographical studies of leaders of the modern missionary movement.* Edited by Gerald Anderson et al. (American Society of Missiology series, 19). Maryknoll, NY: Orbis Books, 1994. 0-88344-964-1.

Biographical essays preserve the stories of a selection of nineteenth- and twentieth-century pioneers of mission, men and women, Catholic and Protestant. The work is divided into several generic categories: promoters and interpreters, theologians and historians, theorists and strategists and administrators. There are also three regional groupings: Africa, China and Southern Asia. Indexes to names, subjects and places. In all, substantial accounts of key figures.

THE OXFORD MOVEMENT

Bibliographies

268. Crumb, Lawrence N. *The Oxford Movement and its leaders: a bibliography of secondary and lesser primary sources.* (American Theological Library Association bibliography series, 24). Metuchen, NJ: American Theological Library Association and Scarecrow Press, 1988. 0-8108-2141-9.

_____. *Supplement.* Metuchen, NJ: Scarecrow Press, 1993. 0-8108-2700-X.

Crumb defines the Oxford Movement 'as referring to the first, or "Tractarian" generation of the Catholic movement beginning with Keble's Assize Sermon of 1833 and ending with the Gorham Judgment of 1850' (Preface, p. ix). Keble, Pusey and Newman, in his Anglican years, receive full coverage in this lengthy bibliography of 5432 entries. The arrangement is chronological and, within each year, by type of item. There are separate author, periodical and subject indexes. Appendixes add value to a generous volume.

The *Supplement* revises and augments the basic bibliography and includes relevant material issued in connection with the centennial observance of Newman's death in 1990. Certainly the major bibliographic resource for studies on the Oxford Movement.

The Ecumenical Movement

Guides and bibliographies

269. Fahey, Michael A. *Ecumenism: a bibliographical overview.* (Bibliographies and indexes in religious studies, 23). Westport, CT: Greenwood Press, 1992. 0-313-25102-9.

An annotated bibliography of books reflecting the multi-faceted nature of ecumenism. The time frame is largely the years from the 1950s to the early 1990s, but pioneer works are also included. Fahey's comments in every area are precise and discerning. Author, title and subject indexes.

270. 'A Bibliography of interchurch and interconfessional theological dialogues'. In *Centro pro unione.* Rome: Centro Pro Unione, no. 1-, 1969- ; bi-annual. ISSN 1122-0384.

The Centre, conducted by the Franciscan Friars of the Atonement, publishes this comprehensive bibliography as a supplement to Puglisi, James F. *A bibliography of interchurch and interconfessional theological dialogue*, published by the Centre in 1984. The tenth supplement appears in *Centro pro unione* 47 (Spring 1995): 8-44.

This multi-language bibliography concentrates on bilateral and multilateral consultations and indexes reports, texts, papers, reflections and reactions. With the cessation of the *International ecumenical bibliography, 1962-1977* (1967-1983), this has become a most important research tool.

Dictionaries

271. *Dictionary of the ecumenical movement.* Edited by Nicholas Lossky et al. Geneva: WCC Publications, 1991. 2-8254-1025-X; Grand Rapids, MI: Eerdmans, 1991. 0-8028-2428-5.

The most extensive and intensive reference resource covering the issues, institutions, doctrinal themes and personalities associated with the worldwide Christian ecumenical movement. Entries are by Catholic, Orthodox and Protestant contributors. Dialogues between Christian and other major faiths are reviewed. Most entries have bibliographies. The index to subjects (pp. 1121-1155) will normally be the place to begin searching. This is a superb resource.

272. Van der Bent, A. J. *Historical dictionary of ecumenical Christianity.* (Historical dictionaries of religions, philosophies, and movements, 3). Metuchen, NJ: Scarecrow Press, 1994. 0-8108-2853-7.

Fills a gap by providing short entries on significant persons, events, institutions, and topics. Includes an authoritative introduction, lists of meetings and members, a helpful chronology and comprehensive bibliography. Author has been director of the library and archives of the World Council of Churches in Geneva.

Biographies

273. *Ecumenical pilgrims: profiles of pioneers in Christian reconciliation.* Edited by Ion Bria and Dagmar Heller. Geneva: WCC Publications, 1995. 2-8254-1145-0.

The fifty 'pilgrims' chosen from Catholic, Orthodox and Protestant traditions all helped break down the churches' long heritage of division. Among them are

Athenagoras I, Karl Barth, Augustin Cardinal Bea, Dorothy Day and Michael Ramsey. Each entry includes a well-crafted profile, excerpts from speeches or writings and, in most cases, a basic bibliography. The focus is not so much biographical but rather representational of the traditions which coalesce in the ecumenical movement. There is a list of contributors and an index of names.

World Council of Churches

Yearbooks

274. *World Council of Churches yearbook, 1995- .*Geneva: WCC Publications, 1995. 2-8254-1157-4 (1995 volume).

This first yearbook has been launched as a pilot project by the World Council. It reviews highlights in the life of the WCC and the ecumenical movement during 1994 and proceeds to list names, addresses and contact numbers for member churches, national and regional councils and ecumenical bodies, and WCC staff. Recent WCC publications are also listed. May this most useful reference work continue.

Documents

275. *Documentary history of Faith and Order, 1963-1993.* Edited by Günther Gassmann. (Faith and Order paper, 159). Geneva: WCC Publications, 1993. 2-8254-1101-9.

The volume is a sequel to *A documentary history of the Faith and Order Movement, 1927-1963* (1963). Following introductory material on the WCC Assemblies and early Faith and Order conferences, it provides a documentary history of Faith and Order between Montreal (1963) and Santiago (1993). An authoritative guide to a generation of ecumenical thinking.

276. *Growing consensus: documents from church conversations in the United states, 1962-1991.* Edited by Joseph A. Burgess and Jeffrey Gros. (Ecumenical documents, 5). Mahwah, NJ: Paulist Press, 1995. 0-8091-3382-2 (pbk).

The most recent issue in the 'Ecumenical documents' series comprises a collection of documents that have emerged from dialogues between certain US churches. It encompasses a wide variety of themes including the nature of ministry, the order of the church, the Lord's Supper, mission, social witness, the role of Mary, and ethical questions including euthanasia and homosexuality. There is an index to names, denominations and subjects. This whole series of documents may well inform church conversations in other countries.

Indexes

277. *Index to the World Council of Churches' official statements and reports, 1948-1994.* Compiled by Pierre Beffa, et al. Geneva: WCC Publications, 1995. 2-8254-1151-5.

This volume comprises three indexes to the statements and reports of the WCC, for the periods 1948-1967, 1968-1977 and 1978-1994. The most recent appears first. Note that there is no integration; each series of reports concludes with its own keyword index. A most important tool for those engaged in ecumenical studies.

Ecumenism in Australia

Histories

278. Engel, Frank. *Australian Christians in conflict and unity.* Melbourne: Joint Board of Christian Education, 1984. 0-85819-425-2.

279____. *Christians in Australia.* Volume 2, *Christians in Australia: times of change, 1918-1978.* Melbourne: Joint Board of Christian Education, 1993. 0-85819-855-X.

The author appears to have been an ecumenist before the modern ecumenical movement was formalised. His experiences, particularly as a staff member with the Student Christian Movement and the Australian Council of Churches, have enabled him to interpret the history of sectarianism in Australia and to observe the ways in which churches and Christians responded to calls for union or unity. These two volumes together relate that history from 1825 to 1978. The text is generously supplied with reference notes and both volumes contain extensive bibliographies. A most insightful and valuable reference work.

Documents

280. *Stages on the way: documents from the bilateral conversations between churches in Australia.* Edited by Raymond K. Williamson. Melbourne: Joint Board of Christian Education, 1994. 1-86407-031-5.

The Faith and Order Commission of the Australian Council of Churches has published documents which have issued from national bilateral conversations. Denominations specifically represented are Anglican, Church of Christ, Greek Orthodox, Lutheran, Roman Catholic and Uniting Church. Essential for tracing ecumenical developments in this country.

5

Christianity: Churches in the world

Having dealt with resources related to the history of Christianity in Chapter 4, this present chapter cites material about the development and current state of the churches in various parts of the world. Inevitably, there is some overlapping with the preceding chapter featuring a number of works which relate to the formation of Christian denominations.

Remember also that certain resources in Part 1, especially the encyclopedias of religion, contain information about the denominations of the Christian church.

This chapter has two sections. The first cites material on several Christian denominations. The second deals with Christianity in various countries. That certain denominations appear to have a disproportionate number of entries is due mainly to the extensiveness of their publishing programs. It may also be the case that the events of their recent history have attracted scholarly attention and commentary.

Works which concentrate on theological positions represented by the several denominations are to be found in Chapter 7.

Christian denominations   **96**

  Anglican Communion   96
      British directory
      Documents
  The Catholic Church   96
      Bibliographies
        Jesuitica
      Dictionaries and encyclopedias
      Documents
      Catechisms
  Papacy   99
      Dictionaries
      Papal statements
      Encyclicals
  Canon law   100
      Texts
      Abstracts
  Yearbooks   101
  Statistics   102

Orthodox churches   102
Pentecostal and charismatic   102
        Bibliographies
        Dictionaries
Protestant denominations   103
        Encyclopedias
Baptist   103
Brethren   104
The Church of Jesus Christ of the Latter-Day Saints   104
Lutheran   104
Methodist   104
        Documents and bibliographies
        Encyclopedias
Presbyterian and Reformed   105
        Encyclopedias
        Indexes
Salvation Army   106
        Bibliographies

Christianity in various countries   106
Africa   106
        Overviews
        Bibliographies
        Histories
    South Africa   107
        Bibliographies
        Documents
The Americas   108
        Dictionaries and encyclopedias
        Yearbooks
Asia   108
Australia   109
        Bibliographies
        Yearbooks, directories
        Biographies
        Statistics and interpretation
        Research organisations
Australia and New Zealand   111
    Theological education   111
Great Britain   112
        Directories
Ireland   112
        General history
        Church records
Japan   112
New Zealand   113
        Documents
        Yearbooks, directories

Oceania   113
        Guides
        Histories
Scotland   114
        Dictionaries and encyclopedias

Oceania   113
        Guides
        Histories
Scotland   114
        Dictionaries and encyclopedias

CHRISTIAN DENOMINATIONS

ANGLICAN COMMUNION

British directory

281   *Crockford's clerical directory.* 1858- . Formerly Oxford University Press, now London: Church House Publishing (93rd isssue, 1993/1994).

Biographical entries for clergy of the four Anglican Churches of the British Isles and, in addition, deaconesses, lists of European chaplaincies, theological colleges, their staffs and courses and much more. Note that *Crockford's* no longer includes biographies of clergy in overseas Anglican provinces, apart from the names and addresses of the bishops of each diocese. It does include a list of clergy directories known to be published by provinces.

Documents

282.   *The Anglican tradition: a handbook of sources.* Edited by G. R. Evans and J. Robert Wright. Minneapolis, MN: Fortress Press, 1991. 0-8006-2483-1.

A collection of 600 documents designed 'to show the continuity of the history of the Anglican Communion with that of the whole church through the ages'. Sources are arranged chronologically and each is preceded by a brief commentary. An index to scriptural references and a general index.

THE CATHOLIC CHURCH

Bibliographies

Note particularly *Critical guide to Catholic reference books,* cited in Part 1.

283.   Hansen, Eric C. *Nineteenth-century European Catholicism: an annotated bibliography of secondary works in English.* New York: Garland, 1989. 0-8240-0697-6.

Intends to cover every aspect of the Catholic experience including ecclesiastical structures, theology and spirituality, and religious life in the individual countries during the nineteenth century. Includes books, articles, pamphlets and dissertations published, for the most part, since 1900. Descriptive annotations. An important resource for studying the period of the First Vatican Council and, in particular, developments in Catholicism in England during this period.

Jesuitica

284.   Polgar, László. *Bibliographie sur l'histoire de la Compagnie de Jésus, 1901-1980.* 6 vols. Rome: Institutum Historicum S. I., 1981-1990.

This work continues the monumental bibliography of Sommervogel, *Bibliothèque de la Compagnie de Jésus,* which left off at the close of the nineteenth century. The work is divided into three parts:

I. Toute la Compagnie. [The Society as a whole, its general history.] In one volume;

II. Les pays. [Countries, history of the order in the various countries.] In two volumes;

III. Les personnes. [The individuals, a bio-bibliography of writings about Jesuits from the beginning of the Order, but published since 1901.] In three volumes.

Given the comprehensiveness of this resource, scholars dealing with Jesuit history or the Jesuits in history will find it indispensable. Those working on Jesuits who contributed to the arts, sciences or theology, among them Canisius, Campion, Gerard Manley Hopkins (who attracts 1555 entries), Lonergan and the Rahners, will find the third part, with its bibliographies of secondary sources, to be very useful. Items relating to Ignatius Loyola are in the first part.

Note: Each of the three sections of this bibliography is updated annually in the periodical, *Archivum Historicum Societatis Iesu* (Rome: Institutum Historicum S. I.).

Dictionaries and encyclopedias

Encyclopedic works dealing specifically with Catholic theology are cited in Chapter 7.

The next three works [285-287] continue to be recommended for their coverage of all matters relating to the life and thought of the Catholic Church.

285. *The Catholic encyclopedia: an international work of reference on the constitution, doctrine, discipline, and history of the Catholic Church.* 17 vols. New York: Catholic Encyclopedia Press, 1907-1922 (Vol. 17, Supplement I, 1922).

Although somewhat polemical and, in certain respects, dated, it is still most important for understanding the church's dogmatic positions at the turn of the century and for its surveys and interpretations of art, history, literature and philosophy. The Index volume (16) is an essential ingredient.

286. *New Catholic encyclopedia: an international work of reference on the teachings, history, organization, and activities of the Catholic Church and on all institutions, religions, philosophies, and scientific and cultural developments affecting the Catholic Church from its beginning to the present.* 15 vols. New York: McGraw-Hill, 1967.

Vol. 16: *Supplement, 1967-1974* . Washington, DC: Publisher's Guild, in association with McGraw-Hill, 1974.

Vol. 17: *Supplement, Change in the church.* Washington, DC: Publisher's Guild in association with McGraw Hill, 1979.

Vol. 18: *Supplement, 1978-1988.* Palatine, IL; Washington, DC: Jack Heraty & Assoc.; Catholic University of America, 1989.

As the title implies, this is all but a general encyclopedia. Respected for its scholarship, its comprehensive coverage and genuine openness, it is an essential resource for all things Catholic and useful for much more. The supplements help to relieve the aging process.

287. *Lexikon für Theologie und Kirche (LThK)*. 3rd edn. Edited by Walter Kasper et al. Freiburg: Herder, 1993- .Vol. 1: 'A' - 'Barcelona' (1993); vol. 2: 'Barclay' - 'Damodos' (1994). Projected in 10 volumes with a Registerband. 3-451-22001-6 (vol. 1); 3-451-22002-4 (vol. 2).

The second edition of *LThK* was published in eleven volumes plus three supplemental volumes from 1957 to 1968. Like the earlier sets, this new edition covers biblical theology, church history, systematic theology, practical theology, missions and world religions. Entries range from short paragraphs to essays. An extensive list of abbreviations used in *LThK* was published separately as *Abkürzungsverzeichnis* (Herder, 1993). This is the major German Catholic encyclopedia.

The following are recently published one-volume encyclopedias:

288. *The HarperCollins encyclopedia of Catholicism.* Edited by Richard P. McBrien et al. San Francisco: HarperSanFrancisco, 1995. 0-06-065338-8.

A compendium of Catholic belief and practice which offers an authoritative guide to the people, doctrines, history, worship, art, spirituality, literature, theological developments and changes which have shaped the Catholic Church over almost two millennia. There are feature-length entries on major doctrines, figures and issues. Numerous tables, lists and illustrations. A reliable source of information regarding every aspect of Catholicism, past and present.

289. *Modern Catholic encyclopedia.* Edited by Michael Glazier and Monika Hellwig. Collegeville, MN: Liturgical Press, 1994. 0-8146-5495-9.

Provides a succinct and contemporary view of the beliefs, practices, and history of the Catholic people. Emphasis is on today's concerns and leading figures and upon recent biblical and theological insights. For example, the role of women receives treatment in two lengthy articles and is also touched on in several shorter ones. Includes a selection of classical works of art depicting the life of Jesus, as well as 200 illustrations embedded in the entries. An attractive, easy to use resource.

Documents

290. *The Christian faith in the doctrinal documents of the Catholic Church.* Edited by J. Neuner and J. Dupuis. Rev. edn. London: Collins, 1983. 0-00-599706-2.

Gathers professions of faith and then authoritative documents from earliest times to 1981. The thematic arrangement, in chronological order, allows one to trace developments in teaching. Includes a chronological table of documents, an index to biblical passages and an analytical index.

291. Denzinger, Heinrich . *Enchiridion symbolorum, definitionum, et declarationum de rebus fidei et morum.* 36th edn. emendata. Freiburg: Herder, 1973. 84-254-0866-0 (cloth).

Collection of sources and texts, dating from the first century, upon which Catholic teaching on faith and morals is based. Material, arranged in chronological order, is in either Greek or Latin. There are indexes to documents, subjects, names and places.

A German edition, the 37th, edited by Peter Hünermann and with the text expanded to 1988, with a German translation, was published by Herder, in Freiburg, in 1991 (3-451-22442-9).

An English translation of the 30th edition of this work is available as, Denzinger, Heinrich. *The sources of Catholic dogma* (St Louis, MO: Herder, 1957).

Catechisms

The new *Catechism of the Catholic Church* was published in English in June, 1994. This is the first official Catholic catechism since the so-called *Roman Catechism*, issued under the direction of the Council of Trent in 1566, and indeed duplicates the organisational structure of that earlier work.

292. *Catechism of the Catholic Church.* Homebush, NSW: St Pauls - Society of St Paul, 1994. 1-875570-19-5 (hc); 1-875570-29-9 (pbk).

The official edition for Australia and New Zealand of this approved synthesis of Catholic faith and practice. Reference potential is enhanced by a series of indexes to Scripture, creeds, councils and synods, pontifical documents, ecclesiastical documents, canon law, the liturgy and to ecclesiastical writers. There is also a general subject index.

The following titles provide reference and commentary material on the *Catechism*:

293. *The Companion to the Catechism of the Catholic Church: a compendium of texts referred to in the Catechism of the Catholic Church.* San Francisco: Ignatius Press, 1994. 0-89870-481-2 (hc); 0-89870-482-0 (pbk.).

Reproduces, in full, English translations of the references and documents cited in the text of the *Catechism*. The arrangement simply follows the *Catechism's* paragraph numbering.

294. *Commentary on the Catechism of the Catholic Church.* Edited by Michael J. Walsh. Collegeville, MN: Liturgical Press, 1994. 0-8146-2305-0. Published in Great Britain by Geoffrey Chapman.

A set of essays on major sections of the *Catechism* by well-known Catholic scholars who were asked to enter into 'critical dialogue' with the text (p. 4). And they did.

295. *Handing on the tradition: a guide to the Catechism of the Catholic Church.* Edited by T. M. Doyle, F. T. O'Loughlin and C. E. H. Toms. Melbourne: Catholic Education Office, 1994. 0-86407-199-X.

Published by the Catholic Education Office, Melbourne, for the Archdiocese of Melbourne, this work represents the reflections and responses to the *Catechism* by parents, religious, priests, teachers, educationalists and theologians.

Papacy

Dictionaries

The following recently published French work is worthy of special attention.

296. *Dictionnaire historique de la papauté.* Edited by Philippe Levillain et al. Paris: Fayard, 1994. 2-213-02537-1.

This is a massive work of 1776 pages, 912 entries, 70 illustrations in colour and 46 in black and white, with maps, summaries, charts and chronologies. Not simply a history of the popes but of all aspects of the papacy and of its evolution to modern times (from 'automobiles' to 'vêtements'). Entries, contributed by experts, may take up several pages and have substantial bibliographies. Emphasis is on the historical, political and social rather than the theological. A most useful guide for any work on the history of Catholicism and on the papacy in particular.

297. Kelly, J. N. D. *The Oxford dictionary of popes.* Oxford University Press, 1986. 0-19-213964-9.

A distinguished historical theologian presents candid accounts of the popes and anti-popes, with information about their families, society and accomplishments. The arrangement is chronological, which means that each pope can be studied in context and that the volume, in effect, comprises a continuous history. Each entry has a bibliography.

Papal statements

298. Carlen, Claudia. *Papal pronouncements: a guide, 1740-1978.* 2 vols. Ann Arbor, MI: Pierian Press, 1990. 0-87650-266-4 (set).

Includes references to all encyclicals and most addresses from Benedict XIV (1740) through John Paul I (1978), as well as a selection of documents in other categories. Entries, arranged chronologically, give the type of document, estimated word count, occasion or group addressed, a statementof content and an abstract. A section on sources provides references to original texts and cites English translations where available. Volume 2 concludes with a title index and a general index to all subjects, personal and corporate names.

Encyclicals

299. *The Papal encyclicals, 1740-1981.* Compiled by Claudia Carlen. 5 vols. Wilmington, NC: McGrath, 1981. 0-8434-0765-4 (set). Reprinted by Pierian Press (Ann Arbor, MI) 1990 (0-87650-259-1) (set).

Provides full texts, in English, of 280 encyclicals from Benedict XIV to John Paul II. Details for each document include the source (usually Latin) of the original text, citations to other available English translations, reference notes and a valuable bibliography of secondary sources on the text. In the final volume there is an extensive index of titles and subjects.

Canon law

In response to a direction from the Second Vatican Council a revision of the *Codex iuris canonici* was published, originally in Latin, in 1983.

Texts

In Latin and English

300. *Code of Canon Law, Latin-English edition.* Trans. under the auspices of the Canon Law Society of America. Washington, DC: Canon Law Society of America, 1983. 0-943616-20-4.

Following introductory material, the Latin text and English translation are given on opposite pages. There is a glossary of terms and an index to the whole.

English translation

301. *Code of Canon Law in English translation.* Prepared by the Canon Law Society of Great Britain and Ireland in association with the Canon Law Society of Australia and New Zealand and the Canadian Canon Law Society. London, Collins; Grand Rapids, MI: Eerdmans, 1983. 0-8028-1978-8 (Eerdmans).

The approved translation. No commentary and no index. A detailed index to the text, however, was published separately as:

302. *Index to the Code of Canon Law in English translation.* Prepared by the Canon Law Society of Great Britain and Ireland. London Collins, 1984. 0-00-599802-6.

With commentary

303. *The Code of Canon Law: a text and commentary.* Edited by James A. Coriden et al. London: G. Chapman, 1985. 0-225-66424-0; New York: Paulist Press, 1985. 0-8091-0345-1.

This massive work, authorised by the Canon Law Society of America, includes the full text of the Code in English and a commentary on each canon. Bibliographies on each section emphasise sources in English. The work concludes with a table of corresponding canons, that is those of the 1983 Code with those of the previous codification of 1917, and an extensive index.

Abstracts

The following abstracting service is intended for specialists, or intending specialists:

304. *Canon Law abstracts.* Published by the Canon Law Society of Great Britain. Melrose, Scotland 1959- .

A half-yearly review of periodical literature on Canon Law by members of the Canon Law Society of Great Britain and Ireland. Presents lengthy abstracts of important recently-published articles. Divided by sections - general subjects and historical subjects - then the following arrangement corresponds with the Code.

Yearbooks

305. *Catholic almanac.* Huntington, IN: Our Sunday Visitor, 1971- . ISSN 0069-1208.

With several predecessors, the present title was adopted in 1969. This is the most complete one-volume source of facts and basic information on the Catholic Church. Each annual volume offers special reports, articles on subjects of current Catholic interest, and includes reprints or excerpts of key texts issued during the year. Numerous summaries and listings and an extensive index make this an accessible *vade mecum* for historical inquiry. Well regarded for its accuracy and comprehensiveness.

Statistics

306. *Annuarium statisticum ecclesiae. Statistical yearbook of the Church.* Secretaria Status, Rationarium Generale Ecclesiae. Vatican City: Polyglottis Vaticanis, 1977- . Now an annual. (Note a minimal delay in publication; the volume for 1992 being published in 1994.)

> The authoritative gathering of the most significant data on the life and activity of the Catholic Church. Statistics relate to the population of the faithful by area, the church's work force, educational institutions, religious practices including the sacraments, welfare institutions, papal-jurisdiction, institutes and diocesan tribunals. Australia, New Zealand and the Pacific Islands are gathered under the heading 'Oceania'. This is the only source available for certain of the Church's statistics.

ORTHODOX CHURCHES

The term, Orthodox, is associated with the story of Eastern Christendom and with two great ecclesial communities. There are the Eastern Orthodox families of churches in communion with the See of Constantinople, the so-called 'Chalcedonian' churches. These include the Russian, Romanian, Serbian, Ukrainian and the several Greek Orthodox churches. In the second grouping are the five Oriental Orthodox churches, the so-called 'non-Chalcedonian' churches - Coptic, Syrian, Armenian, Ethiopian and the Malankara Syrian (Indian). The schism, over christological issues, dated from the Council of Chalcedon (451). After some 1,500 years of separation a series of conversations between leaders of the two groups was initiated in 1964. This Oriental Orthodox-Orthodox dialogue has effectively removed many of the theological and historical obstacles and given hope that communion will be restored.

Another important ecumenical conversation is the Orthodox-Roman Catholic dialogue, officially begun in 1979. Having erased the memory of the mutual excommunications of 1054, the two churches are now able to explore those issues which unite or continue to divide.

There are few reference works devoted to the life, liturgy and thought of the Orthodox churches and one may need to turn to monographs by authorities such as Vladimir Lossky, John Meyendorff, Alexander Schmemann and Kallistos (Timothy) Ware. For authoritative summaries of the ecumenical dialogues in which the Orthodox churches are engaged, see relevant entries in the *Dictionary of the Ecumenical Movement* [271].

Until recently, little more than pamphlets had been published about the Orthodox churches in Australia . There are now useful chapters on 'Eastern Orthodox' and 'Oriental/Ancient Eastern Christians' in *Religious bodies in Australia* [109]. See also the essay by Miltiades Chryssavgis, a priest of the Greek Orthodox Church, entitled, 'Orthodoxy in Australia', in *The Shape of belief: Christianity in Australia today*, edited by D. Harris et al. (Sydney: Lancer Books, 1982).

PENTECOSTAL AND CHARISMATIC

Bibliographies

307. Jones, Charles Edwin. *The charismatic movement: a guide to the study of Neo-Pentecostalism with emphasis on Anglo-American sources.* 2 vols. (American Theological Library Association bibliography series, 30). Metuchen, NJ: American Theological Library Association and Scarecrow Press, 1995. 0-8108-2565-1.

This bibliography is divided into four parts: 1, The Charismatic Movement; 2, Denominational and organisational responses (in the first volume); 3, Schools (Bible schools, colleges, universities); 4, Biography (in the second volume). Given its total 10,910 entries, this is the most comprehensive register of the personalities and literature of the movement to date. There is a general index in the second volume.

Dictionaries

308. *Dictionary of Pentecostal and Charismatic movements.* Edited by Stanley M. Burgess and Gary B. McGee. Grand Rapids, MI: Zondervan, 1988. 0-310-44100-5.

The introduction, which deals with definitional matters, is followed by articles on biblical and theological topics and the varieties of Pentecostalism and charismatic renewal. There are biographies of leaders and analyses of the important aspects of these burgeoning movements. The contributors are drawn from the varieties of Protestantism and Catholicism. While the focus is mainly on North America, this work may function as a general resource for understanding this twentieth-century phenomenon.

PROTESTANT DENOMINATIONS

Encyclopedias

309. *Encyclopédie du Protestantisme.* Edited Pierre Gisel et al. Paris: Éditions du Cerf / Labor et Fides, 1995. 2-204-05243-4.

This major French work presents the cultural and historical dimensions of Protestantism from the time of the Reformation until today. Three hundred scholars contribute some 1400 essays and articles on Protestant teachings, teachers and other noted persons who were nurtured or informed by Protestantism - Barth, Bullinger, Calvin, but also Darwin, Le Corbusier, Klee and Van Gogh. A great range of issues and interests are discussed in such disparate fields as the arts, capitalism, ecology, Judaism, the laity, the law, Lutheranism, morality, church music, world religions, sexuality, theology, violence and vocation. This volume of 1700 pages includes some 1500 illustrations.

BAPTIST

310. *Dictionary of Baptists in America.* Edited by Bill J. Leonard. Downers Grove, IL: InterVarsity Press, 1994. 0-8308-1447-7.

Following the well-regarded *Dictionary of Christianity in America* [330], the present work is the first in a series of concise dictionaries on various traditions in American Christianity to be published by InterVarsity Press. Articles survey histories, beliefs and practices of specific Baptist movements. There are entries on institutions and important leaders. The work has a wider reference in that articles on key doctrines, for example 'Baptism', take into consideration other denominational positions. Most entries include bibliographies. A key resource for students of the Baptist tradition and, more generally, for the study of historical theology.

BRETHREN

311. *The Brethren encyclopedia.* Edited by Donald F. Durnbaugh. 3 vols.
     Philadelphia, PA: Brethren Encyclopedia, 1983-1984.
     0-936693-00-2 (repr. set).

Covers Brethren heritage, life, practice. Volumes 1 and 2 contain articles in alphabetical order, while volume 3 contains maps, a chronology, statistics, lists of divisions and major groups, congregations and ministers.

THE CHURCH OF JESUS CHRIST OF THE LATTER-DAY SAINTS

312. *Encyclopedia of Mormonism: the history, scripture, doctrine, and pro-
     cedure of the Church of Jesus Christ of the Latter Day Saints.*
     Edited by D. H. Ludlow. 5 vols. New York: Macmillan, 1992.
     0-02-904040-X.

The first four volumes cover the topics described in the subheading while the fifth
optional volume contains the Scriptures of Mormonism, including the *Book of
Mormon*. Altogether an impressive, objective work which, while centred on the
Church in the United States, also traces the development of Mormonism
throughout the world.

LUTHERAN

313. Bachmann, E. Theodore and Mercia Brenne Bachmann. *Lutheran
     churches in the world: a handbook.* Minneapolis, MN: Augsburg,
     1989. 0-8066-2371-3.

This comprehensive guide to Lutheran church bodies provides geographical,
descriptive and statistical information. There are indexes to organisations and
countries.

Somewhat dated but still useful for its scholarly coverage of Lutheran doctrine,
church history and activities around the world is:

314. *The encyclopedia of the Lutheran Church.* Edited by Julius Bodensieck.
     3 vols. Minneapolis. MN: Augsburg, 1965.

METHODIST

Documents and bibliographies

315. *History of the Methodist Church in Great Britain.* Edited by Rupert
     Davies et al. Volume 4. London: Epworth Press, 1988.
     0-7162-0444-4.

The fourth volume, which completes this set, is devoted to documents and source
material, edited by John A. Vickers, and to an extensive bibliography by Clive D.
Field. The primary documents begin with the experiences of the Wesleys and
then cover the periods from 1791 to 1851 and from 1851 to 1932. The bibliogra-

phy comprises an extensive and well-classified selection of the immense literature available. This volume is essential for work on the Wesleys and the history of Methodism.

316. Rowe, Kenneth E. *Methodist union catalog, pre-1976 imprints.* Metuchen, NJ: Scarecrow Press, 1975- .Volume 1- (in progess). Volume 6 was published in 1985, with the entries for He-I.

A listing of holdings of Methodist material in some 200 libraries, chiefly in the United States, Canada and Great Britain. The arrangement is alphabetical by the main entry of the item and locations are given for holdings. The essential, international finding tool for Methodistica.

317. *United Methodist studies: basic bibliographies.* Edited by Kenneth E. Rowe. 3rd edn. Nashville: Abingdon Press, 1992. 0-687-43165-4.

Designed to provide a selected list of resources for American seminary courses in United Methodism. However, the bibliographic coverage of Methodist history, doctrine and polity, including material on the Wesleys, is broad enough to ensure a wider usage. It includes sections on periodicals and other basic library requirements. The items are arranged topically and there is an author/editor index.

Encyclopedias

The following older work, now out of print, remains valuable for historical questions relating to Methodism.

318. *The Encyclopedia of world Methodism.* Edited by Nolan B. Harmon. 2 vols. Nashville, TN: United Methodist Publishing House, 1974. 0-687-11784-4.

Covers the history, doctrines, leading figures of Methodism throughout the world. Biographies are a feature. Emphasis is on American Methodism, but other area studies are included. Appendixes, at the end of the second volume, include a chronology, lists of bishops of the Episcopal Methodist churches, presidents of the several British conferences, statistics and a bibliography. The whole work is well indexed.

PRESBYTERIAN AND REFORMED

Encyclopedias

319. *Encyclopedia of the Reformed faith.* Edited by Donald K. McKim. Louisville, KY: Westminster/John Knox Press, 1992. 0-664-21882-2. Also published by Saint Andrew Press, Edinburgh. 0-7152-0660-5.

Reflects the perceptions of faith rooted in the sixteenth-century Reformation and expressed by Calvin and other Protestant leaders in Zurich and Geneva. Entries from 'Accommodation' to 'Zwingli' covers persons, events and theological issues and the histories of Reformed churches around the world. Particularly useful for the treatment it affords lesser-known figures and for its clear summaries of theological positions.

Indexes

320. *World Alliance of Reformed Churches: general index, 1875-1992.* Edited by Edmond Perret. Geneva: World Alliance of Reformed Churches, 1994. 92-9075-017-0.

This index provides access to major documents kept in the Alliance's Archives. Following a table of indexed documents, the work is arranged by subject. This massive volume (some 2000 pages) will assist those studying the history and development of Reformed churches around the world and their Alliance. Includes sections on Presbyterian churches in Australia and New Zealand.

SALVATION ARMY

Bibliographies

321. Moyles, R. G. *A bibliography of Salvation Army literature in English, 1865-1987.* (Texts and studies in religion, 38). Lewiston, NY: Edwin Mellen Press, 1988. 0-88946-827-3.

This bibliography attempts, for the first time, to list and categorise all the publicly available literature produced by the Army and written about it, in English, since 1865. Items are arranged in sections which include history, social service, music, biography and portraits. There is coverage of the Army in Australia from 1880 and in New Zealand from the late 1880s (pp. 29-30; 38). A well-articulated work and of obvious value to anyone researching the Army's history and present status.

A useful bibliographical essay is included in the following critical history:

322. Murdoch, Norman H. *Origins of the Salvation Army.* Knoxville, TN: University of Tennessee Press, 1994. 0-87049-858-4.

See pages 215-220. Murdoch points up particularly the 'tension between the Army's early revivalism and later social reform impulses' (p. 220).

CHRISTIANITY IN VARIOUS COUNTRIES

AFRICA

Overviews

323. Isichei, Elizabeth. *A history of Christianity in Africa.* Grand Rapids, MI: Eerdmans, 1995. 0-8028-0843-3 (pbk).

Begins with an historical survey from early Egyptian Christianity to the churches of the Middle Years (1500-1800) and on to the missionary enterprise of the 1900s. Then there are chapters on changes in Southern Africa since 1900 and on independent black Africa since 1960. Maps and index. This work fills a real gap in church history.

Bibliographies

Note the extensive bibliographical essay in the following history by Adrian Hastings, *The Church in Africa* (pp. 621-685). The essay covers material published, within the last thirty years, on the historical development and character of the Christian church in Africa as a whole.

Histories

324. Hastings, Adrian. *The Church in Africa, 1450-1950.* (Oxford history of the Christian Church). Oxford: Clarendon Press, 1994. 0-19-826921-8.

The first major volume to consider the historical development and character of the Christian Church in Africa as a whole, linking together Ethiopian Orthodoxy, Roman Catholicism, Protestantism and the numerous independent churches of modern times. There is a particular concentration on the place of the church in African society. Several appendixes include maps, there is an extensive bibliography (see above), and a comprehensive index. A superb volume in a major series.

SOUTH AFRICA

Bibliographies

325. *History of the church in South Africa.* Vol. 1, *A select bibliography of published material to 1980.* Edited by J. W. Hofmeyr and K. E. Cross, Pretoria: University of South Africa, 1986. 0-86981-435-4.

326. *History of the church in South Africa.* Vol. 2, *A select bibliography of published material 1981 to 1985.* Edited by J. W. Hofmeyr and K. E. Cross. Pretoria: University of South Africa, 1988. 0-86981-540-7.

327. *History of the church in South Africa.* Vol. 3, *A select bibliography of published material 1985 to 1989.* Edited by J. W. Hofmeyr, J. H. Rykheer and J. M. Nel. Pretoria: University of South Africa, 1993. 0-86981-798-1.

These bibliographies cover the area south of the Cunene and the Zambezi. This includes South Africa, Botswana, Lesotho, Swaziland, Namibia and Zimbabwe. Although particularly strong on denominations and missions, it also attends to non-denominational subjects, for example, church and state, theological trends, ecumenicity, other faiths, race relations, war and education. Entries are limited to books, pamphlets and items in composite works. Periodical literature is covered separately in the following work:

328. *A Select bibliography of periodical articles on South African church history.* Vol. 1, *1975-1989.* Edited by J. W. Hofmeyr, J. H. Rykheer and J. M. Nel. Pretoria: University of South Africa, 1991. 0-86981-738-8.

Documents

329. *History of the church in South Africa: a document and source book.* Edited by J. W. Hofmeyr, J. A. Millard and C. J. J. Froneman. Pretoria: University of South Africa, 1991. 0-86981-727-2.

Documents range from the early beginnings in the sixteenth century to the modern period and appear in chronological order. They are recorded in their original languages, whether English, Afrikaans or Dutch. The introductions are in English.

THE AMERICAS

Dictionaries and encyclopedias

330. *Dictionary of Christianity in America.* Edited by Daniel G. Reid et al. Downers Grove, ILL: InterVarsity Press, 1990. 0-8308-1776-X.

Attempts to convey in an objective manner the history, beliefs and practices of the major and minor Christian traditions in North America (especially the US). Signed articles cover biographies, events, religious bodies, movements and theologies. Perspective is mainly historical although contemporary issues and their advocates do receive attention. The only reference dictionary of its kind to date.

Yearbooks

331. *Yearbook of American and Canadian churches, 1916-.* Edited for the National Council of the Churches of Christ in the USA. Nashville, TN: Abingdon, 1916- . (Title, publisher and frequency have varied.) ISSN 0195-9034.

The sixty-third issue was published in 1995. This is the standard directory providing data about cooperative organisations, religious bodies, ecumenical agencies, theological seminaries and Bible schools, religious periodicals, international congregations and depositories for church history materials. Other major religions are represented but sects, cults and small groups are excluded. There is a statistical section and numerous other aids. Indexes are to organisations and individuals. This is the key resource for current information about religious organisations, leaders and schools and their postal addresses.

ASIA

This guide is glaringly lopsided in barely hinting at the existence of the East. While the encyclopedias of religion adequately cover the major religions of Asia, there are very few reference books, published in English, that provide current information about Christianity in Asia and Southeast Asia.

Instructors and students should be aware that the following periodicals provide interpretations of theological developments in this area and also reviews of current literature. Note that each of the following titles is fully cited in Chapter 14.

332. *The Asia journal of theology.*

The organ of the North East Asia Association of Theological Schools, the Board of Theological Education of the Senate of Serampore College and the Association for Theological Education in South East Asia (ATESEA). Features scholarly articles on the Asian church scene and prevailing theological issues. Also substantial book reviews. At the end of each issue are the names and addresses of the members of the Boards and Colleges and a directory of member institutions of ATESEA.

The Association for Theological Education in South East Asia also publishes the series, *ATESEA occasional papers*. Each quite substantial issue deals with a particular aspect of theological awareness in the area.

333. *East Asian pastoral review.*

A Catholic periodical dealing with theology, mission and pastoral developments in Asia and the Pacific.

334. *PTCA bulletin.*

Published in conjunction with the Programme for Theology and Cultures in Asia. Essential for its bibliographies and reviews of monographs on Asian Christian theology.

AUSTRALIA

Reference resources on religions in Australia, including Christianity, are included in Chapter 2. See, particularly, Humphreys, Robert and Rowland Ward. *Religious bodies in Australia* [109], and *Many faiths, one nation*, edited by Ian Gillman [110]. Items on the ecumenical movement in Australia are cited in Chapter 4.

Bibliographies

The first work, edited by Michael Mason, has already been cited and annotated in Chapter 2 [111]. It remains crucial for research on Christianity and the churches in the Australian setting.

335. *Religion in Australian life: a bibliography of social research.* Edited by Michael Mason; compiled by Georgina Fitzpatrick, Bedford Park, SA: National Catholic Research Council and the Australian Association for the Study of Religions, 1982. 0-908083-09-2.

336. Hynd, Douglas. 'Christianity in Australia: a bibliography'. In *The shape of belief: Christianity in Australia today.* Edited by D. Harris et al. Sydney: Lancer Books, 1982, pp. 201-228.

An extensive bibliography providing comprehensive coverage of material published during the period 1960-1980. There are three sections: 'Australian theology', 'Australian church history' which is divided denominationally, and 'Religion in Australian society' which has entries covering sociological perspectives. This resource remains important as a retrospective survey of the literature.

The authors of the following monograph sources provide valuable bibliographical coverage and effectively help update the previous two items.

337. Breward, Ian. 'Bibliography'. In *A history of the Australian churches.* St Leonards, NSW: Allen & Unwin, 1993. 1-86373-446-5. Pages 257-281.

338. O'Farrell, Patrick. 'Guide to further reading'. In *The Catholic Church and community: an Australian history.* Third rev. edn., with Afterword. Kensington, NSW: University of New South Wales Press, 1992. 0-86840-225-7. Pages 453-466.

This splendid bibliographic guide has been updated by the author in, 'The writing of Australian Catholic history, 1980-1990'. *Australasian Catholic record* 68 (1991): 131-145.

See also Thompson, Roger C. 'Bibliography'. In *Religion in Australia: a history* [112]. This bibliography has mainly to do with Christianity.

For an annual update see the section, 'Selected bibliography of religious books', in *Yearbook of Australian religious organisations* [113] (formerly *Yearbook for Australian churches*). This bibliography lists books published in Australia across the broad spectrum of religion, but with a concentration on Christianity and the churches.

Yearbooks, directories

339. *Yearbook for Australian churches, 1991- 1995.* Edited by Peter Bentley et al. Hawthorn, Vic.: Christian Research Association, 1990-1995. ISSN 1035-8137.
     Superseded by *A Yearbook of Australian religious organisations, 1996- .* [113]

An annual which provided an overview of church-life and religious activities in Australia. Contains directories of churches and other religious groups and organisations, an annual bibliography of religious books, diaries of past and future events and an ecumenical calendar and lectionary. Each volume features reviews on aspects of church life. Note the change of title for 1996.

In additions to magazines, journals and newspapers, certain denominations publish yearbooks which may provide directory information, information about committee structures, clergy appointments, educational institutions, statistical data and lectionary material. Examples are:

Australian Catholic Bishops Conference. *The official directory of the Catholic Church in Australia.* Alexandria, NSW: E. J. Dwyer. ISSN: 1321-4764.

Yearbook of the Lutheran Church of Australia. Adelaide: Openbook Publishers. ISSN: 0726-4305.

Those wishing to identify or subscribe to the directory or yearbook of a particular denomination could contact that denomination's headquarters. *A Yearbook of Australian religious organisations* [113] includes directory information.

Biographies

The *Australian dictionary of biography* [64] and the *Dictionary of New Zealand biography* [66], both cited in Part 1, are major resources for biographies of church persons in the two countries. The following item is more specialised:

340. *The Australian dictionary of evangelical biography.* Edited by Brian Dickey. Sydney: Evangelical History Association, 1994. 0-646-16625-3.

Contains biographical entries for almost 700 persons who have contributed to the making and transmission of evangelical Protestantism in and from Australia. There is a listing by denominational affiliation and another by membership of missionary societies.

See also, *The Blackwell dictionary of evangelical biography* [261], for biographies of evangelicals associated with Australia.

Statistics and interpretation

341. Kaldor, Peter et al. *Winds of change: the experience of church in a changing Australia.* Homebush West, NSW: Lancer published by ANZEA Publishers, 1994. 0-85892-536-2.

Prepared by the staff team of the National Church Life Survey, using data on congregational life and mission, gathered in August 1991, this report represents 'the Anglican/ Protestant section of Australian church life' (Introduction, p. xvii). The survey, in reporting on patterns of faith and participation, includes attitudes to biblical, theological and charismatic teachings, congregational life and service, denominational allegiance, the generation gap and future directions. Statistics for New Zealand Presbyterianism have been included in the denominational tables. Appendixes provide access to statistics and further background material about the survey.

Research organisations

The following research organisations publish material on church life and developments in Australia.

The Christian Research Association, an ecumenical organisation which was formed in 1985, publishes *A Yearbook of Australian religious organisations 1996-* (formerly *Yearbook for Australian churches)* [113, 339]. Also *Pointers: quarterly bulletin of the Christian Research Association* (1991-), which reports on research relevant to faith and church life, overseas research relevant to Australia, new books, articles, conferences and papers. From time to time the CRA also publishes research papers and reports.

The address of CRA is Locked Bag, 23, Kew, Victoria, 3101.

The Zadok Institute for Christianity and Society is a national research body. Its mission statement reads, 'To promote informed theological reflection, especially by lay people, on contemporary issues in Australian culture and society and to bring Christian perspectives into public debate.' It publishes a quarterly, *Zadok perspectives* (1983-), also *Zadok papers* (approximately 8 per year), as well as reading guides and several books, notably *The Shape of belief* (1982) and *Australian Christianity in outline* (1984).

The address of the Zadok Institute is 59 Scotchmer Street, North Fitzroy, Victoria, 3068.

AUSTRALIA AND NEW ZEALAND

Theological education

342. *The Australian and New Zealand Association of Theological Schools. Fact book, 1994-5-6.* Melbourne: Australian & New Zealand Association of Theological Schools, 1994. 0-646-18593-4.

Contains details of the Colleges of Divinity in each State of Australia and the member institutions and faculties of ANZATS. A complete list of the New Zealand Association of Theological Schools is included. Concludes with a printing of the ANZATS constitution. The biographical entries offer the most comprehensive who's who in theological education in the two countries.

Another entry for this title is at item 600.

GREAT BRITAIN

Directories

343. *UK Christian handbook, 1996/97.* Edited by Peter Brierley and Heather Wraight et al. London: Christian Research (formerly MARC Europe - place and publisher have varied), 1995. 1-85321-124-9 (hc); 1-85321-123-0 (pbk).

Covers all aspects and issues of church life in the United Kingdom, the mainstream and minor denominations and the numerous associations and services. Very clearly structured. There is a locations index in alphabetical order by counties and towns and a comprehensive index of titles, names, organisations and subject-areas covered. A veritable gold mine for those seeking information about names and addresses, accommodation, bookshops, theological colleges and a good deal else besides.

IRELAND

General history

344. *A New history of Ireland.* Edited by T. W. Moody et al. Oxford: Clarendon Press, 1976- . (In progress; projected in 10 volumes).

The first seven volumes of text material will cover all periods of political, economic, social and cultural history. There are sections on literature, the arts and the history of the churches.

The final three companion volumes are given to reference material. Volume 8 (1982) comprises a chronology of Irish history to 1976, with index. Volume 9 (1984) provides maps, genealogical tables, succession lists (including bishops and other heads of churches), sessions of parliament and election results. Volume 10, when published, will include illustrations, statistics, bibliographies and documents. Clearly the authoritative history, compiled under the auspices of the Royal Irish Academy, and a most important resource for church history.

Church records

345. *Irish church records: their history, availability and use in family and local history research.* Edited by James G. Ryan. Glenageary, Co. Dublin: Flyleaf Press, 1992. 0-9508466-4-3.

A guide to the content, location and accessibility of records of not only the Roman Catholic Church and the Church of Ireland but also of comparatively minor groups including Presbyterian, Methodist, Baptist and Quaker. Jews are also represented. Each denomination's history in Ireland is summarised, which is a useful contribution in itself, and there is a detailed index.

JAPAN

346. Trevor, Hugh. *Japan's post-war Protestant churches.* Tokyo: Seisho Domei, 1994.

This work, published by Japan's Scripture Union, traces the development of the Japanese Protestant churches since the war and provides information by means of commentary, graphs and statistics. Attention is paid also to the Roman Catholic Church, the sects and other religions of Japan. Certainly a resource which helps fill a gap in library collections.

NEW ZEALAND

A number of the reference resources cited in Part 1 and also in Chapter 2 deal with Christianity and its churches along with the other religions of New Zealand. Note particularly, *Religions of New Zealanders*, edited by Peter Donovan [125].

See also, *The Blackwell dictionary of evangelical biography* [261] for biographies of evangelicals associated with New Zealand.

Documents

347. Davidson, Allan K. and Peter J. Lineham. *Transplanted Christianity: documents illustrating aspects of New Zealand church history.* 2nd edn. Palmerston North: Dunmore Press, 1989. 0-86469-104-1 (pbk).

A comprehensive collection of documents, starting with missionary beginnings and coming through to the 1980's. Editorial introductions provide an overview of New Zealand church history and there is also commentary on particular documents.

Note that the *Yearbook for Australian churches, 1994* (Christian Research Association, 1993) [339], has as a special focus, 'Church life in New Zealand and Australia'. It includes essays, a directory and statistics on the churches in New Zealand.

Yearbooks, directories

Major denominations in New Zealand publish directories and yearbooks. Examples are:

Anglican Church in Aotearoa, New Zealand and Polynesia. *Clerical directory* (Biennial). ISSN 0529-6978.

Presbyterian Church of Aotearoa New Zealand. *Year book and directory* (Annual). ISSN 0110-0416.

Those requiring information about such denominational publications should contact the headquarters of that particular denomination.

OCEANIA

A note on the definition of 'Oceania' is to be found in Chapter 2.

Guides

MARC (Missions Advanced Research and Communication Center), a division of World Vision International, publishes a series entitled 'World Christianity'. Volumes have been issued on the Middle East, Eastern Asia, Central America and the Caribbean, South Africa, Western Europe, Eastern Europe and Oceania. The last is cited here.

348. *World Christianity: Oceania.* Edited by Leonora Mosende Douglas. Monrovia, CA: MARC, 1986. 0-912552-48-4.

Profiles describe the status of Christianity throughout the Pacific area. Coverage includes Australia, Melanesia, Micronesia, New Zealand and Polynesia. Descriptions of history, missionary endeavours and current developments are supported statistically and bibliographically. As with items in this series, this is a basic guide to often-elusive areas.

Histories

The following three items provide new perspectives on Christianity in Oceanic societies. A feature of each is the attention given to bibliographic coverage.

349. *Christianity in Oceania: ethnographic perspectives.* Edited by John Barker. (ASAO monograph, 12). Lanham, MD: University Press of America for the Association for Social Anthropology in Oceania, 1990. 0-8191-7906-X (hc); 0-8191-7907-8 (pbk).

Scholarly essays are contributed by anthropologists, church and mission historians and other specialists on religious movements in the Pacific, including New Zealand. 'While not neglecting historical roots, the authors here are primarily interested in Christianity as an established and developing Pacific island religion in its own right. We explore, in a diversity of circumstances, how islanders understand, live, reproduce and modify their Christian ideas and institutions in the post-mission era' (Editor's preface). The essays are well referenced (pp. 265-306).

350. Forman, Charles W. *The island churches of the South Pacific: emergence in the twentieth century.* (American Society of Missiology series, 5). Maryknoll, NY: Orbis, 1982. 0-88344-218-3 (pbk).

Covers the whole range of the Pacific churches, Catholic and Protestant, English and French. While giving the nineteenth-century background, the concentration is upon the twentieth-century story including a review of the independent churches in an ecumenical age. The work is characterised by a skilful use of sources. There is an extensive bibliography with a note on the location of archives (pp. 231-275).

351. Garrett, John. *To live among the stars: Christian origins in Oceania.* Geneva and Suva: World Council of Churches in association with the Institute of Pacific Studies, University of the South Pacific, 1982. 2-8254-0692-9.

A most experienced, reliable account of Catholic and Protestant origins in Oceania to 1900 and slightly beyond. Chapters deal with the various island groups, district missions and with church growth, paying particular attention to the role of islanders. There is a glossary of names and terms, and an extensive bibliography of sources consulted (pp. 319-339). An intense array of footnotes provide additional references (pp. 340-381). An index, maps and pictures. No other source matches this detailed history of Christianity's progress across Oceania.

SCOTLAND

Dictionaries and encyclopedias

352. *Dictionary of Scottish church history and theology.* Edited by Nigel M. de S. Cameron. Edinburgh: T & T Clark, 1993. 0-567-09650-5.

A comprehensive, balanced account of Christianity in Scotland. Covers Celtic, medieval, Reformation and modern history. Signed entries range from a few lines to essay-length. They encompass geography, theology, biography, art, architecture, hymnology and missions. An exceptionally fine, scholarly work and the first place to go for information about religion in Scotland.

353. Donnachie, Ian and George Hewitt. *A companion to Scottish history: from the Reformation to the present.* London: Batsford, 1989. 0-7134-5739-2.

A guide to major events and personalities that have shaped Scotland's history since the sixteenth century. Particularly important for historical debates. Appendixes include a chronology, acts and statutes, population data, a list of monasteries and there is also a section of clearly-annotated maps. The work provides directly-related as well as contextual material for church history.

6

The Bible and related literature

Within the wide-ranging field of religion no area receives the amount of reference support that is granted biblical studies. Even a cursory examination of the contents of this chapter reveals that biblical scholarship is a multifaceted engagement invoking many disciplines - textual, linguistic, historical, geographical, sociological and theological. The whole gamut of reference works is used to assist with tasks of interpretation and understanding.

Whole Bible	**120**
Guides to the literature	
Bibliographies	
Histories	
Versions	122
Bibliographies	
Ancient	122
Vulgate	122
Modern English versions	123
Modern Catholic versions	123
Evangelical Protestant versions	124
Concordances	
Dictionaries and encyclopedias	
Pronunciation	
Atlases	
Archaeology - the Holy Land	127
Biblical criticism and interpretation	128
Bibliographic surveys	
Bibliographies	
Dictionaries	
Commentaries	129
Hebrew Scriptures	**131**
Bibliographies	
Indexes and abstracts	
Introductions	

Texts and textual criticism 132
Hebrew text 132
Introductions
Texts
Modern Jewish versions 133
Hebrew grammars 134
Hebrew and Aramaic lexicons 134
Concordances
The Septuagint 136
Guides
Texts
English versions
Lexicons
Concordances
Commentaries 138
Theology of the Hebrew Scriptures 139
Theological dictionaries

Intertestamental period: Apocrypha, Pseudepigrapha, Dead Sea Scrolls and other writings. 139

Apocrypha and Pseudepigrapha 140
Guides
Texts in English
Series
The Dead Sea Scrolls 141
Guides
Catalogues
Bibliographies
Texts
Concordances

New Testament 144

Bibliographies
Indexes and abstracts
Introductions
Textual studies 147
Guides
Texts
Greek grammars 148
Greek lexicons 149
Concordances
Dictionaries
Literary forms 151
Commentaries 152
Guides
Series
The Gospels 152
The Synoptic problem 152
Bibliographies
Parallels

Jesus research   153
  Bibliographies
Pauline material   153
  Parallels

New Testament Apocryphal literature and Gnostic writings   **154**

  Guides
  Texts
  Series
Nag Hammadi codices   155
  Texts
 Relation to the Bible   156

WHOLE BIBLE

Guides to the literature

354. Danker, Frederick W. *Multipurpose tools for Bible study*. Rev. and expanded edn. Minneapolis, MN: Fortress Press, 1993. 0-8006-2598-6.

Bibliographic essays present a most comprehensive selection of resources, their history and effective use. Particularly valuable for advice on the choice of versions of the Bible and on the uses of lexicons and biblical commentaries. There are chapters also on Judaica and the Dead Sea Scrolls. In all, a very helpful literature guide.

355. Fitzmyer, Joseph A. *An introductory bibliography for the study of Scripture*. 3rd edn. (Subsidia biblica 3). Rome: Editrice Pontificio Istituto Biblico, 1990. 88-7653-592-6.

Critically annotated bibliography covering all aspects of serious biblical study. Asterisks are used to denote comparative importance and references are given to reviews of the book in question. The work of a major scholar in the field.

The above resources will be cited as 'Danker' and 'Fitzmyer' as they are invoked on several topics in later sections of this chapter.

See also Edward Starkey, *Judaism and Christianity* [9] for a section on the Bibles of the two traditions.

Bibliographies

The most comprehensive annual bibliographic resource for biblical studies is:

356. *Elenchus of Biblica*, 1985 -. Rome: Pontifical Biblical Institute Press, 1988 Annual.

This work superseded *Elenchus bibliographicus biblicus*, 1920-1984. Vols. 1-48 (1920-1967) of that index formed part of the journal, *Biblica*. From volume 49 (1968) it was published as a separate bibliography. The present series with this title, *Elenchus of Biblica*, began with the 1985 volume.

Covers books and periodicals in all major European languages and is most thorough. No annotations, but detailed indexes. Note a delay in publication of some three years.

The gap is filled, to some extent by the following item.

357. *Internationale Zeitschriftenschau für Bibelwissenschaft und Grenzgebiete: International review of biblical studies 1951/1952- .* Düsseldorf: Patmos, 1952- . Annual.

Abbreviated as *IZBG*, this is an annual index to periodical articles, Festschriften, reports and book reviews covering the Bible and related areas. Its prompt publication means that it complements the *Elenchus* (above). Citations are arranged in classified order, with the table of contents at the end of each issue. The items are usually accompanied by abstracts which are in one of several languages, including English. There is an author index. Students without German will still be able to find value in this work.

Covering biblical scholarship from 1930 to 1983 inclusive is the following three-volume set:

358. Langevin, Paul Émile. *Bibliographie biblique. Biblical bibliography. Biblische Bibliographie. Bibliografia biblica. Bibliografiabíblica. 1930-1983.* 3 vols. Quebec: Presses de l'Université Laval, 1972, 1978, 1985. 0-7746-6476-2; 0-7746-6793-1; 2-7637-7060-6.

Introductory material is in the five languages featured in the title. The work began as an index to Roman Catholic periodicals but, with the second volume, other denominational material was included as was the indexing of the contents of books. Because of the additional titles indexed in volumes 2 and 3 it may be necessary to use all three volumes in searching. The classification system is precise (note especially the five cumulative tables of headings at the end of the third volume) and this, together with the indexes, make for easy access. Indispensable for biblical and related research to 1983.

Individual books

The bibliographic series, Books of the Bible, is edited by Henry O. Thompson and published by Garland Publishing, New York. To date volumes include:

359. Thompson, Henry O. *The book of Daniel: an annotated bibliography.* (Books of the Bible, 1). New York: Garland, 1993. 0-8240-4873-3.

360. Muse, Robert L. *The Book of Revelation: an annotated bibliography.* (Books of the Bible, 2). New York: Garland, 1994. 0-8240-7394-0.

361. Mills, Watson E. *1 Corinthians: an annotated bibliography.* (Books of the Bible, 4). New York: Garland, 1994. 0-8153-0890-6.

362. Wittstruck, Thorne. *The book of Psalms: an annotated bibliography.* 2 vols. (Books of the Bible, 5). New York: Garland, 1994. 0-8240-4700-1.

363. Caspi, Mishael Maswari. *The book of Ruth: an annotated bibliography.* (Books of the Bible, 7). New York: Garland, 1994. 0-8240-4632-3.

The intention of the series, which also includes bibliographies on the books of both Testaments, is to represent the scholarship of the last fifty years as comprehensively as possible. Annotations are selective, but thorough. Methods of indexing vary from volume to volume within the series.

Subject bibliography. Law

364. Welch, John W. *A biblical law bibliography.* (Toronto studies in theology, 51). Lewiston, NY: Edwin Mellen, 1990. 0-88946-891-5.

A bibliography of books and articles relevant to the study of biblical law which, in addition to materials on Jewish law, includes ancient Near Eastern studies and New Testament items. The arrangement is by subject, from 'Abortion' and 'Adoption' through 'Torts' and 'Usury', and there is an author-title index. Although designed to supplement the surveys of current literature that are published in the *Jewish law annual,* the work functions very well as an independent resource particularly for work in biblical ethics.

Histories

The standard work in this field remains:

365. *The Cambridge history of the Bible.* Various editors. 3 vols. Cambridge University Press, 1963-1970. 0-521-29018-X.

Contents: Vol. 1, From the beginning to Jerome (1970); vol. 2, The West from the fathers to the Reformation (1969); vol. 3, The West from the Reformation to the present day (1963).

Essays comprehensively cover all matters concerning texts, versions, translations and the transmission and influence of the Bible. Illustrated with plates. Separate bibliographies and indexing in each volume.

VERSIONS

Bibliographies

366. Chamberlin, William J. *Catalogue of English Bible translations: a classified bibliography of versions and editions including books, parts, and Old and New Testament Apocrypha and Apocryphal books.* (Bibliographies and indexes in religious studies, 21). Westport, CT: Greenwood Press, 1991. 0-313-28041-X.

Chamberlin attempts to list complete Bibles, Testaments, portions, single books, single chapters, commentaries with their own translation, theology books that contain the respective author's own translation of biblical quotations, children's Bibles, Apocryphal books, the Dead Sea scrolls, Josephus (whose *Antiquities* can be classified 'as a padded paraphrase of the historical portions of the Old Testament' (Preface p. xvi), early church fathers and the Koran. Within each section the titles are listed chronologically and some are annotated. Index of known translators, editors and named translations. Augments and updates but does not supersede A. S. Herbert's, *Historical catalogue of printed editions of the English Bible, 1525-1961* (1968). Most useful for those engaged in translating (and collecting).

Ancient

The most important editions of the ancient versions of the Bible - Aramaic, Latin, Syriac, Coptic, Targumic - are described in the two guides cited at the beginning of this section, Danker [354], chapter 10, and Fitzmyer [355], chapter vii.

Vulgate

367. *Biblia sacra iuxta vulgatam versionem.* Edited by Robert Weber. 2 vols. Stuttgart: Württembergische Bibelanstalt, 1969 (3rd rev. edn, 1983).

Valuable with respect to text and apparatus. Includes Jerome's prefaces. Text is based on critical editions. The Psalms are presented in both the Septuagint and the Hebrew text.

368. *Nova Vulgata bibliorum sacrorum editio.* Vatican City: Libreria Editrice Vaticana, 1979.

A new revised edition, ordered particularly for use in the revision of Catholic liturgy. A more recent edition (1986) has additional prefatory material.

Modern English versions

Once again Danker (chapters 10, 11) and Fitzmyer (chapter vii) provide descriptions of English versions. See also Keith R. Crim, 'Modern English versions of the Bible.' In *The New interpreter's Bible* [406], vol. 1, pp. 22-32.

369. *NRSV - The Holy Bible containing the Old and New Testaments with the Apocryphal/Deuterocanonical Books: New Revised Standard Version.* Oxford University Press, 1989. Numerous editions.

'To summarise in a single sentence: the New Revised Standard Version, of the Bible is an authorized revision of the Revised Standard Version, published in 1952, which was a revision of the American Standard Version, published in 1901, which, in turn, embodied earlier revisions of the King James Version, published in 1611.' In terms of text, exegesis and language the *NRSV* is likely to succeed the *RSV* (1946-1952) as the most widely accepted English translation for our time.

The quotation above is from page ix of the following work:

370. *The New Oxford annotated Bible with the Apocryphal / Deutero-canonical books. Edited by Bruce M. Metzger and Roland E. Murphy.* New York: Oxford University Press, 1991. 0-19-528356-2.

Contains the full text of *NRSV* with an authoritative, multi-denominational team contributing introductory essays and annotations to the several books.

371. *REB - Revised English Bible with the Apocrypha.* Oxford University Press; Cambridge University Press, 1989. Numerous editions.

A radical revision of the *New English Bible* (1970) reflecting more recent scholarship. The work of a multi-denominational committee which may help to account for a conservative restraint evident in textual and linguistic decisions. The following item is a companion to this version:

372. *The Oxford study Bible: Revised English Bible with the Apocrypha .* Edited by M. Jack Suggs et al. Oxford University Press, 1992. 0-19-529001-1.

Leading Jewish and Christian scholars provide introductory essays. The full text of the *REB* is printed with explanatory and interpretative notes to the text. Plates and maps add to the comprehensiveness.

Modern Catholic versions

373. *NAB - The New American Bible: translated from the original languages with critical use of all the ancient sources by Members of the Catholic Biblical Association of America, with textual notes on Old Testament readings.* Paterson, NJ: St Anthony Guild Press, 1970. Numerous editions.

The translation of the Old Testament was applauded but that of the New Testament was deemed to be seriously defective. Subsequently, the translation of the New Testament was redone and published as:

374. *The New American Bible: the New Testament revised edition.* New York: Catholic Book Publishing Co., 1987. Numerous editions.

Altogether, this is the first version to provide Catholics with a translation from the original texts rather than from the Vulgate. It has been published by other companies, but not always with the pages of textual notes which formed part of the 1970 edition. The following item is a companion to this version.

The full text, with the revised translation of the New Testament is to be found in:

375. *The Catholic study Bible: The New American Bible.* Edited by Donald Senior et al. New York: Oxford University Press, 1990. 0-19-528389-9.

Scholarly introductions, essays and notes to the full text of the *NAB*. In all, more than six hundred pages of study material contributed by Catholic biblical scholars.

376. *NJB - New Jerusalem Bible.* London: Darton, Longman & Todd; Garden City, NY: Doubleday, 1985. Numerous editions.

A revised edition of the *Jerusalem Bible* of 1966. The introductions and helpful footnotes of the *NJB* are drawn from the French revision of 1973, but the translation of the text itself is now made directly from the original languages. A significantly improved version.

Evangelical Protestant versions

377. *NIV - The Holy Bible: New International Version.* Grand Rapids, MI: Zondervan, 1978. Numerous editions.

A group of evangelical scholars who viewed the so-called 'liberalism' of the *Revised Standard Version* (1952) with some suspicion prepared this more cautious translation. The preface affirms that 'the translators were united in their commitment to the authority and infallibility of the Bible as God's Word in written form'. The Apocrypha is not included.

It is interesting to note that the *New Interpreter's Bible* [406] presents the text of the *NIV* and that of the *NRSV* in parallel columns.

Concordances

There are concordances for most of the major versions of the Bible. Should there be need to track down a text in the King James (KJV) or Authorised version of the Bible (1611) one needs:

378. Cruden, Alexander. *A complete concordance to the Holy Scriptures of the Old and New Testaments.*

First published in 1737, but revised and enlarged by various hands and published in many editions. Cruden dealt only with the English text of the KJV.

Best-known examples of concordances citing the various Hebrew, Aramaic and Greek words that are translated are:

379. Strong, James. *Exhaustive concordance of the Bible.* New York: Hunt and Eaton; Cincinnati: Cranston and Curts, 1894 (often reprinted).

380. Young, Robert. *Analytical concordance to the Bible.* New York: American Book Exchange, 1879, 1880 (numerous editions and revisions from several publishers).

Be warned that certain recent editions of Young suffer from abridgments.

Vulgate

381. Dutripon, Francois Pascal. *Concordantiae bibliorum sacrorum vulgatae editionis.* Paris: E. Belin, 1853 (numerous editions and reprints, and with varying titles).

The best of the earlier one-volume concordances to the Latin Vulgate, but superseded by:

382. Fischer, Boniface. *Novae concordantiae bibliorum sacrorum iuxta Vulgatam versionem critice editam.* 5 vols. Stuttgart/Bad Cannstatt: Frommann-Holzboog, 1977.

A completely new computer-generated concordance to Weber's edition of the Vulgate [367].

Recent English versions

The following two volumes have been praised by biblical scholars as well as representatives of the computer industry. Both are excellent tools and the choice, of course, depends upon whether the *NIV* or *NRSV* is being used.

383. *NIV* - Goodrick, Edward W. and John R. Kohlenberger (eds). *The NIV exhaustive concordance.* Grand Rapids, MI: Zondervan, 1990. 0-310-43690-7.

Not to be confused with the *NIV complete concordance* (1981) which it expands.

384. *NRSV* - Kohlenberger, John R. *The NRSV concordance unabridged: including the Apocryphal/Deuterocanonical books.* Grand Rapids, MI: Zondervan, 1991. 0-310-53910-2.

Dictionaries and encyclopedias

General

385. *The Anchor Bible dictionary (ABD).* Edited by David Noel Freedman and associates. 6 vols. New York: Doubleday, 1992.

Some 1,000 scholars represent recent developments in the many areas of biblical research. This set generally updates the highly-regarded *Interpreter's dictionary of the Bible* (*IDB*), edited by George Arthur Buttrick. 4 vols. (Nashville, TN: Abingdon Press, 1962), and its Supplementary volume edited by Keith Crim (New York: Abingdon, 1976). This older work, however, is assumed at many points and will remain valuable. The entries in *ABD* are cross-referenced but the set desperately calls for a general index. A monumental work and, for most topics, the first place to search.

386. *International standard Bible encyclopedia.* Rev. edn. Edited by Geoffrey Bromiley. 4 vols. Grand Rapids, MI: Eerdmans, 1979-1988. 0-8028-8160-2.

A complete reconstruction of a work whose first edition was published in 1915 and second in 1930. Covers terms, topics, people and places with entries ranging from a few lines to several pages. The contributors are evangelical scholars and the general perspective is one of 'reasonable conservatism'. So it tends to complement *ABD* and confirms the adage that, on any given topic, it is best to consult more than one dictionary.

387. *The Oxford companion to the Bible.* Edited by Bruce M. Metzger and Michael D. Coogan. New York: Oxford University Press, 1993. 0-19-504645-5.

Ranging beyond the scope of a traditional dictionary this distinctively academic resource includes interpretative essays which trace the influence of the biblical message on the arts, law, literature, politics and social issues. Short entries provide data on the expected topics. Includes maps and a detailed subject index. This is a rich compendium of information and reflection.

Deities and demons

388. *Dictionary of deities and demons in the Bible (DDD).* Edited by Karel van der Toorn, Bob Becking and Pieter W. van der Horst. Leiden: E. J. Brill, 1995. 90-04-10313-9.

A reference source on the gods, angels, demons, spirits and humans having acquired semi-divine status whose names occur in the Bible. More than four hundred names are treated in entries which discuss the pertinent name, its meaning and religio-historical background and relevant biblical passages. Some entries include extensive bibliographies. The contributors are well-qualified scholars and the whole work promises to be an authoritative guide to the spiritual world which shadowed the biblical records.

Bible and literature

389. *A Dictionary of biblical tradition in English literature.* Edited by David Lyle Jeffrey. Grand Rapids, MI: Eerdmans, 1992. 0-8028-3634-8.

Intends to show how biblical motifs, concepts, names, quotations and allusions have been transmitted through the Jewish and Christian exegetical tradition and then used by authors of English literature from the Anglo-Saxon to the modern. Scholarly essays and articles cover biblical studies, history of interpretation and the Bible in literature. Detailed, annotated bibliographies are at the end of the volume. A most versatile research tool.

Pronunciation

390. *Harper's Bible pronunciation guide.* Edited by William O. Walker et al. San Francisco, CA: Harper & Row, 1989. 0-06-068951-X.

Although some biblical encyclopedias provide the pronunciation of names in the English Bible, this authoritative resource, endorsed by the Society of Biblical Literature, is for those needing a more comprehensive and accessible guide. It is divided into two sections: 'Biblical terms' (both proper and common names) and 'Nonbiblical terms' (covering terms that are important for biblical study, for example 'eschatology' and 'hermeneutics'). Hebrew and Greek words (such as *torah* and *agape*), now currently in use in English, are also included. An easy-to-use pronunciation key is reproduced across the bottom of each page. The work is as definitive as such a project allows.

Atlases

During the last decade a number of biblical atlases have been published. In terms of cartography, illustrative material and commentary the following two works may be regarded as outstanding.

391. Aharoni, Yohanan and Michael Avi-Yonah. *The Macmillan Bible atlas.* 3rd edn. New York: Macmillan, 1993. 0-02-500605-3.

Updates the second edition (1977) with the commentary material being thoroughly revised. Emphasis is on the Holy Land. The text material is accompanied by well-crafted territorial maps and illustrations of costumes, tools, artefacts, coins and weapons. A highly-regarded, scholarly work.

392. *The Harper atlas of the Bible.* Edited by James B. Pritchard. New York: Harper & Row, 1987. 0-06-181883-6. Published in Great Britain as *The Times atlas of the Bible* (1987). 1-86256-055-2.

A brilliant attempt to detail the land, events, people, wars, and customs of the Bible. Includes colour photographs, drawings, graphs and excellent maps with an informative text by some fifty scholars who include archaeologists, historians and theologians. A detailed chronology extending from the beginnings to 150 CE provides a structure and context for the map work. Several indexes, include a listing, with scriptural references, of eminent biblical characters and of place names, with variants.

See also the next section, 'Archaeology'.

ARCHAEOLOGY - THE HOLY LAND

393. *The New encyclopedia of archaeological excavations in the Holy Land.* Edited by Ephraim Stern et al. 4 vols. New York: Simon & Schuster, 1993. 0-13-276288-9 (set).

Effectively replaces the *Encyclopedia of archaeological excavations in the Holy Land,* edited by Michael Avi-Yonah (1975-1978). The text covers some four hundred sites and is accompanied by over four thousand illustrations, maps, charts and drawings. The fourth volume concludes with chronological tables, a glossary, an index to persons, places and biblical references. A major achievement.

394. *The Archaeological encyclopedia of the Holy Land.* Rev. edn. Edited by Avraham Negev. Nashville, TN: Nelson, 1986. 0-8407-7523-7.

A useful one-volume work which improves considerably on the first English edition of 1972. Its task is to comment on 'the majority of the geographical names mentioned in the Bible, both places in the Holy Land and countries and cities in other parts of the Middle East, identifying them as far as possible, describing the excavations that have been carried out at or near them, and analyzing the importance of the finds they have yielded' (Preface). Well-illustrated.

395. Murphy-O'Connor, Jerome. *The Holy Land: an archaeological guide from earliest times to 1700.* 2nd edn. Oxford University Press, 1986. 0-19-285158-6 (pbk).

A deservedly popular work, especially with tourists. O'Connor presupposes little knowledge and provides clear directions to sites and monuments. Excellent on Jerusalem.

BIBLICAL CRITICISM AND INTERPRETATION

Bibliographic surveys

A trilogy of volumes, The Bible and its modern interpreters, published under the auspices of the Society of Biblical Literature, effectively presents scholarly opinion on research work in the numerous subdisciplines since the 1940s. The volumes are:

396. *The Hebrew Bible and its modern interpreters.* Edited by Douglas A. Knight and Gene M. Tucker. Philadelphia, PA: Fortress Press; Atlanta, GA: Scholars Press, 1985. 0-8006-0721-X (Fortress Press).

397. *Early Judaism and its modern interpreters.* Edited by Robert A. Kraft and George W. E. Nickelsburg. Philadelphia, PA: Fortress Press; Atlanta, GA: Scholars Press, 1986. 0-8006-0722-8 (Fortress Press).

398. *The New Testament and its modern interpreters.* Edited by Eldon Jay Epp and George W. MacRae. Philadephia, PA: Fortress Press; Atlanta, GA: Scholars Press, 1989. 0-8006-0724-4 (Fortress Press).

Each volume contains quality bibliographic essays, contributed by an international and ecumenical array of specialists, who review and evaluate the 'state of the art' of each area of studies. They comprise valuable texts and, given the strength of the bibliographies, major reference works.

Bibliographies

399. Powell, Mark Allan et al. *The Bible and modern literary criticism: a critical assessment and annotated bibliography.* (Bibliographies and indexes in religious studies, 22). Westport, CT: Greenwood Press, 1992. 0-313-27546-7.

Following an introductory essay outlining the nature of literary criticism, there is an extensive critically-annotated bibliography on the basis, theory and method of this mode of criticism. Then individual biblical books are covered and finally possible implications for homiletics, theology and literary studies. Indexes are to authors and editors, titles and an all-important subject index.

400. Watson, Duane F. and Alan J. Hauser. *Rhetorical criticism of the Bible: a comprehensive bibliography with notes on history and method.* (Biblical interpretation series, 4). Leiden: Brill, 1994. 90-04-09903-4.

A division into two parts accommodates the Hebrew Scriptures and the New Testament. Each part is introduced by an essay surveying the history and method of rhetorical criticism as pertinent to that Testament. Then follows bibliographic coverage of the Hebrew Scriptures and extra-canonical books, on the one hand, and of Greco-Roman rhetoric and selected topics of New Testament rhetoric, including individual New Testament books, on the other. Essential for all who contemplate using rhetorical criticism as a methodology for biblical interpretation.

Dictionaries

401. *A Dictionary of biblical interpretation.* Edited by R. J. Coggins and J. L. Houlden. London: SCM Press, 1990. 0-334-00294-X (hc); 0-334-00314-8 (pbk).

Not a normal Bible dictionary. The emphasis is on interpretation rather than biblical content. How have biblical books, characters and terms been interpreted? It covers the influential schools of interpretation, leading scholars and the varieties of biblical criticism. Attractively produced and deservedly popular.

402. Soulen, Richard N. *Handbook of biblical criticism.* 2nd edn. Atlanta, GA: John Knox Press, 1981. 0-8042-0045-9.

Defines terms associated with critical methodologies, summarises the work of scholars in this field and comments on research tools and texts. A well-regarded and accessible resource.

COMMENTARIES

Note: for discussions on commentaries and their uses, see Danker [354], chapter 15, and Fitzmyer [355], chapter xiii.

One-volume

403. *The New Jerome biblical commentary.* Edited by R. E. Brown, J. A. Fitzmyer and R. E. Murphy. Englewood Cliffs, NJ: Prentice Hall; London: Chapman, 1990. 0-13-614934-0.

A major revision and updating of the *Jerome biblical commentary* (1968), this work by some seventy North American Catholic scholars reflects a range of exegetical techniques as well as participation in ecumenical dialogue. In addition to a commentary on each book of the Bible including, of course, the so-called 'deutero-canonical books, there are important thematic articles. Note the extensive index of subjects and persons.

404. *Harper's Bible commentary.* Edited by J. L. Mays. San Francisco: Harper & Row, 1988. 0-06-065541-0.

Members, Jewish and Christian, of the Society of Biblical Literature contribute introductory essays and commentaries on individual books. The intention is 'to make the best current scholarship available to general audiences for reading and studying the books of the Bible' (Preface).

405. *Women's Bible commentary.* Edited by Carol A. Newsom and Sharon H. Ringe. Louisville, KY: Westminster/John Knox, 1992. 0-664-21922-5.

Several articles introduce feminist perspectives for biblical study, then individual commentary-chapters on each book point up the importance of these perspectives for the interpretation of the text. A selective commentary, but one bristling with insights.

Multi-volume

406. *New interpreter's Bible: general articles and introduction, commentary, and reflections for each book of the Bible, including the Apocryphal/Deuterocanonical books.* Edited by Leander Keck et al. 12 vols. Nashville, TN: Abingdon Press, 1994- . 0-687-27814-7 (vol. 1).

Projected in 12 volumes, the *NIB* provides general articles, particularly in volumes 1 and 8 (the beginning of the coverage of the Old and New Testaments respectively). Treatment of each book includes an introduction, bibliography and outline. Then the texts of the New International Version and the New Revised Standard Version are presented in parallel columns. Units of the text are followed by a commentary section with exegetical analysis and there is a further section called 'Reflections'. This ecumenical work is designed to support teaching and preaching, study and reflection.

Series

It is customary to introduce series of biblical commentaries with a caution. The quality of scholarship, within a series, may vary considerably. The search should not be for the best series but rather the best commentary on a particular biblical book. With this caution, the following are regarded as major series.

407. Anchor Bible. Garden City, NY: Doubleday, 1964 - .

Catholics, Jews and Protestants have contributed to this still incomplete series. Basically a new translation with notes. The format and quality of the earlier volumes varied considerably, but certain recent entries, for example Raymond Brown's volumes on John and the Johannine epistles, have added some necessary prestige. Note that the series includes the extra-canonical books.

408. Continental commentaries. Minneapolis, MN: Variously Augsburg and Fortress Press, 1984- .

A series of sophisticated, yet accessible, commentaries representing the finest in European scholarship. Claus Westermann on Genesis, Hans-Joachim Kraus on the Psalms and Ulrich Luz on Matthew are but some of the outstanding volumes.

409. Hermeneia: a critical and historical commentary on the Bible. Minneapolis, MN: Fortress Press, 1971- .

Features both original works in English and translations of major German commentaries. This is the most scholarly series available and, in spite of the datedness of certain German inclusions, still invaluable for serious study.

410. International critical commentary on the Holy Scriptures of the Old and New Testaments (ICC). Edinburgh: T. & T. Clark. 1895 - .

Many of the older volumes are seriously outdated but new editions of certain existing volumes are being published and commentaries on books which have not appeared in ICC are in preparation. The new series, beginning with C. E. B. Cranfield's two-volume work on Romans (1975, 1979), and including a major commentary on Matthew by W. D. Davies and D. Allison (1988, 1991-) continues the tradition of sound exegetical scholarship. Note that original texts are cited without translation.

411. Interpretation: a Bible commentary for preaching and teaching. Louisville, KY: Westminster/John Knox, 1983- .

Noted biblical scholars, James L. Mays and Patrick D. Miller edit the Old Testament volumes while Paul J. Achtemeier directs the New Testament contributions. The series intends to represent 'the integrated result of historical and theological work with the biblical text', and to transpose this research in order to assist preachers and educationalists. The series reveals the usual unevenness, but some of the volumes, by well-known authorities, are outstanding.

412. New Century Bible commentary. London, Marshall Pickering; Grand Rapids, MI: Eerdmans, 1966- .

Scholarly and moderately critical, this series has earned wide respect across the Christian traditions. To date it is based on the Revised Standard Version and presents a middle-of-the-way, verse-by-verse exposition of the text. Contributors have been carefully chosen and their work reflects recent exegetical developments.

413. Word biblical commentary (WBC). Waco,TX: Word Books, 1982 - .

With a comprehensive mandate to serve the needs of professional scholars and teachers, seminary students and working ministers, this series aims to present 'the best in evangelical critical scholarship'. For each unit of text there is usually an introduction, then a bibliography, translation, notes on the text, analysis of form structure and setting and then, finally, commentary. Perhaps best described as a preacher's commentary.

HEBREW SCRIPTURES

The term, 'Hebrew Scriptures' is chosen rather than the historical Christian designation, 'Old Testament', to acknowledge that this larger portion of the Bible is, in every respect, Jewish.

Bibliographies

414. *Book list, 1946-* . London: The Society for Old Testament Study, 1946- . ISSN 0309-0892.

The chief marks of this annual are its comprehensiveness, authority and immediacy. Using a classified arrangement, it reviews major publications relating to the Hebrew Bible and associated areas. The 1995 issue contains reviews of more than 500 titles. These reviews, by contributing scholars, are descriptive and critical. There are indexes to authors, periodicals and series. A most important bibliography and reviewing medium.

Indexes and abstracts

415. *Old Testament abstracts.* Vol. 1, no.1- , Feb. 1978- . Washington, DC: Catholic Biblical Association of America, 1978- . 3 issues per year. ISSN 0364-8591.

OTA cites and abstracts articles from periodical literature and, separately, notes and describes the contents of recent books published on the Hebrew Scriptures and related areas. Annual indexes, in the third issue of a year, are to authors, scriptural passages and to words in Hebrew and other ancient languages.

Note: The Catholic Biblical Association and the American Theological Library Association began jointly producing *OTA* on CD-ROM in July/August 1995.

Introductions

Remembering that the kind of reference question one would put to an introduction could well be satisfied by a comprehensive Bible dictionary.

416. Anderson, B. W. *Understanding the Old Testament.* 4th edn. Englewood Cliffs, NJ: Prentice Hall, 1986. 0-13-935925-7. The British title is *The living world of the Old Testament* (London: Longman).

Since the first edition in 1957, an excellent introductory text by an eminent scholar. Emphasis is on the history and religion of Israel. Joseph Fitzmyer regards this work as 'the best introductory textbook for college-students and seminarians'. *Introductory bibliography for the study of Scripture* [355], p. 107.

417. Soggin, J. A. *Introduction to the Old Testament: from its origins to the closing of the Alexandrian Canon.* 3rd edn. London: SCM Pr., 1989. 0-334-00702-X.

Authored by a member of the Waldensian Faculty of Theology in Rome this work has been highly regarded since its first appearance in 1967. This translation, based on the fourth Italian edition (1987), has been substantially rewritten and completely reset. It clearly reflects recent scholarship.

Texts and Textual Criticism

Hebrew text

Introductions

418. Würthwein, Ernst. *The text of the Old Testament: an introduction to the Biblia Hebraica.* 2nd edn. Grand Rapids, MI: Eerdmans, 1995. 0-8028-0788-7.

Translation of the fifth edition of *Der Text des Alten Testaments* (1988). This work, regarded as a classic introduction to the textual criticism of the Hebrew Scriptures, is here updated in the light of new editions of the texts and recent contributions to research. Included are chapters on the methods of textual criticism, its theological significance and a most useful appendix containing further resources for textual research.

For a brief but helpful bibliographic note on the development of an authoritative Hebrew text, see Danker, *Multipurpose tools* [354], pp. 46–47, note 4.

Texts

419. *Biblia Hebraica Stuttgartensia (BHS).* 4th rev. edn. Edited by K. Elliger and W. Rudolph et al. Stuttgart: Deutsche Bibelgesellschaft, 1990. 3-438-05219-9.

The standard critical edition. Usually the text preferred by examining bodies. For an orientation to *BHS* see:

420. Wonneberger, Reinhard. *Understanding BHS: a manual for the users of Biblia Hebraica Stuttgartensia.* 2nd rev. edn. (Subsidia biblica, 8). Rome: Editrice Pontificio Istituto Biblico, 1990. 88-7653-578-0.

Enables beginning students to gain access to the language of both the text and Masoretic apparatus of *BHS*. Another simple and straightforward guide is:

421. Scott, William. *A simplified guide to BHS.* 2nd edn. Berkeley, CA: Bibal Press, 1990. 0-941037-14-2.
   Bound with *An English key to the Latin words and abbreviations and the symbols of Biblia Hebraica Stuttgartensia*, by H. P. Rüger.

Concise guide to the system of Masoretic notation and to the symbols and abbreviations.

Interlinear texts

An interlinear version can be helpful in providing beginning students with a grammatically literal word-for-word translation of the Hebrew. An edition based on *BHS*, and now in one volume is:

422. *The NIV interlinear Hebrew-English Old Testament.* Edited by John R. Kohlenberger. Grand Rapids, MI: Zondervan, 1987. 0-310-44220-6.

Originally published in four volumes (1979-1985). The Hebrew text is the *Biblia Hebraica Stuttgartensia* and the English text is the *New International Version*.

Pentateuch

423. Campbell, Antony F. and Mark O'Brien. *Sources of the Pentateuch: texts, introductions, annotations.* Minneapolis, MN: Fortress Press, 1993. 0-8006-2701-6.

Presents the complete NRSV text of the Priestly document, the Yahwist narrative, the Elohist texts, and non-source texts of the Pentateuch, with introductions which review the history of source-oriented research and with notes and annotations. An essential aid to studies in Pentateuchal criticism.

Modern Jewish versions

424. *Tanakh: a new translation of the Holy Scriptures according to the traditional Hebrew text.* Philadelphia, PA: Jewish Publication Society, 1985. 0-8276-0252-9.

The one-volume edition of a Jewish version which made its debut in 1962 and which was originally issued in the following three volumes:

The Torah: the five books of Moses: a new translation of the Holy Scriptures according to the Masoretic text: First section. Philadelphia, PA: Jewish Publication Society of America, 1962.
The Prophets Nev'im: Second section, 1978.
The Writings Kethubim: Third Section, 1982.

An authoritative translation by American Jewish scholars; notes indicate textual emendations and variant readings.

Hebrew grammars

The last decade or so has seen the publication of numerous Hebrew grammars and textbooks on the language. There is an extensive discussion of 'Hebrew Old Testament grammars and lexicons' in Danker, *Multipurpose tools* [354], chapter 6. In the present section are listed two classical works and an example of a new entry to the field which has been well received. Keep in mind the distinction between a grammar for beginners and an advanced reference grammar.

425. Lambdin, T. O. *Introduction to biblical Hebrew.* New York: Charles Scribner's Sons, 1971. 0-684-41322-1; London: Darton, Longman & Todd, 1973. 0-232-51202-7.

This thorough and well-tried work is more of a reference grammar than a guide for beginning students.

426. Martin, James D. *Davidson's introductory Hebrew grammar.* Edinburgh: T & T Clark, 1993. 0-567-09642-4.

A complete revision and modernisation of the classic introduction which was first published in 1874. While presupposing no previous knowledge of the grammar, it is designed to enable the student, as soon as possible, to read the Hebrew text.

427. Seow, Choon Leong. *A grammar for biblical Hebrew.* Nashville, TN: Abingdon Press, 1987. 0-687-15683-1.

A course introduction to the fundamentals. All illustrations are from the Hebrew Scriptures.

A companion, providing answer keys and a study guide, is the following:

428. Hamilton, Jeffries M. and Jeffrey S. Rogers. *A grammar for biblical Hebrew: handbook.* Nashville, TN: Abingdon, 1989. 0-687-15685-8.

Hebrew and Aramaic lexicons

429. Koehler, Ludwig, Walter Baumgartner and Johann Stamm. *The Hebrew and Aramaic lexicon of the Old Testament.* 4 vols. Leiden: Brill, 1994- . 90-04-09799-7 (set).
Volume 1, *aleph - Heth,* 1994; volume 2, *Teth - ayin,* due for publication toward the end of 1995, and the remaining volumes by 1997.

This English version of a classic reference tool has been translated from the third German edition (1967-). It uses a strictly alphabetical order of entries rather than arrangement by verbal roots. Long recognised as a monument of biblical scholarship, this translation will ensure its continuing as the standard modern dictionary for biblical Hebrew.

A combination of the third and earlier German editions was used to produce the following:

430. Holladay, W. L. *A concise Hebrew and Aramaic lexicon of the Old Testament, based upon the lexical work of Ludwig Koehler and Walter Baumgartner.* Leiden: Brill, 1971 (numerous reprints).

This is a condensed version of the above work, and a user-friendly resource for the beginning student.

431. Brown, F., S. R. Driver and C. A. Briggs. *A Hebrew and English lexicon of the Old Testament (BDB).* Corr. edn. Oxford: Clarendon, 1952.

Originally published in 1907 with reprints and, from 1953 onwards, with corrections. Hardly for beginners in that the words are arranged by Hebrew roots rather than alphabetically. Although outdated by recent linguistic research and the discovery of additional ancient documents it is still a valuable reference resource if used with caution.

The following item is designed to help a student exploit *BDB*.

432. Einspahr, Bruce. *Index to Brown, Driver & Briggs Hebrew lexicon.* Rev. edn. Chicago: Moody Press, 1977. 0-8024-4082-7.

This *Index*, by going through the Old Testament verse by verse, helps the student find both the root and the appropriate contextual nuances of the word being studied.

433. *The Dictionary of classical Hebrew.* Edited by David Clines. Vol. 1, *Aleph.* Sheffield: Sheffield Academic Press, 1993- . 1-85075-244-3 (vol. 1); vol. 2, *Beth-Waw*, 1995. 1-85075-544-2.

Sponsored by the (British) Society for Old Testament Study this work will appear in eight volumes. It is announced as the first dictionary ever compiled of the classical Hebrew language as a whole, that is, including the Hebrew Scriptures, Ben Sira, the Dead Sea Scrolls and other Hebrew texts down to around 200 CE. Citations are given for all the occurrences of a given word in the extant literature. Biblical Aramaic is not included. Appears as a promising replacement for Brown, Driver and Briggs.

434. Andersen, Francis I. and A. Dean Forbes. *The vocabulary of the Old Testament.* Rome: Editrice Pontificio Istituto Biblico, 1989. 88-7653-575-6.

Designed 'to provide easy and accurate access to vocabulary distribution' (p. vii). It presents the entire Hebrew and Aramaic vocabulary in several distinct ways. The text used is that of the Leningrad Codex. There are cross-references to Brown, Driver, to Mandelkern and Even-Shoshan and indexes to deities, persons, places and general terms. J. A. Emerton, in a review, writes, 'This book offers a new tool for the study of the Hebrew Bible, and is one of the most valuable aids to biblical study to be published for many years.' *Vetus Testamentum* 43 (1993): 130.

435. Owens, John Joseph. *Analytical key to the Old Testament.* 4 vols. Grand Rapids, MI: Baker Book House, 1989-1992. 0-8010-6713-8 (vol. 4).

Should help those with a modicum of Hebrew. Using the text of *Biblia Hebraica Stuttgartensia* , Owens moves through the Old Testament verse by verse, giving each word or phrase its grammatical identification, the page number in Brown, Driver where the word appears, and an English translation. For verb forms it also supplies the root.

Concordances

436. Lisowsky, Gerhard and Leonhard Rost. *Konkordanz zum Hebräischen Alten Testament.* 3rd rev. edn. Stuttgart: Deutsche Bibelgesellschaft, 1993.

First published in 1958, this is the reduced-format edition of the 1990 edition. Gives German, Latin and English translations of the Hebrew word. Introductory material is also printed in English. Because the arrangement is simply by words it is useful for quick reference.

437. Mandelkern, Solomon. *Veteris Testamenti concordantiae hebraicae atque chaldaicae.* 3rd edn. Jerusalem/Tel Aviv: Schocken, 1959 (numerous editions, reprintings from several publishing houses).

A comprehensive concordance to the Hebrew and Aramaic text of the Hebrew Scriptures first published in 1896. The entries are arranged by Hebrew roots, with each related form in sub-entries. In later editions, with the collaboration of Margolin, Goshen-Gottstein and other scholars, certain imperfections in the early work were corrected.

438. Even-Shoshan, Abraham, compiler. *A new concordance of the Bible: thesaurus of the language of the Bible, Hebrew and Aramaic roots, words, proper names, phrases and synonyms.* 2nd edn. Jerusalem: Kiryat Sefer, 1989. 965-17-0167-6. This edition distributed by Baker Book House, Grand Rapids, MI. 0-8010-3417-5.

A work for Hebraists. First issued by Kiryat Sepher in three volumes (1977-1980). Each entry-word is followed by lists, in Hebrew, of basic meanings, related words and combined forms in which the word appears. Then, in canonical order, comes the listing of each appearance of the word, with context. This edition includes an introduction and guide to use in English, prepared by John Sailhammer.

The Septuagint

The earliest Greek translation of the Old Testament, the Septuagint, contains material of an exegetical and interpretative nature distinct from the Masoretic text of the Hebrew Bible. It is abbreviated as LXX (the reference being to the 70 (or 72) Hebrew elders who, according to tradition, prepared the translation). The twentieth century has witnessed major developments in the critical reconstruction of the text.

Guides

For a recent overview, with an extensive bibliography, see the article by Melvin Peters, 'Septuagint' in the *Anchor Bible dictionary* [385], vol. 5, pp. 1093-1104.

Texts

439. *Septuaginta: Vetus Testamentum graecum : auctoritate Academiae Scientiarum Gottingensis editum* (various editors). Göttingen: Vandenhoeck & Ruprecht, 1931- (name of issuing body changes during the course of the series; many of the volumes have been published in later editions).

Begun under the direction of Alfred Rahlfs, the Göttingen project is not yet complete. It aims to produce a reconstructed text for each book. The result, thus far, is a series of excellent critical editions.

Should the biblical book required not be among the Göttingen volumes now published the following Cambridge LXX, which is also incomplete, may be of assistance.

440. *The Old Testament in Greek according to the text of the Codex Vaticanus.* Edited by A. E. Brooke, N. McLean and H. Thackery. 3 vols. Cambridge University Press, 1906-1940.

Cambridge University Press published three volumes between 1906 and 1940. Included were the texts of the books from Genesis through Tobit in the LXX order. No further volumes are planned. Still highly valued for its critical apparatus.

Lexicons

441. *A Greek-English lexicon of the Septuagint.* Compiled by J. Lust, E. Eynikel and K. Hauspie with G. Chamberlaine. Part I, A-I. Stuttgart: Deutsche Bibelgesellschaft, 1992. 3-438-05125-7.

A companion to the edition of the Septuagint based on the only complete critical edition of the LXX, Rahlf's edition (*Septuaginta.* 2 vols. Stuttgart, 1935; numerous reprints) but modified to agree with the Göttingen text. The work uses the files of the Computer Assisted Tools for Septuagint Studies (CATSS) project which has produced a computerised database for Septuagint studies. This volume constitutes an important step towards a full-scale lexicon.

More modest in intention is:

442. Rehkopf, Friedrich. *Septuaginta-Vokabular.* Göttingen: Vandenhoeck & Ruprecht, 1989. 3-525-50172-2.

Designed especially for theological students. This is a simple alphabetical list of almost every word in the LXX with its basic German meaning and an indication of its occurrences. Frequencies in the New Testament and early Christian literature are noted in a separate column. This work could be exploited by those able to manage a standard German dictionary.

Minor prophets

443. Muraoka, T. *A Greek-English lexicon of the Septuagint (Twelve prophets).* Louvain: Peeters, 1993. 90-6831-495-5.

This first volume is intended as a prelude to a full-scale, scientific Septuagint lexicon. Each entry includes the morphology of the head word, definition, semantically associated words and details of the relationship between the LXX and Hebrew original. A delightfully constructed and most useful resource.

Concordances

444. Hatch, Edwin and Henry. A. Redpath. *A concordance to the Septuagint and the other Greek versions of the Old Testament (including the apocryphal books).* 2 vols. and supplement. Oxford: Clarendon, 1897-1906. Reprinted in 2 vols., Graz, Austria: Akademische Druck, 1954, 1983.

Provides the presumed Hebrew word equivalents for each Greek word at the head followed by numbered equivalents. Indispensable, although recent textual work calls some equivalences into question. Note its inclusion of apocryphal books.

COMMENTARIES

Series

See also the listing of commentaries on the whole Bible in the first section of this chapter.

445. Old Testament library. Louisville, KY: Westminster/John Knox Press; London: SCM Press, 1961- .

This series includes both monographs on Old testament themes and also commentaries on individual books. The commentaries include some translated from the German. Generally the emphasis is on the historical, literary and theological. No knowledge of biblical languages is assumed. The series continues with Norman Habel's commentary on Job (1985), R. P. Caroll on Jeremiah (1986), J. Blenkinsopp on Ezra-Nehemiah (1989) and J. Limburg on Jonah (1993) being among the more recent entries.

Another series, the aim of which is fundamentally exegetical is,

446. The Forms of Old Testament literature. Grand Rapids, MI: Eerdmans, 1981- .

Designed as a series of twenty-four volumes that will present a form-critical analysis of each book and each unit of the Hebrew Bible. Each volume will examine the structure, genre, setting and intention of the text and also the history behind the form-critical discussion of the material. A bibliography heads each chapter and a shorter bibliography appears at the end of each unit. While several volumes have appeared, the publication schedule appears to be somewhat delayed.

The Torah

447. The JPS Torah commentary. Philadelphia, PA: Jewish Publication Society, 1989- . 0-8276-0331-2 (set). To this date four volumes have been published with *Deuteronomy* pending.

Includes original Hebrew text and the JPS's English translation of the Pentateuch and of the traditional Haftarot. The commentators, Nahum Sarna (Genesis and Exodus), Baruch Levine (Leviticus) and Jacob Milgrom (Numbers) invoke traditional Jewish learning as well as recent biblical scholarship and their work generally reflects 'a liberal point of view' (Preface, p. vii). An essential resource for pentateuchal studies.

Note: These volumes complement the similarly oriented, *The Torah: a modern commentary*, edited by W. G. Plaut et al. (New York: Union of American Hebrew Congregations, 1981). This work includes the Hebrew text, a translation and commentary. It remains an accessible, valuable resource.

THEOLOGY OF THE HEBREW SCRIPTURES

Theological dictionaries

Theological dictionaries deal with the meaning and implications of biblical vocabulary. There are such dictionaries for both Old and New Testaments, but attention is drawn also to the major Bible dictionaries and encyclopedias already cited in the first section of this chapter. Further, it is worth noting that Kittell's *Theological dictionary of the New Testament* [502] provides background material on Old Testament terms where they have equivalents in the New Testament.

448. *Theologisches Wörterbuch zum Alten Testament (TWAT)*. Edited by G. J. Botterweck and H. Ringgren. Stuttgart: Kohlhammer, 1970- .

> This highly-valued multi-volume German work is still in process. By the end of 1993 seven volumes had been completed through *skn*. It presents an essay-format treatment of the Hebrew and Aramaic words giving their background and theological meaning. An English translation is appearing as:

449. *Theological dictionary of the Old Testament*. Edited by G. J. Botterweck and H. Ringgren. Grand Rapids, MI: Eerdmans, [1974] 1977- . 0-8028-2338-6 (set).

> Translation of *TWAT* (above). Note that volume numbers do not correspond to the German sequence. By the beginning of 1995 seven volumes had been issued, with volumes 1 and 2 having been revised and reissued. The main purpose of the work is 'to present the fundamental concepts intended by the respective words and terms, the traditions in which they occur, and the different nuances of meaning they have in each tradition' (Editor's preface to vol. 1). Attention is given to the Septuagint, New Testament and extracanonical usages. Certainly a major resource.

INTERTESTAMENTAL PERIOD: APOCRYPHA, PSEUDEPIGRAPHA, DEAD SEA SCROLLS AND OTHER WRITINGS

The Hebrew canon of Scripture comprises the Law, Prophets and Writings. During the period between the production of these canonical writings and the emergence of the books of the New Testament, some three to four hundred years in all, there were other Jewish writings which reflect the history, culture and religion of the various Jewish groupings during those times. These documents are critically important also for the contribution they are likely to make to New Testament research.

The 'Apocrypha' (Greek: hidden) consists of books, written during the last two centuries BCE and the first century AD which were not included in the Jewish canon.

(Note that these Jewish writings are to be distinguished from a cluster of New Testament apocryphal writings which date from the second century.)

The designation, 'Pseudepigrapha' (Greek: a writing with a false title) is applied to Jewish writings which were not included either in the canon or the Apocrypha.

Yet another important deposit are the scrolls discovered, mostly between 1947 and 1960, in several sites close to the Dead Sea and near the ruins of Qumran. The scrolls provide unique and invaluable information on the history of Judaism in this intertestamental period and on the early roots and background of Christianity. The recent release of photographs of some previously unpublished manuscripts has increased scholarly interest in this field

APOCRYPHA AND PSEUDEPIGRAPHA

Guides

450. Charlesworth, James H. *The Pseudepigrapha and modern research, with a supplement.* Society of Biblical Literature. (Septuagint and cognate studies 7S). Chico, CA [now Atlanta, GA]: Scholars Press, 1981. 0-89130-441-X.

Reports on research from 1960 to 1979. Introduces each document and provides a rich bibliography on its literary and doctrinal content.

451. McNamara, Martin. *Intertestamental literature.* (Old Testament message, 23). Wilmington, DE: Glazier, 1983. 0-89453-256-1.

A lucid introduction to most of the noncanonical Jewish writings of the period. Of particular reference use are the detailed table of contents, careful definitions of Apocrypha/ Pseudepigrapha/ Deuterocanonical (pp. 16-17) and a chronological chart of the literary compositions.

See also Craig Evans, *Noncanonical writings and New Testament interpretation* [519], which includes this literature.

See also: the coverage of this literature in Fitzmyer, *An introductory bibliography* [355], chapter xviii, 'Literature of the intertestamental period'. The chapter covers the writings of Philo Alexandrinus, Flavius Josephus, the pseudepigrapha of the Old Testament and other Jewish writings that emerged in the last centuries prior to Christianity.

Texts in English

452. *The Apocrypha and Pseudepigrapha of the Old Testament.* Edited by R. H. Charles. 2 vols. Oxford: Clarendon, 1913.

Still important for its introductions, translations and notes. The volumes, *Old Testament Pseudedipgrapha*, edited by Charlesworth [453], supersede the second volume of Charles.

The following two collections reflect developments in the study of early Judaism after the close of the Hebrew Bible and also the beginnings of the Christian religion.

453. *The Old Testament Pseudepigrapha.* Edited by James H. Charlesworth. 2 vols. Garden City, NY: Doubleday, 1983-1985. 0-385-09630-5 (vol. 1); 0-385-18813-7 (vol. 2).

English translations of some 52 works of Jewish and Christian origin and the fragments of 13 others. Introductions and notes. Extensive index in volume 2. The most accessible and instructive source for these texts.

454. Sparks, H. F. D. *The Apocryphal Old Testament.* Oxford: Clarendon Press, 1984. 0-19-826166-7 (hc.); 0-19-826177-2 (pbk).

A volume of translations of the more important texts but not the deuterocanonical books. There are 25 works included, 16 of them not in Charles [452], therefore the work is not as inclusive as Charlesworth [453]. Each text is introduced and there are notes and a bibliography. Indexes are to scriptural passages, ancient and modern authors and subjects. A valuable work designed for general, rather than strictly academic use.

Series

An important and accessible series providing extracts of texts of the literature of the period is:

455. Cambridge commentaries on writings of the Jewish and Christian world, 200 BC to AD 200. Cambridge University Press, edited by P. R. Ackroyd, A. R. C. Laney and J. W. Packer.

Eight titles in this series cover Jews in the Hellenistic world, with particular attention to Josephus and Philo; Qumran community, early Rabbinic writings, writings outside the Old Testament and the New Testament, Jews and Christians and an overview of the Jewish and Christian world from 200 BCE to 200 CE. Each piece of literature is introduced, the extracts given are accompanied by commentary.

THE DEAD SEA SCROLLS

The last few years have witnessed a radical change in studies in this area. The releasing of once-hoarded Scrolls, the computerisation of records and the more liberal rights of publication have meant that, increasingly, this material is attracting both scholarly and popular attention. Among the proliferation of books on Qumran and the Scrolls, the following recently published guides represent a range of perspectives, Jewish and Christian.

Guides

456. Fitzmyer, Joseph A. *Responses to 101 questions on the Dead Sea Scrolls.* Mahwah, NJ: Paulist Press, 1992. 0-8091-3348-2.

A member of the international team which has been working on the scrolls, provides a set of responses which deal with the discovery of the scrolls, the Qumran community, and the importance of the scrolls for a study of first-century Judaism and early Christianity. In a final set of questions the author covers recent developments and controversies. There is a select bibliography and three indexes. This volume would be useful to the novice as well as to the scholar requiring a summary of the state of the 'scrolls debate'.

457. Schiffman, Lawrence H. *Reclaiming the Dead Sea Scrolls.* Philadelphia, PA: Jewish Publication Society, 1994. 0-8276-0530-7.

A Jewish scholar argues that the scrolls contain a mine of information about the history of Judaism as well as the early roots of Christianity and demonstrates their thorough-going Jewish character. A persuasive, up-to-date discussion of the circumstances and importance of these writings. Includes an extensive bibliography.

458. *Understanding the Dead Sea Scrolls: a reader from the Biblical archaeology review.* Edited by Hershel Shanks. New York: Random House, 1992. 0-679-41448-7.

A collection of lively articles, by authorities, culled from the periodical, *Biblical archaeology review*, provides a fascinating source book for understanding the scrolls and the controversies that have raged around them. Illustrated and well-indexed. Very good value for the non-specialist.

459. VanderKam, James G. *The Dead Sea Scrolls today.* Grand Rapids, MI: Eerdmans, 1994. 0-8028-0736-4.

Another member of the international team charged with editing and translating the unpublished scrolls has written an up-to-date, authoritative and comprehensive book for students. An attractive, reliable guide.

Catalogues

460. *The Dead Sea Scrolls catalogue: documents, photographs, and museum inventory numbers.* Compiled by Stephen A. Reed. (SBL Resources for biblical study, 32). Atlanta, GA: Scholars Press, 1994. 0-7885-0017-1 (hc); 0-7885-0018-X (pbk).

This catalogue and index to the scrolls material was supported financially by a number of biblical associations and endowment foundations. Arrangement is by documents, from Qumran and Masada, then by photographs and finally by museum inventory numbers. An appendix (pp. 543-558) provides a list of abbreviations and codes used, which is essential for the decipherment of the entries, and also an extensive bibliography. This is a valuable identification and location tool designed for advanced work in this field.

Bibliographies

461. Fitzmyer, J. A. *The Dead Sea Scrolls: major publications and tools for study.* Rev. edn. Society of Biblical Literature. (Resources for biblical study, no. 20). Atlanta, GA: Scholars Press, 1990. 1-55540-510-X (hc.); 1-55540-511-8 (pbk).

First published 1975. Attempts to be exhaustive in the listing of the eight sites and the texts from them which have been published to date. The bibliography of secondary literature is, understandably, selective but covers all types of material including reference tools. The first section explains the system of abbreviations used for the scrolls.

Texts

462. Eisenman, Robert and James M. Robinson. *A facsimile edition of the Dead Sea Scrolls, prepared with an introduction and index.* 2 vols. Washington, DC: Biblical Archaeology Society, 1991. 1-880317-00-1(set).

A collection, limited to some 1785 photographs of texts from Cave 4 and other sites. Accessible, but the following collection is more extensive.

463. *The Dead Sea Scrolls on microfiche: a comprehensive facsimile edition of the texts from the Judean Desert.* Edited by Emanuel Tov and Stephen J. Pfann. Leiden: Brill, 1993. 134 positive halide microfiches in a binder.

Published under the auspices of the Israel Antiquities Authority. Contains some 6,500 photographs of good quality. The two accompanying volumes, identify the sources and provide a sequential list of photographic numbers. Note the following companion to this edition.

464. *Companion volume to the Dead Sea Scrolls microfiche edition.* Edited by Emanuel Tov and Stephen Pfann. 2nd rev. edn. Leiden: Brill, 1995. 90-04-10288-4.

Meant as a general aid to the study of the texts, this edition effectively updates the *Companion volume* of 1993 by supplying revised lists and bibliography. Essays cover all aspects of the history and nature of the texts, the photography and the archival deposits. There are instructions on the use of the microfiche edition. To stress, however, that libraries not holding the microfiche edition could still find considerable value in this volume.

Text with English translation

465. *The Dead Sea Scrolls: Hebrew, Aramaic, and Greek texts with English translations.* Edited by James H. Charlesworth et al. Vol. 1- . Tübingen: Mohr 1994- . 3-16-146199-1 (vol. 1); Louisville, KY: Westminster/ John Knox Press, 1994- . 0-664-21994-2 (vol. 1).

A planned series of volumes issued as part of the Princeton Theological Seminary Dead Sea Scrolls Project. It intends to present a definitive text of all the non-biblical documents found in the eleven Qumran caves. A literal English translation is accompanied by notes to help the scholar understand the text, the variants, philological subtleties, and explain the translation.

The first volume contains the *Rule of the Community* and related documents.

English translations

Here the rule of consulting more than one translation is particularly important, given the options available for both the establishment of the text and its translation.

466. García Martínez, Florentino. *The Dead Sea Scrolls translated: the Qumran texts in English.* Leiden: Brill, 1994. 90-04-10088-1 (hc.); 90-04-10048-2 (pbk).

A substantial introduction precedes a translation of the texts, including the full texts of the multiple copies of works such as the *Rule of the Community*. For this reason it is the most comprehensive translation available to this date. The work concludes with a complete listing of the Qumran manuscripts. The author promises a companion commentary volume.

467. Vermes, G. *The Dead Sea Scrolls in English.* 4th edn. London: Penguin Books, 1995. 0-14-023730-5

Earlier editions of this work have been valued for the clear, accurate translations. This new edition includes additional texts which have become accessible since 1991. Introductory chapters treat the background, history and beliefs of the sectarian community and the significance of the writings.

Concordances

468. Charlesworth, James H. et al. *Graphic concordance to the Dead Sea Scrolls*. Tübingen: Mohr, 1991. 3-16-145797-8; Louisville, KY: Westminster/John Knox Press, 1991. 0-664-21969-1.

Designed for specialists, this concordance claims to be the only one available to editions of all Qumran sectarian texts published before 1990. Being a *graphic* concordance means that it is arranged alphabetically by each graphic unit (rather than by root). The volume shows signs of being a preliminary work and the editors promise a standard analytical concordance which will incorporate the more recently released texts.

NEW TESTAMENT

A number of concerns have characterised New Testament scholarship during recent decades. Textual critics have continued to examine variants and the possibilities of errors or deliberate changes in the transmission of the text. Older critical methodologies have been joined by newer forms - redaction, rhetorical and social scientific criticism, with structural analysis also being invoked.

Considerable importance has been attached to the social history and character of the early Christian communities. Recognition is being paid to their diversity and to the distinctive ways in which they may have informed the developing perspectives and theologies of the New Testament. Another area concerns the very genre of the Gospels and this has meant comparative literary studies using ancient biographical accounts.

Beginning around 1965 there has been a renewal of interest in the so-called New Testament Apocryphal and Pseudepigraphal writings. This literary context has been enlarged to include the Nag Hammadi material. The final section of this chapter is given to this literature and to its relatedness to biblical studies.

Bibliographies

Modes of criticism

469. May, David M. *Social scientific criticism of the New Testament: a bibliography*. (NABPR bibliographic series, 4). Macon, GA: Mercer University Press, 1991. 0-86554-392-5.

May provides a useful introduction to the methodology of social scientific criticism and then a classified bibliography of works utilising this analytical method. An index to authors.

See also *Rhetorical criticism of the Bible: a comprehensive bibliography with notes on history and method* [400], which includes coverage of selected topics of New Testament rhetoric, including an examination of individual New Testament books.

Women

470. Lindboe, Inger Marie. *Women in the New Testament: a select bibliography*. (Bibliography series, 1). Oslo: University of Oslo, Faculty of Theology, 1990. 82-991913-1-9.

Covers material, published in several languages from 1970 to 1987, relating broadly to the social and religious status of women in the New Testament period. Arrangement is alphabetical by author and there are indexes to subjects and to New Testament passages.

Individual books

Note: some of the following bibliographies cite material from books, periodicals and other sources, while others are indexes to periodical literature only.

471. *An Exegetical bibliography of the New Testament.* Edited by Günther Wagner:

> *Matthew and Mark.* Macon, GA: Mercer University Press, 1983. 0-86554-013-6.

> *Luke and Acts.* Macon GA: Mercer University Press, 1985. 0-86554-140-X.

> *John and 1, 2, 3 John.* Macon GA: Mercer University Press, 1987. 0-86554-157-4.

These volumes up-date the *New Testament exegetical bibliographical aids* which were produced in card format at the Baptist Theological Seminary at Rüschlikon, Switzerland, from 1973. Not only periodical literature but also, and unusually, monographs and commentaries, in many languages, have been culled. The items are arranged by chapters and verses or a gathering of verses. For example, the passage, 1 John 5: 13-21, yields seven entries and the particular verse, 1 John 5: 13, another seven entries. The comprehensive coverage, particularly of monograph and commentary material, makes this an effective exegetical tool. A fourth volume on the Pauline letters is in preparation.

Since 1988, the following bibliographic volumes covering three of the Gospels have been published in the series, Bibliotheca Ephemeridum Theologicarum Lovaniensium (BETL), published by Leuven University Press.

472. Van Belle, Gilbert. *Johannine bibliography, 1966-1985.* (BETL, 82). 1988. 90-6186-285-X.

473. Van Segbroeck, Frans. *The Gospel of Luke: a cumulative bibliography, 1973-1988.* (BETL, 88). 1988. 90-6186-327-9.

474. Neirynck, F. *The Gospel of Mark: a cumulative bibliography, 1950-1990.* (BETL, 102). 1992. 90-6186-502-6.

Each comprises a major reference resource. Note that introductory material is in English but that each volume covers English and continental material most thoroughly. The indexing apparatus varies from volume to volume.

A new series of bibliographies on the books of the Hebrew Scriptures and the New Testament, as well as the deutero-canonicals, has been launched by the Mellen Biblical Press. Thirty-five to forty volumes are to published over the next 4-6 years.

The first title in the New Testament series is:

475. Mills, Watson E. *The Gospel of Luke.* (Bibliographies for biblical research. New Testament series in twenty one volumes, 3). Lewiston, NY: Mellen Biblical Press, 1994. 0-7734-2385-0.

The arrangement for this volume on Luke's Gospel is typical of most being planned for the series. There are three divisions: scriptural citations, subjects and commentaries. Entries are to books, essays, articles, dissertations, and commentaries published from 1900-1993. The scriptural citation section, with items arranged verse by verse, is a particularly useful feature. There is an author index.

Johannine scholars should be aware of the following Spanish bibliography:

476. Espinosa, Ricardo Rábanos and Domingo Muñoz Léon. *Bibliografia Joanica: Evangelio, Cartas y Apocalipsis, 1960-1986.* (Bibliotheca Hispana Biblica, 14). Madrid: Consejo Superior de Investigaciones Científicas, 1990. 84-00-07033-X.

Covers the Gospel, Johannine epistles and the Apocalypse. Main section is arranged by subject - 'Abraham' to 'Yo soy'. A further section deals with the texts. Indexes are to biblical passages, subjects, abbreviations, authors and compilations.

477. Mills, Watson E. *A bibliography of the periodical literature on the Acts of the Apostles, 1962-1984.* (Supplements to Novum Testamentum, 58). Leiden: Brill, 1986. 90-04-08130-5.

Straightforward listing of periodical articles (only), in alphabetical order by author, with an index to scriptural passages and to subjects.

478. Mills, Watson E. *An index to periodical literature on the Apostle Paul.* (New Testament tools and studies, 16). Leiden: Brill, 1993. 90-04-09674-4.

Reprints the entries in Bruce Metzger's earlier bibliography with this title (1960, 1966, 1970) and proceeds to update and enlarge on that work. Periodical literature, in a wide spectrum of languages, covers studies on Paul's life, Pauline literature generally, individual epistles and theological studies. Index to authors. An essential tool for Pauline studies.

479. Mills, Watson E. *1 Corinthians: an annotated bibliography.* (Books of the Bible, 4). Hamden, CT: Garland Publishing, 1994. 0-8153-0890-6.

A comprehensive, annotated bibliography which examines articles, books and dissertations, including work in languages other than English. An author and subject index is included.

480. Muse, Robert L. *The book of Revelation: an annotated bibliography.* (Books of the Bible, 2). Hamden, CT: Garland Publishing, 1994. 0-8240-7394-0.

Encompassing the period from 1940-1990, this bibliography covers books and articles in English, French and German along with selected Italian and Spanish titles. Following an introduction to the study of this book the seven chapters are arranged thematically. Cross-references and an author index.

Indexes and abstracts

481. *New Testament abstracts.* Vol. 1- , 1956- . Cambridge, MA: Weston Jesuit School of Theology, 1956- . 3/year. [Publishing details vary.] ISSN 0028-6877.

NTA cites and abstracts periodical articles, from Christian and Jewish journals, on all matters relating to the New Testament, biblical theology and the New Testament world. It also lists and details books published in these areas. The third issue of each volume includes indexes of scriptural passages, authors of articles and book reviews, books reviewed and of book notices. Coverage is of Catholic, Jewish and Protestant journals.

Introductions

482. Kümmel, W. G. *Introduction to the New Testament*. Translated by Howard Clark Kee. London: SCM Press, 1975. 0-334-00705-4.

With an ancestry stretching back to Feine's German edition of 1913, the work has been much revised over the years. This is the translation of the seventeenth edition (1973). The great work is a model of thoroughness and judiciousness for the serious student.

TEXTUAL STUDIES

Guides

483. Aland, Kurt.*The text of the New Testament: an introduction to the critical editions and to the theory and practice of modern textual criticism*. 2nd rev. edn. Grand Rapids, MI: Eerdmans; Leiden: Brill, 1989. 0-8028-3662-3; 90-04-08367-7.

This translation, which represents a revision of the original German edition of 1982, describes and analyses recently published editions of the Greek text and incorporates data from newly examined texts. An authoritative, attractive introduction to textual criticism.

Texts

484. *The Greek New Testament*. Edited by Barbara Aland et al. 4th rev. edn. Stuttgart: Deutsche Bibelgesellschaft, United Bible Societies, 1993 (2nd printing, 1994). 3-438-05110-9.

The essential text. The former edition of the *GNT* (the 3rd corrected) was published in 1983. There are numerous changes in this new edition reflecting an editorial promise to improve on the reliability and clarity of the work. A companion volume is:

485. Metzger, Bruce M. *A textual commentary on the Greek New Testament*. 2nd edn. Stuttgart: Deutsche Bibelgesellschaft, United Bible Societies, 1994. 3-438-06010-8.

Updates the first edition of 1970 and is adapted to the fourth revised edition of *The Greek New Testament* [484]. Metzger comments on the United Bible Societies' Committee decisions to adopt or reject various readings. Valuable for establishing the text.

The Gospels

486. *The Complete Gospels: annotated Scholars Version*. Edited by Robert J. Miller. 3rd rev. and expanded edn. Sonoma, CA: Polebridge Press, 1994. 0-944344-45-3 (hc); 0-944344-49-6 (pbk).

Presents all twenty of the known Gospels from the early Christian era. Includes the Bible's four Gospels plus the Gospel of Thomas and Mary, the Sayings Gospel Q, the Secret Gospel of Mark, and twelve other Gospels from the first three centuries. Four new pieces have been added to this third edition: the three Jewish-Christian Gospels and the Greek fragments of the Gospel of Thomas. Translations are into contemporary English, and are accompanied by cross-references, notes on the original text and exegetical comments. The contributors include well-known experts in this field and all are fellows of the Jesus Seminar. An accessible, comparatively inexpensive guide to these ancient texts.

Greek grammars

First, two major reference grammars:

487. Blass, F. and A. Debrunner. *A Greek grammar of the New Testament and other early Christian literature.* Translated by Robert. W. Funk. Chicago, IL: University of Chicago Press, 1961.

Revises and augments the 9th-10th edition of the authoritative and advanced German grammar. Includes detailed indexes to subjects, Greek words and literary forms. Complex and technical, this remains the best reference grammar.

488. Moulton, J. H. , W. F. Howard and Nigel Turner. *A grammar of New Testament Greek.* 4 vols. Edinburgh: T & T Clark, 1976. 0-567-09492-8 (set).
Vol. 1: Prolegomena (1906), 3rd edn (1949); vol. 2: Accidence and word-formation with an appendix on Semitisms in the New Testament (1929); vol. 3: Syntax (1963); vol. 4: Style (1976).

In spite of its age, Moulton is still regarded as a most comprehensive resource for reference purposes.

As for class grammars or grammars for beginners, there are a host of options and professorial preferences. They range from 'do-it-yourself Greek' grammars to those requiring the assistance of a tutor. The following list represents a mixture of tried and trusty tools along with some recent contenders. It does not claim to be exhaustive. A helpful discussion of Greek grammars for beginners is in Danker, *Multipurpose tools* [354], pp. 128-129, and a listing of more advanced grammars is in Fitzmyer, *An introductory bibliography for the study of Scripture* [355], pp. 83-86.

489. Efird, J. M. *Grammar for New Testament Greek.* Nashville, TN: Abingdon Press, 1990. 0-687-15678-5.

Not for self-study.

490. Greenlee, J. Harold. *A concise exegetical grammar of New Testament Greek.* Rev. edn. Grand Rapids, MI: Eerdmans, 1987. 0-8028-0173-0.

Since 1953, a well-tried work with an insistence on learning the principles of grammar. Now thoroughly revised.

491. Jay, Eric G. *New Testament Greek: an introductory grammar.* London: SPCK, 1958, 1974. 0-281-02806-0 (pbk). A key to assignments is:

_____. *New Testament Greek: key.* London: SPCK, 1961. 0-281-00664-4.

In order to observe the ways in which the language is being used, the author concentrates on the Gospel of Mark and details its grammatical structures.

492. Wenham, J. W. *The elements of New Testament Greek.* Cambridge University Press, 1965. 0-521-09842-4 (reprint, 1991). The key to assignments is:

_____. *Key to elements of New Testament Greek.* Cambridge University Press, 1965.

Based on H. P. V. Nunn's *Elements of New Testament Greek*, this is one of the best-known introductions.

493. Whittaker, Molly. *New Testament Greek grammar.* Rev. edn. London: SCM Press, 1980. 0-334-01128-0. The key was published with the first edition in 1969. 0-334-00830-1.

Features a more interesting teaching methodology than most of the grammars and proves quite popular with students.

494. Zerwick, M. *Biblical Greek: illustrated by examples.* 5th reprint edn. Rome: Pontificio Istituto Biblico, 1990. 88-7653-554-3.

Works on comparisons between New testament syntax and that of classical Greek. Assumes some knowledge of the latter and therefore is hardly for beginners.

495. Zerwick, M. and M. Grosvenor. *A grammatical analysis of the Greek New Testament.* 4th rev. edn. Rome: Pontificio Istituto Biblico, 1993. 88-7653-588-8.

Not so much a grammar as a running commentary on the text, identifying Greek forms and supplying lexical and grammatical analysis.

Greek lexicons

496. Bauer, W., F. W. Gingrich and F. W. Danker. *A Greek-English lexicon of the New Testament and other early Christian literature.* 2nd edn. Chicago: University of Chicago Press, 1979. 0-226-03932-3.

Based on Bauer's fifth German edition of 1958, this augmented work includes extensive revisions of an earlier English translation (1957). This standard work is both usable and useful.

Besides Bauer there are two classical dictionaries which are worthy of mention:

497. Liddell, H. G. and R. Scott. *A Greek-English lexicon with revised supplement.* 9th edn., revised by H. S. Jones, with the assistance of R. McKenzie. *Supplement* edited by P. G.W. Glare. Oxford: Clarendon, 1995. *Supplement* available separately.

Not limited to classical Greek only, it has references to a broad range of Greek literature down to AD 600, covering every surviving Greek author and including the Septuagint and the New Testament. Fully cross-referenced, the new *Supplement* updates the dictionary with words and forms discovered after 1940.

498. Lampe, G. W. H. (ed.). *A Patristic Greek lexicon.* Oxford: Clarendon, 1961.

Aims to 'interpret the theological and ecclesiastical vocabulary of the Greek Christian authors from Clement of Rome to Theodore of Studium (died AD 826)'. Therefore this work is a mine for patristic comment on the Scriptures as it shows the developments in the church fathers' use of New Testament terms.

Concordances

499. Aland, Kurt et al. *Vollständige Konkordanz zum griechischen Neuen Testament: unter Zugrundelegung aller modernerkritischen Textausgaben und des Textus Receptus.* 2 vols. in 3. Berlin: de Gruyter, 1975-1983.

The first volume, in two parts (published in 14 Lieferungen and completed in 1983), provides the concordance in full to every word of the New Testament, including *de* and *kai*! The second volume (1978) analyses the data statistically. Computer-generated, this work is based on Nestle ^{26} and gives variant readings from major modern critical editions of the Greek New Testament. A great achievement; simply the best available.

500. *Computer-Konkordanz zum Novum Testamentum graece von Nestle-Aland, 26. Auflage und zum Greek New Testament.* 3rd edn. Edited by H. Bachmann and W. A. Slaby. Berlin: de Gruyter, 1980. 3-11-007313-7.

A one-volume concordance which anticipates the first volume of *VK* above, in a somewhat abridged form. It lacks citations to variants. A slightly revised edition, with the same editors and with only slight variations, was published with a change of title as *Konkordanz zum Novum Testamentum Graece von Nestle-Aland.* Berlin: de Gruyter, 1987.

501. *Concordance to the texts of the Greek New Testament.* Edited by William F. Moulton and A. S. Geden. 5th edn, revised by H. K. Moulton with a supplement. Edinburgh: T & T Clark, 1978. 0-567-01021-X.

For all but a century the most widely used concordance in the field. Given the availability of more recent critical editions of the text, Moulton has been outdated by *VK* and *CK* above. While incomplete it can still prove a helpful and reliable resource.

Dictionaries

502. *Theological dictionary of the New Testament.* Edited by Gerhard Kittel. 10 vols. Grand Rapids, MI: Eerdmans, 1964-1976.

Abbreviated as *TDNT.* Translation of the somewhat dated, Kittel's *Theologisches Wörterbuch zum Neuen Testament* (1932-1979), but still important for its treatment of Hebrew antecedents and the classical, biblical and post-biblical meanings of words deemed, by the editors, to have theological significance. Volume 10 provides indexes to English keywords, Greek keywords, Hebrew and Aramaic words and to biblical references.

An abridged version of *TDNT* has been published as:

503. *Theological dictionary of the New Testament.* Edited by Gerhard Kittel; translated by Geoffrey W. Bromiley; abridged in one volume by Geoffrey W. Bromiley. Grand Rapids, MI: Eerdmans, 1985. 0-8028-2404-8.

One-sixth of the length of the parent work, this work emphasises the New Testament usage of each word, transliterates Greek and Hebrew words, but omits all footnotes and bibliographical material. The location (volume and page) of the original article is provided making it possible to consult the more detailed treatment in the complete set. This is the 'user-friendly' version.

TWNT and *TDNT* have, to some extent, been updated by the following:

504. *Exegetical dictionary of the New Testament.* Edited by Horst Balz and Gerhard Schneider. 3 vols. Grand Rapids, MI: Eerdmans, 1990-1993.

Translation of the German edition (1978-1983) which was an ecumenical undertaking by Catholic and Lutheran scholars. This guide to the forms, meaning and usage of New Testament words, while not as detailed as *TDNT* [502], reflects more recent scholarship and is an essential tool.

505. *Dictionary of Jesus and the Gospels.* Edited by Joel B. Green and Scot McKnight. Downers Grove, IL: InterVarsity Press, 1992. 0-8308-1777-8.

Major articles with extensive bibliographies on the Gospel traditions, background issues, Christology, and the range of methodological approaches used in research today. A most helpful guide to this material and to current evangelical scholarship.

506. Rousseau, John J. and Rami Arav. *Jesus and his world: an archaeological and cultural dictionary.* Minneapolis, MN: Fortress Press, 1994. 0-8006-2903-0 (hc); 0-8006-2805-5 (pbk).

The authors, both biblical scholars and archaeologists combine to present locations, artefacts and customs relevant to the life and ministry of Jesus and draw out their implications for research. This attractive work includes maps, tables, chronologies and is well indexed.

507. *Dictionary of Paul and his letters.* Edited by Gerald F. Hawthorne et al. Downers Grove, IL: InterVarsity Press, 1993. 0-8308-1778-6.

The intention of this companion volume to the *Dictionary of Jesus and the Gospels* [505] is to present 'the fruit of evangelical New Testament scholarship at the end of the twentieth century'. It includes major articles on the Pauline corpus, theological themes and other matters relating to history and interpretation. There are indexes to scriptural passages, subjects and to the articles themselves.

LITERARY FORMS

506. Bailey, James L. and Lyle D. Vander Brock. *Literary forms in the New Testament: a handbook.* Louisville, KY: Westminster/John Knox Press, 1992. 0-664-25154-4.

Defines and describes the literary forms present in the three main sections of the New Testament. Analyses the exegetical significance of each form and provides an annotated bibliography.

COMMENTARIES

See also the listing of commentaries on the whole Bible in the first section of this chapter.

Guides

509. Carson, D. A. *New Testament commentary survey.* 4th edn. Grand Rapids, MI: Baker Books, 1993. 0-8010-2579-6.

An up-to-date interpretative survey of commentary resources. Introductory notes provide principles and warnings about the choice of a commentary and then series are listed and evaluated. There is a short section on introductions to the New testament and on New Testament theologies. Then, using the biblical-book order, individual commentaries are examined. Carson's verdict tends to reflect a conservative evangelical position and he 'prefers to be a shade too trenchant than a good deal too bland' (Preface). The comprehensiveness, coverage and provocative judgments make this work, at once, useful and stimulating.

Series

510. New international Greek Testament commentary. Grand Rapids, MI: Eerdmans, 1978- .

The editors of the series, W. Ward Gasque and I. Howard Marshall stress that while engaging the major questions of text and interpretation at a scholarly level, the authors keep in mind the needs of beginning students of Greek. However, in an attempt to be exegetically thorough, the volumes are somewhat intense in style and highly technical. A strong feature is the bibliographic coverage. The theological perspective of the series is generally evangelical.

511. Sacra Pagina. Collegeville, MN: Michael Glazier/Liturgical Press, 1991- .

The editor, Daniel J. Harrington, SJ, has enlisted an international team of Catholic scholars to present fresh translations and commentaries on each book of the New Testament. The series is intended for 'biblical professionals, graduate students, theologians, clergy and religious educators' (Cover). Represents modern critical Catholic scholarship.

THE GOSPELS

The Synoptic problem

Bibliographies

512. Longstaff, Thomas R. W. and Page A. Thomas. *The synoptic problem: a bibliography, 1716-1988.* (New Gospel studies, 4). Macon, GA: Mercer University Press, 1988. 0-86554-321-6.

William R. Farmer contributes an introductory essay which is followed by a bibliography listing some 1,967 titles arranged alphabetically by author. There is a date-of-publication index and an index to keywords. Valuable for its coverage and evaluation of the different solutions to the synoptic problem over some 272 years.

Parallels

513. *Gospel parallels: a synopsis of the first three Gospels, with alternative readings from the manuscripts and noncanonical parallels.* Edited by Burton H. Throckmorton. 5th edn. Nashville, TN: Thomas Nelson, 1992. 0-8407-7484-2.

This well-known work, first published in 1949, is fully revised and updated. It now uses the New Revised Standard Version, with a new, improved system of comparison.

Jesus research

Bibliographies

514. Evans, Craig A. *Life of Jesus research: an annotated bibliography.* (New Testament tools and studies, 13). Leiden: Brill, 1989. 90-04-09180-7.

This work covers scholarly writings concerned with the problem of the historical Jesus, firstly by means of a chronological arrangement of items from 1768. Then it employs a series of related topical headings, for example demythologisation and the life, teaching and miracles of Jesus. There is also a section on noncanonical historical sources. Brief annotations are included with most of the entries. Indexes are to modern authors and to ancient writings.

515. Hultgren, Arland J. *New Testament Christology: a critical assessment and annotated bibliography.* (Bibliographies and indexes in religious studies, 12). New York: Greenwood Press, 1988. 0-313-25188-6.

An introductory essay, 'Literature and trends in the study of New Testament Christology' (pp. 3-19) is followed by an annotated bibliography arranged within four main divisions - orientation and christological foundations, christological titles, christologies of the New Testament writers and christological themes from 'pre-existence' to ' parousia' and 'soteriology'. There is an index of authors and editors, of titles and of subjects. The classified arrangement makes this a most accessible tool.

516. Garland, David E. *One hundred years of study on the Passion narratives.* (NABPR bibliographic series, 3). Macon GA: Mercer University Press, 1989. 0-86554-371-2.

This bibliography cites books and articles in English, French and German. Entries are arranged chronologically under topics relating to the separate sections of the Passion stories in the Gospels. An author index.

PAULINE MATERIAL

Parallels

517. *Pauline parallels.* Edited by Fred O. Francis and J. Paul Sampley. 2nd edn. Minneapolis, MN: Fortress Press, 1984. Paperback edn in 1987, 0-8006-2094-1 (pbk).

1st edition published in 1975. This edition has been redesigned to provide an improved tool for those working on the Pauline corpus. It offers 'a sequential presentation of each of the ten letters attributed to Paul' (Introduction, p. xi), and highlights ways in which Paul treats similar topics in varying contexts. A valuable interpretative aid.

NEW TESTAMENT APOCRYPHAL LITERATURE AND GNOSTIC WRITINGS

Not to be confused with the Jewish apocryphal writings of the intertestamental period, the New Testament apocryphal literature consists of uncanonical writings dating from the second to the sixth centuries. This literature includes gospels, acts, epistles and apocalypses; all in some way related to the stories and sayings of Jesus, the disciples and apostles. Included also are pseudepigraphs or anonymous texts of Christian origins. New Testament scholars are now realising that this body of literature may yield important data, in addition to that supplied by the canonical Gospels, for understanding the historical Jesus and the rise of the early Christian communities.

From the later second century there emerged people who claimed that God had revealed to them the knowledge (gnosis) of their heavenly home and destiny, and otherwise pretended to having received particular revelations. The church fathers thought of Gnosticism as comprising patterns of heresy which took numerous forms and which penetrated both Jewish and Christian communities. The Gnostic writings exhibit a highly eclectic use of different philosophical and religious traditions, including a heavy use of the Hebrew and Christian Scriptures.

A collection of Christian and Gnostic writings, dating from the fourth century, was found in 1945-1946 in a cave near the modern town of Nag Hammadi in Upper Egypt. The library consists of eleven codices, one tractate and the fragments of a twelfth codex. Particularly important are such texts as the Gospel of Thomas, the Secret Book of James and the Dialogue of the Saviour. They are relevant for biblical interpretation and also for studies in the development of doctrine.

Guides

518. Charlesworth, James H. and James R. Mueller. *The New Testament Apocrypha and Pseudepigrapha: a guide to publications, with excurses on Apocalypses.* (ATLA Bibliography series, 17). Metuchen, NJ: American Theological Library Association, 1987. 0-8108-1845-0.

The introduction reports on NTAP research. Two essays follow: the first on the Apocalypse of John and its impact on subsequent apocalypses, and the second on the continuum of Jewish and Christian apocalypses. The main section of the work provides over 5000 bibliographic citations for the 104 publications listed on the NTAP. This coverage is the most complete and definitive to date, although the inaccuracy of a number of references has been noted (see a review by J. K. Elliott in the periodical, *Novum Testamentum* 31 (1989): 182-185).

519. Evans, Craig A. *Noncanonical writings and New Testament interpretation.* Peabody, MA: Hendrickson, 1992. 0-943575-95-8.

Intended 'to serve the needs of students who aspire to become New Testament interpreters' (Preface), this comprehensive survey introduces the diverse bodies of ancient literature which are in various ways cognate to biblical literature. The categories range from the Old Testament Apocrypha and Pseudepigrapha and the Dead Sea scrolls through to the writings of the early fathers and the Gnostic texts. Each category is described, the writings are summarised and the themes enunciated (with bibliography). There are useful appendixes, mainly lists of parallels, and indexes to modern authors, ancient writings and writers, and ancient sources. A particularly important manual for those engaged in New Testament exegesis.

Texts

520. *The Apocryphal New Testament: a collection of apocryphal Christian literature in an English translation.* Edited by J. K. Elliott. Oxford: Clarendon Press, 1993. 0-19-826182-9.

This collection supersedes the best-selling, similarly-titled, edition of M. R. James which was originally published in 1924, and regularly reprinted. Elliott presents new translations in modern English, providing each document with an introduction and a bibliography of primary and secondary sources.

521. *New Testament apocrypha.* Edited by Wilhelm Schneemelcher. English translation edited by R. McL. Wilson. Rev. edn. 2 vols. Cambridge: James Clarke & Co; Louisville, KY: Westminster/John Knox Press, 1991-1992. 0-664-21878-4 (vol. 1); 0-664-21879-2 (vol. 2).

Schneemelcher revised and augmented the work of Edgar Hennecke; this revised edition being a translation of the German sixth edition (1989-1990). The volumes incorporate the most recent discoveries and research. Will prove a valuable resource for both specialist and non-specialist alike.

Series

Note. Scholars should be aware of the 'Series Apocryphorum' within the major series, 'Corpus Christianorum', published by Brepols of Turnhout. The series, which began in 1983, is in process. The intention is to collect all the Christian apocryphal literature, including the pseudepigraphal, into one series and to supply the best texts, translations and reliable introductions. The first volume in the series was, E. Junod and J. -D. Kaestli. *Acta Johannis.* (Corpus Christianorum, Series Apocryphorum 1-2). 2 vols. Turnhout: Brepols, 1983. The series will exclude the Nag Hammadi codices (see below) because of their having been well-treated in separate collections and series.

Nag Hammadi Codices

Texts

522. *The facsimile edition of the Nag Hammadi codices.* 12 vols. Leiden: E. J. Brill, 1972-1984.

Facsimiles of writings, most of them Gnostic in character, dating from the 4th century AD, which were discovered in 1945. Between 1972 and 1977 the entire library was published. Then followed the *Cartonnage* volume (1979) and an *Introduction* (1984).

A complete critical edition of the texts is:

523. *The Coptic Gnostic library: edited with English translation, introduction and notes; published under the auspices of the Institute for Antiquity and Christianity.* Leiden: E. J. Brill, 1975- .
   [The volumes are included in the series, Nag Hammadi studies, which has been published by E. J. Brill since 1971.]

Comprises a critical text and English translation of the codices and includes related manuscripts held in Berlin, Oxford and London. This edition is essential for detailed work.

Somewhat more accessible, and with translations in conformity with the critical edition noted above is:

524. *The Nag Hammadi Library in English: translated by members of the Coptic Gnostic library project of the Institute for Antiquity and Christianity.* Edited by J. M. Robinson. 3rd edn. San Francisco: Harper & Row; Leiden: E. J. Brill, 1988. 90-04-08856-3.

A comprehensively revised edition of a work first published in 1978. A fine introduction and 'Afterword' on this literature and the first full translation into English of all the codices. A major resource.

Relation to the Bible

525. *Nag Hammadi texts and the Bible: a synopsis and index.* Edited by Craig A. Evans et al. (New Testament tools and studies, 18). Leiden: E. J. Brill, 1993. 90-04-09902-6.

Presents, in 'synopsis' format, parallel texts from Nag Hammadi documents and from the Hebrew and Christian Scriptures. This allows comparisons and a determination of possible relationships and indebtedness between these two bodies of material. Includes an extensive bibliography covering general items and particular tractates and a Scripture index. Essential for those studying the tractates and it will prove invaluable to those concerned with the interpretative history of given scriptural passages.

7

Christian theology

The task of theology is to reflect upon and to interpret the content of faith for the contemporary situation.

Christian theology has been characterised by diverse traditions, denominational, liberal, conservative and, particularly in the last two centuries, by major paradigm shifts. New contextual perspectives have been brought to the theological task. We now have 'black theology', 'feminist theology,' the 'theology of liberation' and 'political theology', to name but some alternative models. The wide-ranging area is also informed by inter-faith and ecumenical dialogues; a new openness contrasts with the absolute claims once made for certain theological propositions.

Resources which deal with theological thinking about certain practices of the church, for example the sacraments, are included in relevant subject chapters. Theological perspectives, as they have emerged in Christianity's dialogue with Judaism, are represented in Chapter 3.

General resources	**158**
Bibliographies	
Dictionaries and encyclopedias	
Documents	
Handbooks and wordbooks	
Greek and Latin theological terms	
Denominational perspectives	**160**
Catholic	160
Dictionaries and encyclopedias	
Liberation theology	161
Bibliographies	
Orthodox	162
Protestant	162
Dictionaries and encyclopedias	
Theologians	**163**
Biographies	
Bibliographies	

GENERAL RESOURCES

Bibliographies

526. Hadidian, D. Y. *Bibliography of British theological literature, 1850-1940.* Pittsburgh, PA: Pittsburgh Theological Seminary, 1985. 0-931222-11-7.

Begins with a valuable essay, 'Introduction to the British theological scene, 1850-1940', and then lists, in author order, the titles by that author, along with the place and date of the first edition of each work. All entries are British imprints. The bibliography is, of necessity, selective but this particular coverage helps fill a gap.

Dictionaries and encyclopedias

It is sometimes difficult to distinguish a 'general' religious encyclopedia from a 'theological' encyclopedia. Certain of the encyclopedic titles cited in Part 1 are concerned, at least in part, with theology, whether historical, systematic or dogmatic. It is also difficult to distinguish a general denominational encyclopedia (found in Chapter 5) from a theological encyclopedia which reflects denominational perspectives. The items treated in this section are concerned with defining theological terms and movements, with developments in theological thinking and with major theologians.

527. *The Blackwell encyclopedia of modern Christian thought.* Edited by Alister McGrath. Oxford; Cambridge, MA: Blackwell, 1993. 0-631-16896-6.

Covers theology from the dawn of the Enlightenment to the present. Substantial essays on central themes, articles on philosophical movements as well as the leading branches of the sciences. Major denominations of the church and influential theologians feature prominently. Includes useful bibliographies, a glossary of terms and is well indexed. The work is ecumenical; the predominant ethos tending toward theological conservatism.

528. *Companion encyclopedia of theology.* Edited by Peter Byrne and Leslie Houlden. London: Routledge, 1995. 0-415-06447-3.

An international team of forty-eight theologians and practitioners contribute essays reflecting the present state of theology in its Western academic context. They do this within six divisions: the Hebrew and Christian Bible, the tradition, the contribution of philosophy, spirituality, contemporary ethics and, finally, issues in present-day theological construction. Each essay concludes with references and a guide to further reading. This apparatus and an extensive index to the whole work ensures that this will be a most useful reference resource.

529. *A New dictionary of Christian theology.* Edited by Alan Richardson and John Bowden. London: SCM Press, 1983. 0-334-02206-1(hc); 0-334-02208-8 (pbk).

Published in the US as *The Westminster dictionary of Christian theology* (Philadelphia: Westminster Press, 1983. 0-664-21398-7).

Effectively builds upon and updates the 1969 edition edited by Richardson. This is a comprehensive, ecumenical work which describes developments in theological thinking since the Enlightenment. Includes material on political and feminist theology, cultural relativism and religious pluralism. No biographies, but an index of names. An excellent place to go for concise definitions and for the clarification of theological themes and questions.

See also *Dictionary of ethics, theology and society* [652].

Documents

530. *The Christian theology reader.* Edited by Alister E. McGrath. Oxford: Blackwell Publications, 1995. 0-631-19584-X (hc); 0-631-19585-8 (pbk).

Although a companion to the editor's *Christian theology: an introduction* (1994), the present work can stand independently and with considerable reference potential. It makes available some 280 seminal texts from Ignatius of Antioch to the *Catechism of the Catholic Church* (1994). Each subject chapter has an introduction outlining particular historical and theological interests and noting the key contributors. Each reading is also introduced and its source identified. Appended are sections detailing the theologians, the conciliar and confessional material, providing a glossary of theological terms and suggestions for further reading. There is a comprehensive index.

Handbooks and wordbooks

531. *A New handbook of Christian theology.* Edited by Donald W. Musser and Joseph L. Price. Nashville, TN: Abingdon, 1992. 0-687-27802-3.

Catholic and Protestant theologians contribute articles on the current scene. Ecumenicity and pluralism are assumed. A good place to look for an overview of theologies which have emerged since the 1950s.

Greek and Latin theological terms

532. Muller, Richard. *Dictionary of Latin and Greek theological terms: drawn principally from Protestant scholastic theology.* Grand Rapids, MI: Baker Book House, 1985. 0-8010-6185-7.

The terms are taken from the Lutheran and Reformed theological traditions of the late sixteenth and seventeenth centuries. The work is valuable for research in historical theology and expressions of Protestant orthodoxy.

533. Stelten, Leo F. *Dictionary of ecclesiastical Latin: with an appendix of Latin expressions defined and clarified.* Peabody, MA: Hendrickson Publishers, 1995. 1-56563-131-5.

Not a research dictionary but a practical manual designed particularly for Catholic students. A listing of words from Scripture, the Code of Canon Law, the liturgy and from the documents of Vatican II, with other philosophical and theological words added. Cases, parts of verbs and declensional forms are given as appropriate. An appendix provides definitions or explanations of some legal and theological terms. There is a bibliography listing linguistic sources. A clearly-prepared guide.

The following more general work is also useful for deciphering Latin phrases which creep (or sweep) into theological discourse:

534. Ehrlich, Eugene. *Nil desperandum: a dictionary of Latin tags and useful phrases.* London: Robert Hale, 1986. 0-7090-2631-5.

(First published in the USA as, *Amo, amas, amat and more,* by Harper & Row, 1985.)

Treats some 1200 Latin phrases, from *ab absurdo* to *vultus est index animi* and provides correct spelling, literal meaning and notes on usage. There is an index connecting English translations to the Latin phrases. As entertaining as it is useful.

(Incidentally, the given translations are 'from the absurd' and 'the face is mirror of the soul'.)

DENOMINATIONAL PERSPECTIVES

CATHOLIC

Dictionaries and encyclopedias

An older work, still of great importance, is:

535. *Sacramentum mundi: an encyclopedia of theology.* Edited by Karl Rahner et al. New York: Herder & Herder; London: Burns and Oates, 1968-1970. 6 vols.

Long, signed articles by Catholic scholars generally reflect post-Vatican II theological positions. Some datedness is now evident, for example this work preceded liberation theology and the emergence of issues concerning women's roles in the church. Yet it remains an important historical compendium. The final volume concludes with a general index and a list of contributors. This roster draws attention to the thought of major theologians on given topics - Klaus Berger, Henri Crouzel, Waldemar Molinski and, notably, Karl Rahner, to name but a few.

536. *Dictionary of fundamental theology.* Edited by René Latourelle and Rino Fisichella. New York: Crossroad, 1994. 0-8245-1395-9.

The English edition of the Italian that was originally published in 1990. A major work which reflects the paradigm shift in Catholic apologetics over the past fifty years. Thirty essay-length entries serve as keys to the structure of the whole, for example on christology, church, history, religion and revelation. Some 222 articles deal with apologetic concerns including the credibility of revelation and the response of faith, interchurch and interfaith relations, the relationship of Christian revelation to the humanities, social sciences and sciences. The work is characterised by liberality, it is well structured, most entries have extensive bibliographies and there is an analytic index.

537. *Handbook of Catholic theology.* Edited by Wolfgang Beinert and Francis Schüssler Fiorenza. New York: Crossroad, 1995. 0-8245-1423-8 (hc).

The English version of *Lexikon der katholischen Dogmatik* (1987), this resource concentrates on Roman Catholic systematic theology. A dictionary arrangement includes substantial articles, by leading theologians, ranging from 'absolution' to 'worldview'. Each article is divided into five sections: biblical background, history of theology, church teaching, ecumenical perspectives and systematic reflections. Numerous tables and charts help crystallise the text. Bibliographies refer mainly to English works and there is a subject index. An objective introduction to the basic categories and topics in Catholic theology.

538. *The New dictionary of theology.* Edited by Joseph A. Komonchak, Mary Collins and Dermot A. Lane. Wilmington, DE: Michael Glazier, 1987. 0-89453-609-5; Dublin: Gill and Macmillan, 1987. 0-7171-1552-6.

Reflects developments in the Catholic Church since Vatican II by concentrating on twenty-four topics and amplifying these through a series of entries. The articles, by some 175 scholars, present positions in Catholic theology, including moral and social issues, while demonstrating ecumenical sensitivity. Cross-referenced with extensive bibliographies.

Theological doctrines

Several reference works have been compiled on specific theological doctrines by Michael O'Carroll, C.S.Sp. Each volume has entries in dictionary order, which survey biblical teaching, historical events and the insights of theologians, past and present, Catholic and Protestant, on a particular doctrine. A feature is the bibliographic coverage for each entry. The five volumes to date, which cover Mariology, the Trinity, the Eucharist, the Holy Spirit and Christology, are as follows:

539. O'Carroll, Michael. *Theotokos: a theological encyclopedia of the Blessed Virgin Mary.* Rev. edn. with supplement. Wilmington, DE: Michael Glazier, 1983. 0-89453-268-5.

540._____. *Trinitas: a theological encyclopedia of the Holy Spirit.* Wilmington, DE: Michael Glazier, 1987. 0-89453-595-1.

541._____. *Corpus Christi: an encyclopedia of the Eucharist.* Wilmington, DE: Michael Glazier, 1988. 0-89453-687-7.

542._____. *Veni creator Spiritus: a theological encyclopedia of the Holy Spirit.* Collegeville, MN: Liturgical Press, 1990. 0-8146-5785-0.

543._____. *Verbum Caro: an encyclopedia on Jesus, the Christ.* Collegeville, MN: Liturgical Press, 1992. 0-8146-5017-1.

Liberation theology

Bibliographies

544. Musto, Ronald G. *Liberation theologies: a research guide.* New York: Garland, 1991. 0-8240-3624-7.

A bibliography of monographs and essays (but not periodical articles) on varieties of liberation theology. There are chapters on biblical roots, Catholic history, area studies, Latin American configurations and feminist theology. Annotations are often extensive and may be critical. There is an index of titles and of authors and editors. An important work for the study of Catholic responses to varying forms of oppression.

ORTHODOX

Few major resources have appeared in English in recent years. For material on Orthodox theologies consult *The new dictionary of Christian theology* [529].

PROTESTANT

Dictionaries and encyclopedias

545. *Evangelical dictionary of theology.* Edited by Walter A. Elwell. Grand Rapids, MI: Baker Book House, 1984. 0-8010-3413-2.

Contributions by evangelical Protestants cover developments in all fields of theology. Every effort has been made to be fair to the traditions that comprise evangelicalism or that affirm non-evangelical theologies. Includes biographies. Most entries are followed by helpful bibliographies.

546. *New dictionary of theology.* Edited by Sinclair B. Ferguson and David F. Wright. Downers Grove, IL, 1988. 0-8308-1400-0; Leicester, England: Inter-Varsity Press. 0-85110-636-6.

Designed to provide an introduction to the world of theology, the work concentrates on its biblical basis, systematic expression and historical development. The common standpoint of the editors and contributors is 'allegiance to the supreme authority of the Scriptures' (Preface). Strong on biographies. Thorough cross-referencing; brief bibliographies.

German

547. *Evangelisches Kirchenlexikon: internationale theologische Enzyklopädie (EKL).* 3rd edn. Edited by Erwin Fahlbusch et al. Göttingen: Vandenhoeck & Ruprecht, 1986- . (In progress).

A new edition to be complete in four volumes (Volume 3: L-R, published in 1992; volume 4, with index, promised for 1995). Extensive articles on the life and work of the churches. Generally a German Protestant perspective but reflects ecumenical concerns. Focuses on contemporary issues but there is no separated biographical coverage of modern theologians.

548. *Evangelisches Lexikon für Theologie und Gemeinde.* Edited by Helmut Burkhardt and Uwe Swarat. 3 vols. Wuppertal: R. Brockhaus Verlag, 1992-1994. 3-417-24641-5 (vol. 1); 3-417-24642-3 (vol. 2); 3-417-24643-1 (vol. 3).

Some 2,800 signed articles deal with theologians and theological issues throughout the world. Themes included are biblical theology, church history and historical theology, dogmatics, ethics, missiology, confessional literature and practical theology. The recency of the work, the authoritative entries and its bibliographic coverage make this a valuable set for those with German.

549. *Theologische Realenzyklopädie (TRE).* Edited by Gerhard Müller. Berlin: de Gruyter, 1977- (In progress. Vol. 25: Ochino-Parapsychologie, was published in 1995.) 3-11-002218-4 (set).
Abkürzungsverzeichnis. Edited by Siegfried Schwertner. 2nd edn. (1993); *Register zu Band 1-17* (1990).

Projected in 30 volumes. Examines the entire spectrum of Christian faith with an emphasis on theology rather than history, and from an ecumenical perspective. Strong on biographical material. Each volume has its own index; a general index will complete the set. The added volume by Schwertner provides a listing of abbreviations of periodicals, series, encyclopedias and other sources used throughout the set. The index volume cited is an interim cumulative guide to the contents of the first seventeen volumes.

THEOLOGIANS

Biographies

In addition to biographical accounts in encyclopedias:

550. Bowden, John. *Who's who in theology.* London: SCM Press, 1990. 0-334-02464-1.

> This handbook presents brief and basic information about the leading figures in Christian history and theology. Contemporary theologians are well represented. An appendix covers the popes of Rome.

551. *Handbook of evangelical theologians.* Edited by Walter A. Elwell. Grand Rapids, MI: Baker Books, 1993. 0-8010-3212-1.

> The accounts of thirty-three theologians, deemed to have had a lasting impact on twentieth-century evangelical thought, reflect the breadth and diversity of the modern church. They range in date from Augustus H. Strong (1836-1921) to Alister McGrath who was born in 1953. Entries for each are well documented and usually include bibliographies of both primary and secondary sources.

Bibliographies

> The entries under this heading are limited to items published since 1980. They are in alphabetical order according to the theologian's name.

Balthasar, Hans Urs von.

552. *Hans Urs von Balthasar: Bibliographie, 1925-1990.* Hrsg. von Cornelia Capol. Freiburg: Johannes Verlag, 1990. 3-89411-029-5.

> Includes primary sources only, that is Balthasar's books, articles, essays, reviews and other publications. Translations into other languages are noted. The arrangement is chronological. An index to persons about whom Balthasar wrote.

> The secondary literature on Balthasar is effectively updated annually in the Jesuit periodical, *Archivum Historicum Societatis Iesu* [284n].

Barth, Karl

553. *Bibliographie Karl Barth.* Erarb. von Hans Markus Wildi. Theologischer Verlag Zurich, 1984; 1992. 3-290-11552-6; 3-290-10082-0.

> Bd 1: Veröffentlichungen von Karl Barth [Primary sources]
> Bd 2: Veröffentlichungen über Karl Barth [Secondary sources]
> I. A-Z; II. Register.

The authoritative bibliography of writings by and about Barth and essential for research on his life and thought. The Register (index) volume includes titles subdivided by language, periodicals and series, biblical passages, persons and places. There is also a chronological index. In all a magnificent, albeit expensive (c. DM 1630), production.

Bonhoeffer, Dietrich

554. Floyd, Wayne Whitson and Clifford J. Green. *Bonhoeffer bibliography: primary source and secondary literature in English.* Evanston, Il: American Theological Library Association, 1992. 0-9604960-6-8.

Part I contains all of Bonhoeffer's writings that, to this date, have been translated into English. Part II contains books, articles, chapters and occasional pieces about Bonhoeffer that appear in English. There are indexes to names and works. Essential for all involved in Bonhoeffer studies.

The updating mechanism is the *Newsletter* of the Bonhoeffer Society, English Language Section (see Introduction to the above work, p. viii).

Merton, Thomas

555. *Thomas Merton: a comprehensive bibliography.* Edited by Marquita Breit and Robert E. Daggy. New edn. (Garland reference library of the humanities, 659). New York: Garland, 1986. 0-8240-8920-0.

Updates the Breit bibliography of 1974 and is intended to be as complete and inclusive a bibliography of writings by and about Merton, through 1985, as is possible. An index covers primary and secondary sources, including book reviews. An essential resource for the study of Merton's life and thought.

Moltmann, Jürgen

556. *Bibliographie Jürgen Moltmann.* Zusammengestellt von Dieter Ising et al. München: Chr. Kaiser Verlag, 1987. 3-459-01709-0.

Prepared in conjunction with a Festschrift to mark Moltmann's sixtieth birthday. His monographs, articles, essays and sermons are listed in chronological order from 1954 to 1987. Works about Moltmann's theology, to that date, are also included.

Schleiermacher, Friedrich

557. Tice, Terrence N. *Schleiermacher bibliography, 1784-1984.* (Princeton pamphlets, 101). Princeton, NJ: Princeton Theological Seminary, 1985.

In 1966 Tice published *Schleiermacher bibliography: with brief introductions, annotations, and index* (Princeton University Press). That inventory of secondary sources is augmented and extended by the present work. Coverage is of material about Schleiermacher's life and writings, subject literature to 1984 and the pedagogical literature. There are indexes to the writings, biographical material, names and subjects. An authoritative resource.

Teilhard de Chardin, Pierre

558. McCarthy, Joseph M. *Pierre Teilhard de Chardin: a comprehensive bibliography.* (Garland reference library of the humanities, 158). New York: Garland, 1981. 0-8240-9783-1.

Comprehensive coverage of works by and about Teilhard to 1980, with subject indexes to the two sections.

The secondary literature in this source is effectively updated annually in the Jesuit periodical, Archivum Historicum Societatis Iesu [284n].

Tillich, Paul

559. Albrecht, Renate et al. *Schlüssel zum Werke von Paul Tillich: Textesgeschichte und Bibliographie sowie Register zu den Gesammelten Werke.* 2., neubearb. u. erw. Aufl. (Gesammelte Werke Bd. XIV). Berlin: de Gruyter, 1990. 3-11-12039-9.

This volume provides an authoritative key to the German edition of the collected works of Paul Tillich which appeared between 1959 and 1983. It has a wider use because of sections dealing with the structuring and textual variations of his writings, a chronologically arranged bibliography of his works, a listing of titles in alphabetical order with translations noted and, finally, several indexes to the other volumes of the *Werke*. An important resource for those engaged in Tillich studies.

A guide to primary and secondary literature, in English, is:

560. Crossman, Richard C. *Paul Tillich: a comprehensive bibliography and keyword index of primary and secondary writings in English.* (ATLA bibliography series, 9). Metuchen, NJ: American Theological Library Association; Scarecrow Press, 1983. 0-8108-1650-4.

Provides bibliographies of Tillich's writings, including reviews by him. Then material about his life and thought including book reviews, relevant dissertations, articles, books and portions of books. There are keyword indexes to subjects and to persons. The whole work, although limited to English language material, functions as a good identification tool for Tillich's writings and provides good coverage of secondary material to the early eighties.

8

Christian worship, liturgy, preaching and music

The public worship of God engages a community of faith in either traditional or experimental forms of praise, thanksgiving and supplication. Usually this involves ritual acts, music and preaching. Most Christians regard the celebration of the sacraments as distinctive acts of worship. However, differing theologies of the sacraments have caused stubborn divisions. In recent times, particularly under the auspices of the ecumenical movement, there have been signs of convergence, an appreciation by the churches of the liturgical richness of other denominational traditions, and a willingness to worship together.

This chapter combines the major elements of Christian worship. The first section covers worship and liturgy; it is followed by sections on preaching and church music.

Worship and Liturgy   **169**
    Bibliographies
    Dictionaries and encyclopedias
    Handbooks
  Liturgical texts   171
  Church calendars and lectionaries   172
    Holy days   173
  Prayers   173

Preaching   **173**
    Encyclopedias
  The Lectionary   174
    Commentaries
  Communication   174
    Bibliographies

Church music   **174**
  General works   175
    Dictionaries
  On church music   175
    Dictionaries

Plainchant   175
        Handbooks
Hymnology   176
        Dictionaries
        Companions
        Concordances

WORSHIP AND LITURGY

The distinction is a fine one but 'worship' is the more general term for the reverence or homage tendered a divine being, and 'liturgy' for the form which that worship takes in a public service. Liturgics is the study of rites, observances or prescribed services in the Christian churches. Reference resources include both general or ecumenical works and denominational material.

Bibliographies

561. *A Bibliography of Christian worship.* Edited by Bard Thompson. (ATLA bibliography series, 25). Metuchen, NJ: American Theological Library Association/ Scarecrow Press, 1989. 0-8108-2154-0.

This large work (some 786 pages) is the most comprehensive bibliography of books and articles in this field. It covers worship and liturgy in the Christian tradition, developments from the early church to the Eastern and Latin churches, the elements of the Mass, the contributions of the Reformers, and so on, to worship in contemporary denominations and ecumenical communities. The detailed table of contents provides a subject guide and there are indexes to authors/editors, denominations and organisations. A fundamental resource for studies in the history and expressions of worship.

562. Zitnik, Maksimilijan. *Sacramenta: bibliographia internationalis.* 4 vols. Rome: Editrice Pontificia Università Gregoriana, 1992. 88-7652-641-2 (set).

Four volumes: I *Introductio*, A-G; II H-Q; III R-Z, *Supplementum A-Z;* IV *Indices.*

The introduction which is printed in German, English, Italian and French is followed by a bibliography covering not only the seven sacramental rites of the Catholic Church but also a wide range of related topics - theological, sociological, pastoral and ecumenical. Protestant teachings are well represented as are opposing views, for example on intercommunion and the ordination of women. The entries include books, articles from Catholic, Protestant and non-denominational periodicals, and reviews. While works published prior to 1960, but not before 1900, are included, the major proportion of entries are for items published since Vatican II. This work, by a well-known Jesuit scholar, is an exceptional achievement and will repay careful scrutiny. Begin with the index volume.

Dictionaries and encyclopedias

563. Pfatteicher, Philip H. *A dictionary of liturgical terms.* Philadelphia, PA: Trinity Press International, 1991. 1-56338-026-9.

Concise glossary of terms and practices. Covers the various liturgical books, vestments, architectural forms, ornaments and the titles given to ministers. The scope includes Eastern and Western, Catholic, Orthodox and Protestant.

564. *New dictionary of liturgy and worship.* Edited by J. G. Davies. London: SCM Press, 1986. 0-334-022070-X. (Published in US as *The New Westminster dictionary of liturgy and worship.)*

Many articles have been updated from the earlier edition (1972) to reflect a period of liturgical revision. Useful for definitions, and introductions to liturgical practices in major and minor denominations. Some 90 black-and-white, well-chosen illustrations. For those with German:

565. *Handbuch der Liturgik: Liturgiewissenschaft in Theologie und Praxis der Kirche.* Edited by Hans-Christoph Schmidt-Lauber and Karl-Heinrich Bieritz. Göttingen: Vandenhoeck & Ruprecht, 1995. 3-525-57191-7. Also published by Evangelische Verlagsanstalt, Leipzig (3-525-57191-7).

A massive (1023 pages) one-volume work with essay-length articles contributed by world authorities. These cover the history of Christian worship, ecumenical perspectives, the forms of worship including the sacraments, and the relation of worship to culture, education, evangelisation and the diaconate. A feature is the amount of attention paid to the Orthodox, Roman Catholic, Lutheran, Reformed, Anglican and Free Church traditions. Extensive bibliographies. Indexes to names mentioned in the text, subjects and authors.

Catholic

566. Lang, Jovian. *Dictionary of the liturgy.* New York: Catholic Book Publishing Co., 1989. 0-89942-273-X.

The author is a Franciscan priest, an experienced liturgist and a theological librarian. The *Dictionary* makes available explanations of everything relating to Catholic liturgy - words, gestures, rites, prayers, service books, sacred vessels, vestments, art, music and much more. The dictionary proper is followed by a series of appendixes - a table of Mass prayers, a comparison of the 1570 Mass with the 1970 Mass, a select chronology of major events in the history of liturgy, the Roman calendar and Latin texts for the people's parts of the Ordinary of the Mass. In all, a thorough and authoritative guide which integrates the liturgical reforms of Vatican II and the Post-Conciliar Documents on the Liturgy.

567. *New dictionary of sacramental worship.* Edited by Peter Fink. Collegeville, MN: Liturgical Press, 1990. 0-8146-5788-5.

Intends to reflect and support the task of liturgical reform and renewal, particularly as informed by the vision framed by Vatican II. The dictionary is structured as a theological and pastoral resource and entries cover the range of activities constitutive of a sacramental church, including material on the church and the arts.

568. Walsh, Michael. *Dictionary of Catholic devotions.* New York: HarperCollins, 1993. 0-06-069271-5.

Devotions are defined as 'the private pieties of individuals' and these include special prayers, the invocation of the saints in specific situations, pilgrimages, the wearing of medals, the veneration of relics and much more. This attractive, informative compendium concludes with the calendar of the Roman Rite, a table of moveable feasts, a bibliography and a very detailed index.

Orthodox

569. Day, Peter D. *The liturgical dictionary of Eastern Christianity.* Collegeville, MN: Liturgical Press, 1993. 0-8146-5848-2; Tunbridge Wells, Kent: Burns & Oates, 1993. 0-86012-216-6.

Straightforward explanations of ecclesiastical and liturgical terms with coverage of the various Eastern churches. A reference guide at the end of the book provides a list of familiar Western terms with equivalent terms for the Eastern rites, which then can be located within the dictionary. Comprehensive, concise and accurate.

Note: a classic work providing theological perspectives on worship in the Orthodox tradition, is Alexander Schmemann, *An introduction to liturgical theology* (Crestwood, NY: St Vladimir's Press, 1986. 0-913836-18-4). It was first published in English in 1966. A recent, introductory guide is:

570. Wybrew, Hugh. *The Orthodox liturgy: the development of the Eucharistic liturgy of the Byzantine Rite.* London: SPCK, 1989. 0-281-04416-3.

A succinct, clearly written, history of the shaping of the Orthodox liturgy from the Last Supper to the present. A good place to begin.

See also David Coomler, *The icon handbook* [607].

Inter-denominational

571. *The Complete library of Christian worship.* Edited by Robert E. Webber. 7 vols. in 8. Nashville, TN: Star Song Publishing, 1994-1995.

The declared purpose of this set is 'to make biblical, historical and contemporary resources on worship available to pastors, music ministers, worship committees and the motivated individual worshipper.' (Introduction to each volume). The volumes are given to the following areas: the biblical foundations of worship, historical and theological development of worship, then resources for worship and preaching, for music and the arts, for the services of the Christian year, for sacraments, ordinances and other sacred acts and, finally, for worship and related ministries. The mass of contributors are representative of numerous denominations and include Catholic and Orthodox scholars. The work, as a whole, however, is predominantly American Protestant in orientation and tone. Subject bibliographies are particularly well developed and each volume is indexed. Depending upon one's liturgical position, this ambitious set could well bristle with reference possibilities.

Handbooks

572. Perry, Michael. *Preparing for worship: the essential handbook for worship leaders.* London: Marshall Pickering, 1995. 0-551-02895-5.

The author is an Anglican priest with much experience in creating resources for contemporary worship. This volume contains extensive listings of music and other worship material, clear guidelines on creating patterns of worship and helpful advice on practical matters such as 'leadership and change' and the hoary issue of 'musicians and ministers'. (Note that the chapter on copyright relates to the laws of the UK.) This volume is a mine of information and a creative resource for those who plan and lead worship services.

LITURGICAL TEXTS

An older work which remains valuable for liturgical texts and expert commentary and which is still in print is:

573. *Liturgies of the Western Church.* Edited by Bard Thompson. Cleveland, OH: World Publishing Company, 1961. Reprinted Philadelphia, PA: Fortress Press, 1980. 0-8006-1428-3.

A selection, and in some cases a fresh translation of liturgies of Word and Sacrament ranging from the church fathers, Justin Martyr and Hippolytus through the Roman Mass (both in Latin and English), to the Reformation liturgies of Luther, Zwingli, Calvin, Knox, the First and Second Prayer Books of Edward VI, the Middleburg Liturgy of the English Puritans and the Westminster Directory, and finally the Savoy Liturgy of Richard Baxter and the Sunday Service of John Wesley. Each text is accompanied by a lucid introduction and there are explanatory notes. A highly-regarded reference work, by no means supplanted.

574. *Baptism and Eucharist: ecumenical convergence in celebration.* Edited by Max Thurian and Geoffrey Wainwright. (Faith and Order paper, 117). Geneva: World Council of Churches, 1983. 2-8254-0783-6 ; Grand Rapids, MI: Eerdmans, 1983. 0-8028-0005-X.

This volume brings together a wide selection of liturgies of Baptism and the Eucharist, with commentaries on the traditions and texts included. The work is divided into liturgies of Baptism, introduced by Max Thurian, and of the Eucharist, introduced by Geoffrey Wainwright. A third section, devoted to the pastoral setting, includes the Eucharistic Liturgy of Lima (see below). The rites of all major traditions - Catholic, Orthodox and Protestant are represented. In addition there are significant texts from the early fathers and texts which have emerged from new contexts, including the *Eucharistic Prayer for Australian Aborigines* (1973). The purpose of the collection is ecumenical - to help church leaders understand each other's theological positions and sacramental practices and to assess the importance of the differences that remain. It comprises a key liturgical resource.

The Lima liturgy

An important recent eucharistic liturgy, known as the Lima liturgy, was compiled by Max Thurian for a session of the Faith and Order Commission of the World Council of Churches which met at Lima in 1982. This liturgy was generally well received and regarded as an expression of the ecumenical theology which informed the document, *Baptism, Eucharist and Ministry*, published by the Council also in 1982. The text of the liturgy is printed as, 'The Eucharistic Liturgy of Lima', in *Baptism and Eucharist: ecumenical convergence in celebration* [574], pp. 241-255

CHURCH CALENDARS AND LECTIONARIES

A number of denominations publish lectionaries annually, either as separate publications or as insertions in yearbooks. Some examples are:

Australian lectionary for [*1995.*] Sydney: Anglican Press Australia, [1994]. ISSN 0812-0811.

Calendar and lectionary of the Uniting Church: [*Year C - 1994-95*]. Melbourne: Joint Board of Christian Education, 1994. ISSN 0728-9138.

Holy Days

Church calendars and lectionaries list prescribed holy or festival days.

Note that the section 'Ecumenical calendar and lectionary' in the *Yearbook of Australian religious organisations* [113], formerly *Yearbook for Australian churches*, lists major festivals, celebrations, anniversaries and other significant events for churches and other religious groups for the given year.

PRAYERS

575. *The SPCK book of Christian prayer.* London: Society for Promoting Christian Knowledge, 1995. 0-281-04795-2.

Brings together over 1,200 prayers, both classic and contemporary, with more than half from this century. Arranged by subject with a comprehensive index of subjects as well as authors and sources. This work draws on Catholic, Orthodox and Protestant traditions and so is a rich resource for Christians of all denominations.

576. *The Oxford book of prayer.* Edited by George Appleton. London: Oxford University Press, 1985. 0-19-213222-9.

This collection, for private use or public worship, includes prayers from the Bible, the saints and mystics of the past and contemporary prayers from different parts of the world. There is a section of prayers from non-Christian traditions of faith. An index to authors and sources and another to subjects, including particular occasions.

PREACHING

In the Christian tradition preaching is thought of as the proclamation of the good news of God's grace to all people. Sermons or homilies are delivered, usually as elements in services of worship. Reference literature in this area is not prolific. The following titles serve to introduce material on the history and practice of preaching and, connectively, on the nature and means of Christian communication.

Encyclopedias

577. *Concise encyclopedia of preaching.* Edited by William H. Willimon and Richard Lischer. Louisville, KY: Westminster John Knox Press, 1995. 0-664-21942- X.

This most comprehensive reference work on Christian preaching combines concerns for practical preaching with theological themes and the historical tradition. Many entries on influential preachers, from the early church until recent times, include sermon excerpts. Some two hundred contributors, Jewish, Catholic and Protestant, have fashioned this valuable first-of-a-kind resource for preachers and students of preaching. A major resource.

The Lectionary

Commentaries

The following are examples of commentary resources designed particularly to help preachers who use the Revised Common Lectionary. They provide exegetical and commentary material for sermon preparation based on those lectionary readings.

578. *Proclamation 6, Series A: interpreting the lessons of the Church Year.* Minneapolis, MN: Fortress Press, 1994-1995.

579. *Preaching the revised common lectionary: Year A, Year B, Year C.* 12 vols. Compiled by Marion Soards, Thomas Dozeman and Kendall McCabe. Nashville, TN: Abingdon Press, 1992, 1993, 1994.

580. *Texts for preaching: a lectionary commentary based on the NRSV: Year B, Year C, Year A.* 3 vols. [Contributors vary from volume to volume.] Louisville, KY: Westminster John Knox Press, 1993, 1994, 1995.

See also the periodical, *Pulpit resource* (1984- .), edited by William H. Willimon. This is a quarterly journal of biblical interpretation, suggested approaches, and illustrative material for the preparation of sermons. Based on the New Revised Common Lectionary. *Pulpit resource* is distributed by MediaCom Associates, with offices in Australia and New Zealand.

Communication

Bibliographies

581. Soukup, Paul A. *Christian communication: a bibliographical survey.* (Bibliographies and indexes in religious studies, 14). New York: Greenwood Press, 1989. 0-313-25673-X.

Following an introductory section, bibliographic items are listed and annotated under the following headings: communication theory, history, rhetoric, interpersonal communication, mass communication, intercultural communication and other media; homiletics being excluded. The author's experience both in theology and communication is reflected in his choice and careful analysis of the literature.

Church Music

Reference questions about church music usually have to do with service music, and, particularly in the Protestant churches, with the identification and choice of hymns. Some major general works, noted first, are essential for musicological studies.

Further material on church music will be found in the dictionaries of worship cited earlier in this chapter.

GENERAL WORKS

Dictionaries

582. *The New Grove dictionary of music and musicians.* Edited by Stanley
     Sadie. 20 vols. London: Macmillan, 1980. 0-333-23111-2.

     This monumental work includes much material pertinent to research on church
     music. Includes musical history, theory and practice, biographies and lists of com-
     positions. Substantial bibliographies.

     Two well-pedigreed reference works, embracing all aspects of music and providing
     authoritative definitions, descriptions and commentary on musical history, theory
     and practice are:

583. *The New Harvard dictionary of music.* Edited by Don Michael Randel.
     Cambridge, MA: Belknap Press of Harvard University Press, 1986.
     0-674-61525-5.

584. *The New Oxford companion to music.* Edited by Denis Arnold. 2 vols.
     Oxford University Press, 1983. Reprinted with corrections, 1990.
     0-19-311316-3.

ON CHURCH MUSIC

Dictionaries

585. Poultney, David. *Dictionary of Western church music.* Chicago:
     American Library Association, 1991. 0-8389-0569-2.

     Brief definitions of terms used in the several denominational traditions and
     accounts of composers of significant sacred works. In all, a clear, introductory
     work with tables and appendixes adding to its usefulness.

Plainchant

Plainchant is the oldest substantial body of music that has been preserved in any
shape or form. The following recent work is a most authoritative manual.

Handbooks

586. Hiley, David.*Western plainchant: a handbook.* Oxford: Clarendon Press,
     1993. Reprinted 1995. 0-19-816289-8 (hc); 0-19-816572-2 (pbk).

     David Hiley is Professor at the Institut für Musikwissenschaft at the University of
     Regensburg and co-editor of the second volume of the *New Oxford History of
     Music* which deals with the period from the early Middle Ages to 1300 (2nd edi-
     tion, 1990).

     This work provides a clear and concise introduction to plainchant in the liturgy,
     chant genres, liturgical books and plainchant sources, notation, plainchant and
     early music theory, and the history of its performance and mutations. Illustrated
     with 200 musical examples. A feature is the extensive bibliography (pp. xxxiii-
     xcvii). Surely an indispensable resource for this complex subject.

Hymnology

Dictionaries

The following work, first published in 1892, is still the most-used source for information about Christian hymns of all ages and countries.

587. Julian, John. *A dictionary of hymnology setting forth the origin and history of Christian hymns of all ages and nations.* 2nd rev. edn with new *Supplement.* London: Murray; New York: Scribners, 1907. (Repr.: Grand Rapids, MI: Kregel, 1985. 2 vols. 0-8254-2960-9.)

The most comprehensive reference resource which serves historical, biographical and doctrinal interests. Particular attention is paid to hymns appearing in the hymnbooks of English-speaking countries. Note: there are separate indexes to the two appendixes and to the new supplement.

Companions

Companions have been published to several denominational hymnals. For example:

588. Milgate, Wesley. *Songs of the people of God: a companion to the Australian hymn book/ With one voice.* London: Collins, 1982. 0-00-599704-6.

An introduction deals with congregational singing, hymn details and the obligations of those involved in their presentation. Then the entry for each hymn includes notes on the words and tunes. There is a section of biographical notes and finally indexes to first lines and tunes. Given the comprehensiveness of the hymnal itself, this is a valuable reference resource.

Wesley Milgate also authored *A companion to Sing alleluia: a supplement to the Australian hymn book.* Sydney: Australian Hymn Book Pty Ltd, 1988. 0-7316-3319-9 (pbk).

Concordances

People needing to choose hymns for services of one sort or another may be struggling with a few misremembered lines or phrases. Julian (above) may help as well as the work by Katharine Diehl, *Hymns and tunes: an index* (New York: Scarecrow Press, 1960), which provides first-line access to hymns from seventy-eight English-language hymnals as well as an index to authors, tunes and composers. The following concordance functions for the words of hymns in the same way as a Bible concordance functions for the biblical text.

589. Klepper, Robert F. *A concordance of 'The Hymnal 1982'.* Metuchen, NJ: Scarecrow Press, 1989. 0-8108-2250-4.

The official hymnbook of the Episcopal Church in the USA is *The Hymnal 1982* (New York: Church Hymnal Corporation, 1985). This hymnal attempted to retain the best of the past and to incorporate material from the contemporary renaissance of musical activity. It is an ecumenical work, designed also for the use of non-Episcopal congregations. In drawing on the best from many traditions it is regarded as a comprehensive and high-quality collection.

Klepper 's concordance lists every key noun or verb in this *Hymnal* and notes the hymn line in which that word appears. That line directs the user, by hymn number, to the first line or common title of the hymn in the complete listing at the end of the volume. To fully exploit this concordance one would need access to the *Hymnal* itself but, where this is not available, one could check for that first line in other major hymn books.

Spirituality

The word, 'spirituality' has achieved prominence in relatively recent times and is used to describe the dimensions of a person's life in relationship to God and to the world. In the great religions, this life has been described in the writings and witness of spiritual directors. And various disciplines - ascetic, contemplative, mystical, socially active - have provided models for devotion. In the Christian tradition spirituality is thought to involve a lived-discipleship of faith and love. But, once again, the forms are diverse as spirituality comprehends the worship life of Orthodox monks, the faith-quests of charismatic experientialists and the social accents of liberation theologians.

The few reference resources in this field reflect a continuing dependence on the spiritual guides of the ages. It is also clear that, given the twin factors of the ecumenical movement and inter-faith dialogues, contemporary religious leaders are recognising the partial character of their isolated Eastern and Western traditions and are learning and borrowing from each other.

Spirituality   **179**

    Dictionaries
    Documents, histories: series
  Australian Aboriginal   181

Dictionaries

590. *Dictionnaire de spiritualité: ascétique et mystique, doctrine et histoire.*
     Editors vary. 17 vols. Paris: Beauchesne, 1932-1995.

The great resource in this field, begun in 1932 and only recently completed. Lengthy, signed articles cover spiritual theology, the religious history of countries, schools of spirituality and the lives and works of those deemed to have lived the spiritual life. The final volume 17 is an index to the whole work and includes a list of contributors with their articles.

The following one-volume dictionaries are useful:

591. *A Dictionary of Christian spirituality.* Edited by Gordon S. Wakefield.
     London: SCM Press, 1983, 1988. 0-334-01967-2 (pbk).
     (Published in the US as *The Westminster dictionary of Christian
     spirituality.* Philadelphia: Westminster Press, 1983.)

An ecumenical compilation which deals with the spirituality of every school and denomination, Christian and non-Christian, and with the varying forms of spiritual life. Helpful for biographical accounts of the spiritual theologians.

592. *The New dictionary of Catholic spirituality.* Edited by Michael Downey.
     Collegeville, MN: Liturgical Press, 1993. 0-8146-5525-4.

Designed to serve as a reliable theological and pastoral resource, this work treats the subject of spirituality in light of the reform and renewal which emerged from the Second Vatican Council. Entries, ranging from 'abandonment' to 'zeal', include expressions of spirituality in a variety of church groupings. Biographical material is not separated but can be traced in the index of names.

For a brilliant overview and extensive bibliography, see the essay by Geoffrey Wainwright, 'Christian spirituality', in the *Encyclopedia of religion*, edited by Mircea Eliade [51], volume 3, pp. 452-460.

Documents, histories: series

There are two major series, in process of publication. The first features documents and the second, historical analyses. These are:

593. Classics in Western spirituality.

Volumes in the series, 'Classics of Western spirituality', now published by Paulist Press, Mahwah, NJ., feature the writings of acknowledged teachers within the Catholic, Eastern Orthodox, Jewish, American Indian, Islamic and Protestant traditions. Each volume includes selected documents, introduced and translated by scholars in the field. To mention only a few entries in the series, *Augustine, George Herbert, Ignatius of Loyola, Philo of Alexandria, the Talmud, John and Charles Wesley, Zohar*, is to suggest the wide-ranging coverage.

594. World spirituality: an encyclopedic history of the religious quest.

The multivolume series, 'World spirituality', now published by SCM Press, London and Crossroad Publishing, New York, explores the spiritual wisdom of the human race from prehistoric times, through the great religions, to the meeting of traditions in modern times. Titles already published include Christian spirituality (in three volumes), Jewish (in two volumes), Classical Mediterranean, Hindu, Islamic (in two volumes), Modern esoteric and South and Meso-American native spirituality. Each volume contains an introduction and then interpretative essays, by leading authorities, on aspects of the particular subject. There are usually glossaries, bibliographies and indexes.

AUSTRALIAN ABORIGINAL

See, *Aboriginal art and spirituality*, edited by Rosemary Crumlin [602].

Religious and theological education

There are few current reference resources in the field of religious and theological education but those mentioned here, particularly *Harper's encyclopedia* [598], are of major importance.

The student is reminded that material on educational issues, theories, practices and institutions, including aspects of religious education, may be found in encyclopedias of education. For example, the recent edition of the *International encyclopedia of education*, edited by Torsten Husen and T. Neville Postlethwaite. 2nd edn. 12 vols. (Tarrytown, NY: Pergamon Press/ Elsevier Science, 1994. 0-08-041046-4), is a valuable resource for definitional, historical and theoretical material.

A reminder also that the field of education is well supplied with indexing and abstracting services. Australian interests are served by the *Australian education index*, a comprehensive index to literature relevant to Australian education, including religious education. It is published by the Australian Council for Education Research, Private Bag 55, Camberwell, Victoria and is available in print copy (ISSN 0004-9026), or online through Ozline (National Library of Australia).

Religious education   **184**

    Bibliographies
    Dictionaries and encyclopedias
    Histories

Theological education   **185**

    Guides
    Australasian   185

RELIGIOUS EDUCATION

Bibliographies

595. Wyckoff, D. Campbell and George Brown. *Religious education, 1960-1993.* (Bibliographies and indexes in religious studies, 33). Westport, CT: Greenwood Press, 1995. 0-313-28453-9.

Beginning with a critical survey of recent religious education the work proceeds to bibliographic coverage of the foundations of education, theory, administration, program and curriculum. The two settings in which relationships between religion and education are receiving particular attention - the school and higher education - are dealt with separately. The emphasis throughout is on Christian education. In all some 1169 entries, with name, subject and title indexes. An outstanding bibliographic tool.

Dictionaries and encyclopedias

General

596. Lawton, Denis and Peter Gordon. *Dictionary of education.* Sevenoaks, Kent: Hodder & Stoughton Educational, 1993. 0-340-53179-7.

Following a section in which key educational concepts are discussed, there is a dictionary of words which are either peculiar to education or have a specific meaning in an educational context. While there is a definite emphasis on education in the United Kingdom, there is much of a general nature which makes this an accessible resource for those requiring clear definitions and explanations of vocabulary used in educational circles.

Religious

597. *Dictionary of religious education.* Edited by John M. Sutcliffe. London: SCM Press in association with the Christian Education Movement, 1984. 0-334-01968-0.

Covers religious education around the world and as practised by the major faiths, but is particularly strong on developments in Britain. The contributors concentrate on methods of teaching. Major entries include bibliographies.

598. *Harper's encyclopedia of religious education.* Edited by Iris V. Cully and Kendig Brubaker Cully. San Francisco: Harper & Row, 1990. 0-00-606165-6.

Effectively updates and upgrades the well-known *Westminster dictionary of Christian education* (1963). Contributions are from Catholic, Jewish and Protestant scholars who represent the disciplines of education, biblical studies, religion, theology, history and psychology. Members of other faiths also present surveys. Among the 600 entries are essay-length articles, for example on 'Faith development', 'Hinduism', 'Jewish education', 'Theology and education'. Strong on biographies and organisations. A comprehensive resource for the history, theory and practice of religious education and the major encyclopedic work in this field.

Histories

599. Reed, James E. and Ronnie Prevost. *A history of Christian education.* Nashville, TN: Broadman, 1993. 0-8054-6586-3.

Designed both as a textbook for Christian education courses and as a reference tool, this work provides a straightforward historical account which begins with education in ancient Greece and moves to our time. Useful for introductory material and particularly for profiles of educators.

THEOLOGICAL EDUCATION

Guides

The periodical, *Theological education*, published by the Association of Theological Schools in the United States (1964-), is a major source for developments in this field. Note that, from time to time, supplements to this journal deal with specific aspects of theological education.

AUSTRALASIAN

The Colleges of Divinity or Theology throughout Australasia, along with affiliated or independent theological faculties or colleges, publish their own annual handbooks. However, for comprehensive directory information see:

600. *The Australian and New Zealand Association of Theological Schools: fact book, 1994-5-6.* Melbourne, Vic.: Australian and New Zealand Association of Theological Schools, 1994. 0-646-18593-4.

Lists membership of the ANZATS Council, the Colleges of Divinity/Theology, members schools of both ANZATS and NZATS, theological colleges, and a who's who in theological education in the two countries. The ANZATS constitution is also printed.

Another entry for this title is at item 342.

11

Religious art and architecture

The disciplines of art and architecture are well supplied with reference resources covering history, techniques and criticism. Students working in religion studies will need access to the major general and subject encyclopedias and to folios of reproductions. This chapter, however, also features comparatively modest publications which deal most effectively with the history and forms of religious art and of Christian art in particular. Religious myths, stories and sacred happenings come to expression in symbolic form, and there are a number of sources which help with the interpretation of symbolism and iconography. Religious imagery in Australian Aboriginal art forms receives special attention.

The arts in general   **188**
         Encyclopedias

Religious art   **188**
     Australia   188
         Aboriginal art   188
         Comprehensive   189

Christian art   **189**
         Surveys
         Dictionaries, handbooks
         Subject bibliographies

Religious symbolism   **190**
         Guides and dictionaries
     Oceania   192

Religious architecture   **192**
         Surveys

Church architecture   **192**
         Guides
     Asia   193
     Australia   193

THE ARTS IN GENERAL

Encyclopedias

The following great set remains a major reference resource for the fine arts:

601. *Encyclopedia of world art.* 15 vols. New York: McGraw-Hill, 1959-1968, 1983, 1987. 0-07-019467-X.

> Published in Italian and English with the English set being augmented. Signed contributions by specialists make this an outstanding resource in the field. There are substantial sections on the art of the major religions. Note that volumes 1-14 include plates arranged according to the alphabetical sequence of the entries in the respective volumes. Volume 15 contains a very thorough index.
>
> Two supplemental volumes have been published:
>
> Volume 16: 'World art in our time'. Edited by Bernard S. Myers, 1983;
>
> Volume 17: 'New discoveries and perspectives in the world of art'. Edited by Giulio Carlo Argan, 1987.
>
> Note: after many years in production, 1996 should see the publication of the *Dictionary of art*, by Groves Dictionaries, a division of Macmillan Publications, rightly famous for the *New Grove dictionary of music and musicians*. An announcement speaks of a 34-volume, extensively illustrated, edition with over forty thousand articles by art historians and other authorities, covering every aspect of the visual arts throughout the world.

RELIGIOUS ART

AUSTRALIA

Aboriginal Art

602. *Aboriginal art and spirituality.* Edited by Rosemary Crumlin and images curated by Rosemary Crumlin and Anthony Knight. North Blackburn, Vic.: Dove, 1991. Paperback edition, 1995. 0-85924-998-0 (hc); 1-86371-386-7 (pbk).

> The work divides between the presentation of art works by Aboriginals and a set of interpretative essays, by artists and scholars, and gathered under the heading, 'Talking about art'. In all, the volume is an authoritative, beautifully illustrated guide to the spiritual wealth of Aboriginal culture and, particularly, to the transmission of the myths, stories and practices reverenced by particular groups. The volume's reference value is enhanced by a catalogue to the exhibition, a bibliography and index.

603. *Dreamings: the art of Aboriginal Australia.* Edited by Peter Sutton. New York: George Braziller in association with the Asia Society Galleries, 1988. 0-8076-1201-4.

This outstanding work is a catalogue of an exhibition of Australian Aboriginal art presented by the South Australian Museum, in association with the Asia Society Galleries, New York, and four other museums. The collection makes it clear that the traditional art forms of the Aborigines are a manifestation of their religious beliefs. Their images of the Dreaming, its beings, places and ceremonies, reflect both religious knowledge and experience. There are several interpretative essays contributed by experts. The art forms appear in a range of media from bark paintings to acrylic. The catalogue of the collection includes some 103 items, but the volume is lavishly illustrated with many more representations and descriptive illustrations. There are biographies of the artists, notes, a valuable bibliography and general index.

Comprehensive

604. Crumlin, Rosemary. *Images of religion in Australian art.* Kensington, NSW: Bay Books, 1988. 1-86256-291-1.

The artists and paintings in this collection present, in microcosm, the history of Australian painting over the last few decades. Most works draw on the Judaeo-Christian traditions. Some reflect the power of the sacred and of its myths and symbols and raise questions about the meaning of life and death. The text of a section on Aboriginal artists has been written by Judith Ryan. There is a list of the 93 plates, a bibliography and indexes to artists and subjects.

CHRISTIAN ART

Monotheistic religions have had an ambiguous relationship with the arts. The Decalogue's prohibition on the imaging of the divine influenced the attitudes of some early church fathers and, indeed sections of later Christendom. The history of the relationship between the arts and the churches has been one of support and constraint, of lavish patronage and obdurate charges of extravagance and image-worship.

Surveys

605. Dillenberger, Jane. *Style and content in Christian art.* London: SCM Press, 1986. 0-334-02344-0.

A reprint of a work originally published in 1965, this is a highly-regarded guide to great Christian art. Following an introductory chapter which discusses the iconography, form and meaning of art, the work proceeds to consider the main periods of Christian art and the recognised masterpieces. These are discussed in detail and illustrated through some eighty pages of illustrations. The language of the book is non-technical. That this work has endured for some thirty years is a mark of its quality.

For an excellent survey of biblical art see Pamela Tudor-Craig, 'Art, The Bible in', in *A Dictionary of biblical interpretation*, edited by R. J. Coggins and J. L. Houlden [401], pp. 57-65.

Dictionaries, handbooks

606. Apostolos-Cappadona, Diane. *Dictionary of Christian art.* New York: Continuum, 1994. 0-8264-0779-X.

With over 1,000 entries from 'Aaron' to 'Zucchetto', this work identifies and explains the major signs, symbols, figures and subjects which have emerged in European Christian art from its beginnings to today. Profusely illustrated.

Russian Orthodox

607. Coomler, David. *The icon handbook: a guide to understanding icons and the liturgy, symbols and practices of the Russian Orthodox Church.* Springfield, IL: Templegate Publications, 1995, 0-87243-210-6.

A specialist in Russian icons, Coomler designed this work especially for those puzzled by the unfamiliar subjects and mysterious inscriptions. Includes 174 full-page illustrations of icons in black and white and several in colour as well as charts and instructions for reading and understanding the Church Slavonic inscriptions.

Subject bibliographies. History. Reformation

608. Parshall, Linda B. and Peter W. Parshall. *Art and the Reformation: an annotated bibliography.* Boston, MA: G. K. Hall, 1986. 0-8161-8602-2.

A classified bibliography covering Catholic and Protestant reformers and such topics as the image controversy, iconoclasm, the use of illustration in printed propaganda, artists of the period, architecture, decorative and minor arts and the iconography of the reformers. Many entries are extensively annotated. Indexes are to authors, exhibitions and subjects. An important resource for art and church historian alike.

RELIGIOUS SYMBOLISM

Guides and dictionaries

Several older works continue to provide excellent coverage in the area of Christian symbolism.

609. Ferguson, George Wells. *Signs and symbols in Christian art: with illustrations from paintings of the Renaissance.* New York: Oxford University Press, 1954; London: Zwemmer, 1955.

Uses skilful line drawings and art reproductions to explain the incidence and meaning of symbols and to illustrate their use. There is an index of names and subjects.

610. Hall, James. *Dictionary of subjects and symbols in art.* Rev. edn. London: John Murray, 1979. Reprinted 1989. 0-7195-4147-6 (pbk).

The number of editions published since the original in 1974 indicates the popularity and quality of this basic work about the subject-matter of art. It is concerned with recurring themes, persons, objects and attributes in classical and

Christian art. Remarkably good coverage, lucid definitions. It remains an essential tool for work on the history of Christian art.

A major German set is:

611. *Lexikon der christlichen Ikonographie.* Hrsg. von Engelbert Kirschbaum. 8 vols. Rome: Herder, 1968-1976. Reissued in a paperback edition, 1990.
Vols 1-4: Allgemeine Ikonographie [biblical and general themes]; vols. 5-8: Ikonographie der Heiligen [the saints] and Register [index].

For those with some German, this is an authoritative and comprehensive work. Each entry includes a survey of sources, a description of the iconography and finally, a bibliography. There are numerous illustrations. Volume 4 includes an index to English and French equivalents of the topics treated, while the final volume concludes with a list of saints' days and a subject index.

612. Schiller, Gertrud. *Iconography of Christian art.* 2 vols. Greenwich, CT: New York Graphic Society, 1971-1972.

Translation of the first two volumes of *Ikonographie der christlichen Kunst* (1969, 1968).

Vol. 1: Christ's incarnation, childhood, baptism, temptation, transfiguration, works and miracles; vol. 2: The passion of Christ.

Arranged thematically, the excellent text and illustrations describe the treatment of the events and themes of the life of Jesus in art. Index at end of volume 2.

A new work specifically to do with Christian symbols is:

613. Speake, Jennifer. *The Dent dictionary of symbols in Christian art.* London: J. M. Dent, 1994. 0-460-86138-7.

Over 800 entries cover Eastern and Western art forms from Coptic, Orthodox and Catholic traditions and detail the differences in emphasis and presentation. The list includes biblical characters, material from the legends of the saints and from episodes in church history. An interesting visual index, including over 100 illustrations, serves to identify saints and symbols. A clear introductory guide.

See also Metford, J. C. J. *Dictionary of Christian lore and legend* [185].

Covering symbols of Christian origin, but also those from other sources is:

614. Walker, Barbara G. *The women's dictionary of symbols and sacred objects.* New York: Harper & Row, 1988. 0-06-250992-5 (hc); 0-06-250923-3 (pbk).

A guide to the history and mythology of women-related symbols. Entries for the symbols are arranged in twenty-one sections, by shape or type, for example 'four-way motifs', 'deities' signs', 'flowers'. There are introductory essays to each section. The work is well illustrated by line drawings and there is a bibliography and a comprehensive index. A concise guide to this specialised symbol system.

OCEANIA

615. Moore, Albert C. *Arts in the religions of the Pacific: symbols of life.* (Religion and the arts). London: Pinter, 1995. 0-86187-186-3.

This volume fills a real gap by exploring the relationship between religious experience and the diverse art forms of the native peoples of Australia, Melanesia, Polynesia and New Zealand. The focus is on the symbolism expressed in music, dance, masks and carvings and the work enables 'fruitful connections, contrasts and comparisons across the regions of the Pacific' (Preface). Illustrations are in black and white. There is an extensive list of references, a glossary and general index.

RELIGIOUS ARCHITECTURE

Surveys

616. Mann, A. T. *Sacred architecture.* Shaftesbury, Dorset: Element Books, 1993. (Also published in Australia by Element Books for Jacaranda Wiley, Brisbane, 1993.) 1-85230-391-3

From the early astrological and mythical influences which determined the location, form and function of early monuments, this survey traces architectural patterns to the present time. It will be useful particularly for its imaginative text and brilliant illustrations. Well-indexed.

Note the survey article 'Architecture' by J. G. Davies, a well-known scholar in this field, in the *Encyclopedia of religion*, edited by Mircea Eliade [51], vol. 1, pp. 382-392.

CHURCH ARCHITECTURE

Guides

617. Norman, Edward. *The house of God: church architecture, style and history.* London: Thames and Hudson, 1990. 0-500-25108-8.

An authoritative, chronological survey which describes churches as both acts of faith and works of art. Enhanced, quite brilliantly, by photographs. Concludes with a glossary of terms, sources of illustrations and an index.

618. Purdy, Martin. *Church and chapels: a design and development guide.* (Butterworth Architecture design and development guides). Oxford: Butterworth-Heinemann, 1991. 0-7506-1222-3.

Offers guidelines for congregations wishing to construct a building for worship.

Part 1 covers a strategy for design development and a historical survey. Part 2 describes the process itself, including a feasibility study, brief making, design analysis and scheme design. The work is well illustrated with plans, diagrams and photographs. A most practical resource for those engaged in building projects.

ASIA

619. Takenaka, Masao. *The place where God dwells: an introduction to church architecture in Asia.* Hong Kong: Christian Conference of Asia, in association with Auckland: Pace Publishing, 1995. 0-959797-5 -7. Also published by the World Council of Churches (Geneva: WCC Publications, 1995. 2-8254-1164-7).

Not strictly a reference work but a valuable survey of church architecture in Asia. Takenaka, a well-known ecumenical leader and supporter of the arts, provides a lengthy and authoritative introduction. Then the book is divided into Asian regions and countries with church architecture being delightfully illustrated by means of more than 100 photographs, many in colour, and these are accompanied by commentary. Numerous denominations are represented as are indigenous expressions of the gospel.

AUSTRALIA

620. Reed, T. T. *Historic churches of Australia.* South Melbourne: Macmillan, 1978. 0-333-25148-2.

An illustrated study of forty churches built before the discovery of gold in Australia. They are chosen from all States, from city and country, and reflect a cross-section of architectural and denominational styles. The photographs, taken by Richard Beck, are an important feature.

621. *Victorian churches.* Edited by Miles Lewis. Melbourne: National Trust of Australia (Victoria), 1991. 0-909710-42-2.

A comprehensive survey which begins with introductory material on the relationship between the church and state, a history of denominations and a typology of architectural styles. Then there is an illustrated inventory of over 400 church buildings. The work concludes with a glossary, an expansive bibliography and a detailed index.

622. *The future of our historic churches: conflict and reconciliation.* Edited by John Henwood and Tom Hazell. Melbourne: National Trust of Australia (Victoria), 1988. 0-909710-71-6.

This volume comprises a set of papers delivered to a symposium on the future of church buildings. Experts examine attitudes relating to the preservation of the buildings and possible solutions, as proposed in Australia and overseas. They describe the decision-making involved in all the Australian States. Illustrated with 70 plates featuring significant buildings and furnishings.

Pastoral care and counselling

Those working in the fields of pastoral care are usually aware of biblical sources and theological presuppositions, but also of the need to understand and evaluate research in the behavioural sciences, particularly psychology and psychotherapy. With this in mind, the opening entries comprise encyclopedic works which include instructive overviews, definitions and summaries of research developments

Recently there has been a tendency to locate pastoral care and counselling within the context of a theologically-informed ethical framework, a correlation which is reflected in certain reference resources, particularly those relating to specialised areas of pastoral concern.

Psychology   **196**
       Dictionaries and encyclopedias

Pastoral care   **196**
       Dictionaries
  Australia   197
       Histories

Specialised areas   **197**
       Bibliographies
  Aging   197
  AIDS   198
  Death and dying   198

PSYCHOLOGY

Dictionaries and Encyclopedias

623. *Encyclopedia of psychology.* Edited by Raymond J. Corsini. 2nd edn. 4 vols. New York: John Wiley & Sons, 1994. 0-471-55819-2 (set).

The highly-regarded first edition of this encyclopedia (1984) has been effectively updated and augmented. Experts contribute essays in all fields of psychology. The first three volumes contain the subject matter while the final volume includes biographies, a bibliography, name and subject indexes. A quality reference work.

624. *The Encyclopedic dictionary of psychology.* Edited by Rom Harré and Roger Lamb. Oxford: Blackwell Reference, 1983. 0-631-12663-5.

Designed for specialists and advanced students, this work includes entries ranging from concise definitions to substantial articles. Schools of psychology, important practitioners, fundamental concepts and empirical techniques are described. Most articles have bibliographies and there is a detailed index and glossary.

625. Campbell, Robert J. *Psychiatric dictionary.* 6th edn. New York: Oxford University Press, 1989. 0-19-505293-5.

Originally published in 1940, this revised and otherwise updated edition adds new terms and definitions and describes developments in research since the fifth edition of 1981. An authoritative, highly-regarded work which covers all areas of psychiatric interest and is supportive of work in pastoral care and related behavioural fields.

The following item is a practical guide, designed especially for clergy:

626. Ciarrocchi, Joseph W. *A minister's handbook of mental disorders.* (Integration series). New York: Paulist Press, 1993. 0-8091-3403-9.

The author, a clinical psychologist who teaches pastoral counselling at Loyola College, Maryland, fills a void with this resource on adult psychopathology. There are sections on major theories of abnormal behaviour, on interviewing and assessment, and detailed chapters on anxiety and mood disorders, stress, addiction, schizophrenia, sexual problems and dysfunction, and personality disorders. Analyses of pastoral situations and moral issues bring the textual material to life. A detailed person/subject index.

PASTORAL CARE

Dictionaries

627. *A Dictionary of pastoral care.* Edited by Alastair V. Campbell. London: SPCK, 1987. 0-281-04239-X (hc).

A concise but comprehensive guide to the concepts and problems most likely to be encountered in pastoral work. Entries cover theoretical and practical issues and a wide subject range from theology and ethics to psychology and medicine.

More substantial is:

628. *Dictionary of pastoral care and counseling.* Edited by Rodney J. Hunter. Nashville, TN: Abingdon Press, 1990. 0-687-10761-X.

More than 1200 state-of-the-art articles, prepared by experts, cover virtually every topic related to care and counselling. Catholic, Jewish, Orthodox and Protestant perspectives are represented. Entries range from brief treatments to detailed articles and essays and include fulsome bibliographies. The editorial intention of naming important issues and suggesting future directions succeeds admirably. In all, an invaluable sourcebook and the best in the field.

629. *New dictionary of Christian ethics and pastoral theology.* Edited by David J. Atkinson et al. Downers Grove, IL: Inter-Varsity Press, 1995. 0-8308-1408-6

Major sections relating to pastoral theology include those on character, pastoral care, counselling and psychotherapy, life, health and death. For a more extensive annotation see item 654.

AUSTRALIA

Histories

The following work is an important documentary history of pastoral ministry in Australia.

630. Griffin, Graeme M. *They came to care: pastoral ministry in colonial Australia.* Melbourne, Vic.: Joint Board of Christian Education, 1993. 0-85819-879-7.

A well-researched account of the history and development of a pastoral ministry which helped to establish the Protestant churches in Australia. It focuses particularly on the early clergy of the three oldest and largest traditions (apart from Anglicanism) - Congregational, Methodist and Presbyterian. There are chapters on this history and on the pastoral contacts involved in the rites of baptism, marriage and burial. The work includes much primary-source material, is well-illustrated and there are footnotes to each chapter. Indexes are to names and also places.

SPECIALISED AREAS

Bibliographies

AGING

631. Simmons, Henry C. and Vivienne S. Pierce. *Pastoral responses to older adults and their families.* (Bibliographies and indexes in gerontology, 15). New York: Greenwood Press, 1992. 0-313-28039-8.

The authors are well-known directors of the Center for Aging at the Presbyterian School of Christian Education in Richmond, Virginia. The work, designed for practising clergy, educators and lay professionals, organises the field of religion and aging from a pastoral perspective. Areas of gerontology covered include church and synagogue, ethics, spiritual life, death and dying, theology and religious professionalism. 736 entries, including books, articles and dissertations are annotated. There are indexes to authors and subjects. A comprehensive, up-to-date resource.

AIDS

632. *National Church HIV/AIDS: bibliography, 1993.* Compiled by Jillian Murphy. Sydney: National Churches Working Group on AIDS, 1993. 0-646-15896-1.

Subjects covered include education, theology, ethics, the role of the church, experiences of people with HIV/AIDS and the caregivers. Resources cited include books, conference papers, articles, pamphlets and education kits. Entries are annotated. The Working Group is supporting the updating of this data base.

DEATH AND DYING

633. Southard, Samuel. *Death and dying: a bibliographic survey.* (Bibliographies and indexes in religious studies, 19). New York: Greenwood Press, 1991. 0-313-26465-1.

The author, who teaches pastoral theology at Fuller Theological Seminary, has compiled a well-annotated bibliography of books and articles providing a multi-disciplinary coverage of the subject. An introductory essay on the development of the literature of thanatology is followed by sections devoted to the span and style of life, philosophical theology, counselling the dying, grief, the caring professions, education for death, current research and bibliographies. Annotations are both descriptive and critical. Indexes are to authors, titles and subjects. An important pastoral and theological resource.

13

Philosophy and ethics

Were biblical theology to determine, wherever possible, to have nothing to do with reason in things religious, we can easily foresee on which side would be the loss; for a religion which rashly declares war on reason will not be able to hold out in the long run against it.

Immanuel Kant. *Religion within the limits of reason alone.*
Translated by T. M. Greene and H. H. Hudson.
Chicago, Open Court, 1934.
Preface to the first edition, p. 9.

Philosophers, in attending to theological statements, look for conceptual clarity. They examine the ways in which language is being used, inquire about the nature of 'knowledge' in religious discourse, and attempt to evaluate claimed religious experiences. All this in an attempt to keep theology reasonable.

Philosophical disciplines have been particularly well served by subject bibliographies, dictionaries and encyclopedias. These types of resources loom large here.

Two of the several divisions of philosophy, namely metaphysics and ethics, remain most important for theological work. Their subject matter is, of course, well represented in the general encyclopedic resources for the study of philosophy, but there are also specialist items and these are listed under the relevant divisions. Separate treatment is also afforded resources for the study of Christian ethics.

Philosophy   **201**
         Bibliographic guides
         Dictionaries and encyclopedias
   Modern thought   202
         Dictionaries
         Biographies

Metaphysics   **203**
         Handbooks

Ethics   **203**
         Bibliographies
         Dictionaries and encyclopedias
         Companions
         Indexing services

Bioethics   205
        Bibliographies
        Encyclopedias

Christian ethics   **205**
        Dictionaries
        Documents, commentaries

PHILOSOPHY

Bibliographic guides

634. Bynagle, Hans E. *Philosophy: a guide to the reference literature.* Littleton, CO: Libraries Unlimited, 1986. 0-87287-464-8.

Some 400 general and specialised reference works, published through mid-1985, are cited, extensively annotated and critically evaluated. Also chapters on leading journals in the field and on professional associations.

635. Tice, Terrence N. and Thomas P. Slavens. *Research guide to philosophy.* (Sources of information in the humanities, 3). Chicago: American Library Association, 1983. 0-8389-0333-9.

Offers lengthy bibliographic essays on the history of philosophy with sub-sections on individual philosophers, and on subject areas, among them ' Philosophy of religion'. There is an annotated listing of reference works. The whole is well indexed.

Dictionaries and encyclopedias

The following two earlier sets continue to be regarded as major resources:

636. *Dictionary of the history of ideas: studies of selected pivotal ideas.* Edited by Philip P. Wiener. 4 vols plus index. New York: Scribner's, 1973-1974. Reprinted 1980. 5 vols. 0-684-16418-3 (set, pbk).

Written by scholars from many countries, the substantial articles in this interdisciplinary guide trace the development of concepts in intellectual history from antiquity to the present. Religious and philosophical subjects are prominent. In order to exploit this important work it is essential to use the separate index volume.

637. *The Encyclopedia of philosophy.* Edited by Paul Edwards. 8 volumes. New York: Macmillan, 1967. Reprinted 1972, 8 volumes in 4.

A definitive resource which treats Eastern and Western philosophy, major philosophical issues and philosophers by means of substantial signed articles and annotated bibliographies. It includes religious thinkers where these have had an impact on philosophy. The final volume includes an index.

The following two authoritative one-volume dictionaries of philosophy have been published recently by the great university presses. Both are, as one would expect, of high quality, the Cambridge item being the more ambitious.

638. Blackburn, Simon. *The Oxford dictionary of philosophy.* New York: Oxford University Press, 1994. 0-19-211694-0.

The author is responsible for some 2,500 entries which cover the entire span of philosophical endeavour from the Hindu *Vedas* to the most recent terminology. There are biographical entries for nearly 500 philosophers. Cross-references are made to related themes and there is an appendix on logical symbols. A good place to begin a quest for the meaning or significance of a subject, person or movement.

639. *Cambridge dictionary of philosophy.* Edited by Robert Audi. Cambridge University Press, 1995. 0-521-40224-7 (hc); 0 521-48328-X (pbk.).

An edited work containing 4000 entries and cross-references from over 380 specialists in all areas of philosophy. These cover major philosophers, lesser-known figures, surveys of subdisciplines including ethics, epistemology, philosophy of religion and metaphysics. A feature are entries on non-Western thought. There are entries also on related subjects, including theology, science and literature. Cross-referencing enables further searching. An appendix explains symbols used in logic.

See also Geddes Macgregor, *Dictionary of religion and philosophy* [54].

MODERN THOUGHT

Biographical dictionaries, cited under this heading, include not only professional philosophers but also persons whose ideas have informed philosophical thinking.

Dictionaries

640. *Fontana dictionary of modern thought.* Edited by Alan Bullock and Oliver Stallybrass. 2nd rev. edn. London: Fontana Press, 1988. 0-00-686129-6.

Short explanatory accounts by distinguished contributors of some 4,000 'twentieth-century' terms, covering the whole range of the humanities and the sciences. Fields of study, movements, events, theories, -isms and -ologies of every kind are included. The language employed is as simple as possible but without over-simplification or distortion.

Biographies

641. *Biographical dictionary of twentieth-century philosophers.* Edited by Stuart Brown, Diané Collinson and Robert Wilkinson. London: Routledge, 1996. 0-415-06043-5.

Provides detailed accounts of the careers, works, thought and critical reception of the most important philosophers of this century. Bibliographies in each case are divided between 'main publications' and 'secondary sources'. There are indexes to nationality, category (e.g. scholasticism), interests (e.g. history of ideas), influences upon others (e.g. Husserl upon Ricoeur) and, finally, subjects. A most comprehensive resource and of particular value for tracing developments in thought.

642. *Fontana dictionary of modern thinkers.* Edited by Alan Bullock and R. B. Woodings. New edn. London: Fontana Paperbacks, 1989. 0-00-636965-0.

A new edition of the Fontana biographical companion to modern thought (1983). Covers the lives and work of nearly 2000 persons of all professions who have influenced the way we think in the twentieth century. By 'modern' is meant the period from 1900 to the present but there are notable exceptions, for example Kierkegaard and Marx, whose achievements were made available in this century.

643. *Thinkers of the twentieth century: a biographical, bibliographical and critical dictionary.* Edited by Elizabeth Devine et al. 2nd rev. edn. London: St James Press, 1987. 0-912289-83-X.

First published in 1983. This work on twentieth-century thinkers is more selective than the *Fontana dictionary* [642], but also more detailed. Entries provide critical assessments and include extensive bibliographies of primary and secondary sources.

METAPHYSICS

Christian theologians have regarded metaphysical inquiry as both enemy and ally. However, they do share with metaphysicians certain common ground as they attend to questions about the nature of ultimate reality, the structures of existence, and the meaning of revelation.

Handbooks

644. *A Companion to metaphysics.* Edited by Jaegwon Kim and Ernest Sosa. (Companions to philosophy). Oxford: Blackwell Publishers, 1995. 0-631-17272-6.

This volume within Blackwell's well-regarded series, 'Companions to philosophy', insists that the discipline of metaphysics is alive, well and working. The 264 alphabetically arranged, signed entries cover all areas and topics of metaphysics, including ontological, cosmological and teleological interests, and also the contributions of historical and contemporary proponents. Bibliographies.

645. *Handbook of metaphysics and ontology.* Edited by Hans Burkhardt and Barry Smith. 2 volumes. Philadelphia: Philosophia Verlag, 1991. 3-88405-080-X.

Entries, some of essay length, cover the work of the ancient metaphysicians and the development of metaphysical theories. There is a certain concentration on recent criticisms and new departures. Most entries have bibliographies. A highly technical, but valuable resource.

ETHICS

Traditionally, religions have been concerned with the ways in which people live meaningfully with and toward their neighbours with Christianity, for example, prescribing that faith be active through love (Galatians 5:6).

Recent ethical inquiry has embraced issues as diverse as the care of native peoples, environmental concerns and the use of the land, business ethics and economic rationalism, the treatment of animals. What does it mean to live ethically in these situations?

Also, in recent years, bioethical issues have attracted both theological and popular attention. Matters such as artificial insemination, the transplantation of organs, euthanasia, assisted suicide, are debated by philosophers, theologians and professionals who are aware of the widening gap between biotechnology and bioethical inquiry. Resources covering these areas are cited in this section.

Bibliographies

646. *A Bibliographic guide to the comparative study of ethics.* Edited by John Carman and Mark Juergensmeyer. New York: Cambridge University Press, 1991. 0-521-34448-4.

This work, sponsored by the Berkeley-Harvard Program in Comparative Religion features fifteen scholarly bibliographic essays which review ethical writings about the major religious traditions, Eastern and Western. One contribution is devoted to modern philosophical ethics. Essays on Christian ethics cover the early church, medieval, Reformation and modern periods. The accompanying bibliographies are classified and annotated. This global work bristles with devices for examining both discreet and cross-cultural perspectives on ethical issues.

Dictionaries and encyclopedias

The classic and most comprehensive work in this field has been the *Encyclopaedia of religion and ethics*, edited by James Hastings (1908-1926) [50], whose fading maroon volumes have helped identify religious reference shelves for many decades. Old, but in many respects, not out-dated, this turn-of-the-century liberal and irenic Protestant work continues to serve many purposes.

The Encyclopedia of religion, edited by Mircea Eliade [51], is self-avowedly intended to reflect advances in scholarship generally. It does not intend to match *ERE*'s coverage of ethics, however it does devote reasonably substantial articles to such topics as 'Christian ethics', 'The Good', 'Love', 'Morality and religion', 'Natural law' and 'Wealth'. Both these encyclopedias are cited in Part 1.

647. *The Encyclopedia of ethics.* Edited by Lawrence C. Becker. (Garland reference library of the humanities, 925). New York: Garland, 1992. 0-8153-0403-X.

Substantial essays and articles introduce the wide range of ethical issues and cover concepts, periods, problems and trends, as well as the thought of leading ethicists. Numerous entries on aspects of religion and ethics, and on the ethical positions of the major religions and Christian denominations. On certain topics it serves to update *The Encyclopedia of philosophy* [637]. Extensive bibliographies and an excellent subject index. Highly commended.

Companions

648. *A Companion to ethics.* Edited by Peter Singer. (Blackwell companions to philosophy series). Oxford: Blackwell Publishers, 1991; reprinted with corrections, 1993. 0-631-16211-9.

The editor is Professor of Philosophy and Director of the Centre for Human Bioethics at Monash University, Melbourne. Various scholars contribute interpretative essays in several areas - the roots of the ethical traditions, major traditions, including Indian, Chinese, Jewish, Christian and Islamic, a short history of philosophical ethics, ethical theories and applied ethics, the latter embracing poverty, the environment and euthanasia. Finally there are critiques of ethical perspectives. The multi-layered index and the bibliographies of relevant literature mean that this volume may serve as a reference resource both for those who are fresh to the study of ethics as well as the initiated.

Indexing services

649. *Ethics index on CD-ROM. 1994- .* Evanston, IL: American Theological Library Association, 1994- . 3/year into cumulative issues.

The *Index* includes full coverage of major ethics journals, scanning of a variety of other journals, coverage of anthologies, regular series and annuals. It provides access to a wide range of ethical information and expedites research across a number of disciplines, including the environment, criminal justice, the social sciences, religion, education and law-related professions.

BIOETHICS

'Bioethics can be defined as the systematic study of value questions that arise in biomedical and behavioral fields'. *Bibliography of bioethics* 21 (1995): 3.

Bibliographies

650. *Bibliography of bioethics, 1975- .* Currently edited by LeRoy Walters and Tamar Joy Kahn. Publishers have varied. Present publisher is the Kennedy Institute of Ethics, Georgetown University, Washington, DC. ISSN 0363-0161. Volume 21 was published in 1995.

The most comprehensive bibliography in the field, arranged under 76 major subject headings, from 'Abortion' and 'AIDS' to 'War' and 'Wrongful life'. Lists English-language material from books, journals, court decisions and other sources. A finely structured work and of great value to ethicists.

Encyclopedias

The following older work, which has served very well, is about to be replaced:

651. *Encyclopedia of bioethics.* Edited by Warren T. Reich. 4 vols. New York: Free Press, 1978. 0-02-926060-4.

Usually long, signed entries, arranged alphabetically by subject, cover the range of issues, concepts, principles, history, theory and traditions in bioethics. Each article includes a bibliography. Biographies are excluded. An appendix includes codes of medical ethics. There is a systematic classification of articles and an index.

Macmillan of New York have announced that a revised edition of this *Encyclopedia*, edited by Warren Reich, is to be published in 1995-1996. The ISBN assigned is 0-02-897355-0.

CHRISTIAN ETHICS

Dictionaries

652. *Dictionary of ethics, theology and society.* Edited by Paul Barry Clarke and Andrew Linzey. London: Routledge, 1996. 0-415-06212-8.

The 250 substantial entries in this large work provide a survey of the historical and contemporary interrelation between Judaeo-Christian theology and the evolution of Western political, social and ethical structures. The articles, signed by an international team, cover a range of disciplines including theology, political science, economics, philosophy, women's studies, gay and lesbian studies and environmental issues. They represent a full range of Christian denominational as well as atheist and agnostic positions, with no editorial attempt to reconcile disparate positions. Entries include bibliographies and there is a general index. A valuable guide to recent interdisciplinary studies.

653. *A New dictionary of Christian ethics.* Edited by John Macquarrie and James Childress. London: SCM Press, 1986. 0-334-02205-3. Published in the USA as *The Westminster dictionary of Christian ethics.*

An extensive revision and updating of the *Dictionary of Christian ethics* (1967) which reflects changes in the methods, content and context of the discipline. Emphasis is on applied or practical ethics. The contributions of philosophers, doctors, lawyers, and also of an ecumenical team, convey varying ethical perspectives. There are also entries on the teachings of the major religions. Deservedly a standard resource.

654. *New dictionary of Christian ethics and pastoral theology.* Edited by David J. Atkinson et al. Downers Grove, IL: Inter-Varsity Press, 1995. 0-8308-1408-6.

Intended 'for pastors, social workers, doctors and counsellors working in a Christian context' (Preface), this resource breaks new ground by combining material on ethics and pastoral theology. Arranged in two parts. The first comprises keynote articles which introduce major themes from 'God' to 'Christian moral reasoning'. The second consists of alphabetically-arranged articles on specific topics. The coverage ranges widely over areas such as philosophy, systematic theology, psychology, economics and sociology and the complex of issues related to pastoral care, with a theological conservatism informing much of the material. A cross-referencing system enables an easy transition from one part to the other.

Documents, Commentaries

655. Gill, Robin. *A textbook of Christian ethics.* New edn. Edinburgh: T & T Clark, 1995. 0-567-29280-0).

The author makes a systematic survey of subject areas: methodology, politics, economics and social justice, war and peace, the environment and human life and inter-personal relationships. Note that this new edition includes sections on biblical interpretation, environment and feminist theology. Classical and/or modern texts are presented for each area. The ethical positions reflected in these texts are examined along with the social and historical factors which may have shaped their differing perspectives. A reference feature is the extensive bibliography (pp. 567-588). Justifiably, a widely-used textbook.

Religious and
theological periodicals

A section in Part 1, 'Periodical literature' covered directories, union lists of periodicals, and references to the abbreviations used for periodical titles. The section, 'Indexing and abstracting services' described indexing systems that are relevant to religious studies.

The present chapter contains a list of over one hundred periodicals which support studies in religion and theology. Titles are limited to English-language publications (although certain biblical journals, in particular, may include articles in French or German).

The list is designed, primarily, to introduce students to key journals in the various subject areas. A further purpose is library-oriented. With due allowances being made for religious or denominational leanings and curricular interests, this list may help the theological librarian involved in building a core collection of serials. It could also suggest means of enhancing the collections of other-type libraries which support teaching programs in religion and theology. Finally, the identification of Australasian periodicals in the field of religion is intended to assist librarians in other countries.

First, the titles are cited in full in alphabetical order. Then, using a short-title format, those titles are arranged in classified order. The classification all but reflects the structure of this Guide. A final section repeats information about the periodical indexing systems which cover all aspects of the study of religion and theology.

The citation order is as follows:

> title of the serial, frequency, place of publication, issuing or publishing body, year of first issue (or, in certain cases, the first year of publication under its present title) and the International Standard Serial Number - an eight-digit number uniquely allocated to each serial title. (In some cases, no ISSN is printed in the journal.)

Australian and New Zealand titles are designated with an asterisk.

Periodicals	**209**
1. Alphabetical order	209
2. Classified order	215
Religion and religions	215
Church history, including the ecumenical movement	215
Church and society	216
Bible and related literature	216
Theology	216

Liturgy and worship   217
Religious and theological education   217
Ministry, pastoral care and ethics   217
Theological librarianship   218

Indexes to religious periodical literature   218

PERIODICALS

1. ALPHABETICAL ORDER

* Indicates an Australasian-edited title.

Anglican theological review (q.). Evanston, IL: Anglican Theological Review Ltd., 1918- . ISSN 0003-3286.

The Asia journal of theology (semi-ann.). Bangalore, India: North East Asia Association of Theological Schools, Board of Theological Education of the Senate of Serampore College and Association for Theological Education in South East Asia, 1987- . ISSN 0218-0812.

* *Australasian Catholic record* (q.). Strathfield, NSW: Australasian Catholic Record, 1924- . ISSN 0727-3215.

* *Australian and New Zealand Theological Library Association newsletter* (3/year). Parkin-Wesley College, Wayville, SA: Australian and New Zealand Theological Library Association, 1987- . ISSN 1030-701X.

* *Australian biblical review* (ann.). Parkville, Vic.: Fellowship for Biblical Studies, 1951- . ISSN 0045-0308.

* *Australian journal of liturgy* (semi-ann.). Kew Vic.: Australian Journal of Liturgy, 1987- . ISSN 1030-617X.

* *Australian religion studies review* (semi-ann.). Wollstonecraft, NSW: Australian Association for the Study of Religions, 1988- . ISSN 1031-2943.

Biblica (q.). Rome: Pontificium Institutum Biblicum, 1920- . ISSN 0006-0887.

Biblical archaeologist (q.). Atlanta, GA: Scholars Press for the American Schools of Oriental Research, 1938- . ISSN 0006-0895.

The Biblical archaeology review (6/yr). Washington, DC: Biblical Archaeological Society, 1975- . ISSN 0098-9444.

British journal of religious education: the journal of the Christian Education Movement (3/year). Derby, England: Christian Education Movement, 1934- . ISSN 0141-6200.

The Catholic biblical quarterly (q.). Washington, DC: Catholic Biblical Association, 1939- . ISSN 0008-7912.

Catholic historical review (q.). Washington, DC: Catholic University of America, 1915- . ISSN 0008-8080.

Christian century (37/year). Chicago, IL: Christian Century Foundation, 1884- . ISSN 0009-5281.

Christianity today (15/year) Carol Stream, IL: Christianity Today Inc., 1956- . ISSN 0148-3331.

Church history (q.). Chicago: American Society of Church History, 1932- ISSN 0009-6407.

* *Colloquium: the Australian and New Zealand theological review* (semi-ann.). Everton Park, Qld, 1964-1965- . ISSN 1030-6161.

Communio: international Catholic review (q.). Washington, DC: Communio, 1974- . ISSN 0094-2065.

Concilium (m). London: SCM Press; Maryknoll, NY: Orbis Books, 1965- .

East Asian pastoral review (q.). Quezon City, Philippines: East Asian Pastoral Institute, 16- , 1979- . ISSN 0040-0564.

The Ecumenical review (q.). Geneva: World Council of Churches, 1948- . ISSN 0013-0796.

* *Eureka Street* (11/year). Richmond, Vic.: Eureka Street Magazine Pty Ltd., March 1991- . ISSN 1036-1758.

Evangelical quarterly (q.). Carlisle, England: Paternoster Periodicals, 1929- . ISSN 0014-3367.

The Expository times (m.). Edinburgh: T & T Clark, 1889- . ISSN 0014-5246.

* *Faith and freedom* (q.). Bentley, WA: Baptist Peace Fellowship of Western Australia, 1992- . ISSN 1038-9865.

* *Gesher (Bridge): the official journal of the Council of Christians and Jews* (irregular). Kew Vic.: Council of Christians and Jews, Oct 1990- .

The Greek Orthodox theological review (q.). Brookline, MA: Holy Cross Greek Orthodox School of Theology, 1954- . ISSN 0017-3894.

Harvard theological review (q.). Cambridge, MA: Harvard Divinity School, 1908- . ISSN 0017-8047.

Hastings Center report (6/year). Briarcliff Manor, NY: Hastings Center, 1971- . ISSN 0093-0334.

Heythrop journal: a quarterly review of philosophy and theology (q.). Oxford: Blackwell Publishers, 1960- . ISSN 0018-1196

International bulletin of missionary research (q.). New Haven, CT: Overseas Ministries Study Center, 5- , 1981 - . ISSN 0272-6122.

International review of mission (q.). Geneva: World Council of
    Churches, 59- , 1970- . ISSN 0020-8582.

Interpretation: a journal of Bible and theology (q.). Richmond, VA:
    Union Theological Seminary in Virginia, 1947- . ISSN 0020-9643.

Journal for the scientific study of religion (q.). West Lafayette, IN:
    Society for the Scientific Study of Religion, 1961- .
    ISSN 0021-8294.

Journal for the study of the New Testament (q.). Sheffield, England:
    JSOT Press, 1978- . ISSN 0142-064X.

Journal for the study of the Old Testament (q.). Sheffield, England:
    JSOT Press, 1976- . ISSN 0309-0892.

Journal of biblical literature (q.). Atlanta, GA: Scholars Press for the
    Society of Biblical Literature, 1881- . ISSN 0021-9231.

*Journal of early Christian studies: journal of the North American
    Patristics Society,* (q.). Baltimore, MD: Johns Hopkins University
    Press for the North American Patristics Society, 1993- . ISSN
    1067-6341. Continues *The Second century* (1981-1992).

The Journal of ecclesiastical history (q.). Cambridge, England:
    Cambridge University Press, 1950- . ISSN 0022-0469.

Journal of ecumenical studies (q.). Philadelphia: Temple University,
    1964- . ISSN 0022-0558.

Journal of feminist studies in religion (semi-ann.). Atlanta, GA: Scholars
    Press, 1985- . ISSN 8755-4178.

Journal of Near Eastern studies (q.). Chicago, IL: University of Chicago
    Press, 1942- . ISSN 0022-2968.

The Journal of pastoral care (q.). Decatur, GA: Journal of Pastoral Care
    Publications, 1947- . ISSN 0022-3409.

Journal of religion (q.). Chicago: University of Chicago Press, 1893- .
    ISSN 0022-4189.

The Journal of religious ethics (q.). Atlanta, GA: Scholars Press, 1973- .
    ISSN 0384-9694.

* *Journal of religious history* (q.). Oxford: Blackwell Publishers, on behalf
    of the Association for the Journal of Religious History, School of
    History, Macquarie University, NSW, 1960- . (Varied publishers).
    ISSN 0022-4227.

Journal of supervision and training in ministry (ann.). Chicago, IL:
    North Central Region ACPE, and Central Region, AACP, 1978- .
    ISSN 0160-7774.

Journal of the American Academy of Religion (q.). Atlanta, GA: Scholars Press for the American Academy of Religion, 1933- . ISSN 0002-7189.

Journal of theological studies (semi-ann.). Oxford: Clarendon Press, 1899- . ISSN 0022-5185.

Journal of theology for Southern Africa (q.). Cape Town: Journal of Theology for Southern Africa, 1972- . ISSN 0047-2867.

Literature and theology: an interdisciplinary journal of theory and criticism (q.). Oxford University Press, 1987- . ISSN 0269-1205.

* *Lucas: an evangelical history review* (q.). Sydney: Evangelical History Association, 1987- . ISSN 1030-4428.

* *Lutheran theological journal* (3/year). North Adelaide, SA: Faculty of Luther Seminary, 1967- .

* *Ministry, society and theology* (semi-ann.). North Fitzroy, Vic: Association for Supervised Pastoral Education in Australia, Australian Health and Welfare Chaplains Association, Field Education Programme Anglican Diocese of Melbourne, Field Education - Uniting Church in Australia, 1987- . ISSN 1322-8943.

Modern theology (q.). Oxford: Basil Blackwell, 1984- . ISSN 0266-7177.

The Month: a review of Christian thought and world affairs (m.). London: The Month, 1864- . ISSN 0027-0172.

* *Nelen Yubu* (q.). Kensington, NSW: Nelen Yubu Missiological Unit, Australian MSC Province, No. 5- , 1981- . ISSN 0726-0458.

New Testament studies (q.). Cambridge, England: Cambridge University Press, 1954- . ISSN 0029-2176.

Novum testamentum: an international quarterly for New Testament and related studies (q.). Leiden: E. J. Brill, 1956- . ISSN 0048-1009.

Numen: international review for the history of religions (3/year). Leiden: E. J. Brill, 1954- . ISSN 0029-5973.

One in Christ: a Catholic ecumenical review (m.). Turvey, Bedfordshire, England: Vita et pax Foundation, Turvey Abbey, 1965- . ISSN 0030-125X.

* *One voice: a magazine about church music* (semi-ann.). Stafford Heights, Qld: Royal School of Church Music (Queensland Branch), 1986- . ISSN 0816-973X.

PTCA bulletin: programme for theology and cultures in Asia. Hong Kong: Programme for Theology and Cultures in Asia, 1988- .

* *Pacifica: Australian theological studies* (3/year). Brunswick East, Vic.: Pacifica Theological Studies Association, 1988- . ISSN 1030-570X.

Pastoral psychology (6/year). New York: Human Sciences Press, 1950- . ISSN 0031-2789.

* *Phronema: an annual review* (ann.). Redfern, NSW: Faculty of St Andrew's Greek Orthodox College, 1986- . ISSN 0819-4920.

* *Pointers: bulletin of the Christian Research Association* (3/year). Hawthorn, Vic.: Christian Research Association, 1991- .

* *Prudentia: a journal devoted to the thought, literature and history of the ancient world* (semi-ann.). Auckland, NZ: Prudentia, University of Auckland, 1969- . ISSN 0110-487X.

Quarterly review: a journal of theological resources for ministry (q.). Nashville, TN: United Methodist Publishing House, 1980- . ISSN 0270-9287.

Reformed liturgy and music (q.). Louisville, KY: Presbyterian Church (USA), 1967- . ISSN 0362-0476.

* *Reformed theological review* (3/year). Doncaster, Vic.: The Reformed Theological Review, 1942- . ISSN 0034-3072.

Religious education (q.). New Haven, CT: Religious Education Association, 1906- . ISSN 0034-4087.

* *Religious education journal of Australia* (semi-ann.). East Melbourne, Vic: Australian Association for Religious Education, 1985- . ISSN 0815-3094.

Religious studies review (q.). Valparaiso, IN: Council of Societies for the Study of Religion, 1975- . ISSN 0319-485X.

Reviews in religion and theology (q.). London: SCM Press, 1994-. ISSN 1350-7303.

St Mark's review: a journal of Christian thought and opinion (q.). Canberra, ACT: St Mark's, 1955- . ISSN 0036-3103.

Scottish journal of theology (q.). Edinburgh: Scottish Academic Press, 1948- . ISSN 0036-9306.

Second opinion (q.). Chicago, IL: Park Ridge Center for the Study of Health, Faith, and Ethics, 1986- . ISSN 0890-1570.

Semeia: an experimental journal for biblical criticism (q.).Atlanta, GA: Scholars Press for the Society of Biblical Literature, 1974- . ISSN 0095-571X.

The Sixteenth century journal: the journal of early modern studies (q.). Kirksville, MO: Sixteenth Century Journal Publishers, 1970- . ISSN 0361-0160.

Soundings: an interdisciplinary journal (q.). Knoxville, TN: University of Tennessee and the Society for Value in Higher Education, 1918- . ISSN 0038-1861.

* *Stimulus: the New Zealand journal of Christian thought and practice* (q.). Masterton, NZ: Stimulus, 1993- . ISSN 1171-7920.

Studia liturgica: an international ecumenical review for liturgical research and renewal (semi-ann.). Notre Dame, IN: Societas Liturgica, 1962- . ISSN 0039-3207.

Studies in Christian ethics (2/yr). Edinburgh: T & T Clark, 1988- . ISSN 0593-9468.

Studies in religion/Sciences religieuses (q.). Waterloo, Ontario: Wilfred Laurier University Press, 1971- . ISSN 0008-4298.

The Tablet: the international Catholic weekly (London) (weekly). London: Tablet, 1840- . ISSN 0039-8837.

Theological education (semi-ann.). Pittsburgh, PA: Association of Theological Schools, 1964- . ISSN 0040-5620.

Theological studies (q.). Washington, DC: Theological Studies Inc., for the Society of Jesus in the US, 1940- . ISSN 0040-5639.

Theology (6/year). London: SPCK, 1920- . ISSN 0040-571X.

Theology today (q.). Princeton, NJ: Theology Today, 1944- . ISSN 0040-5736.

* *Tjurunga: an Australasian Benedictine review* (semi-ann.). Croydon, Vic: The Benedictine Union of Australia and New Zealand, 1971- . ISSN 1031-6582.

Traditio: studies in ancient and medieval history, thought, and religion (ann.). New York: Fordham University Press, 1943- . ISSN 0362-1529.

* *Trinity occasional papers* (semi-ann.). Toowong, Qld: Trinity Theological College, 1981- . ISSN 0811-2304.

Union Seminary quarterly review (q.). New York: Union Theological Seminary, 1945- . ISSN 0362-0492.

Vetus testamentum (q.). Leiden: E. J. Brill for the International Organization for the Study of the Old Testament, 1951- . ISSN 0042-4935.

Vigiliae Christianae: a review of early Christian life and language (q.). Leiden: E. J. Brill, 1947- . ISSN 0042-6032.

* *Vox Reformata: Australasian journal for Christian scholarship* (semi-ann.). Geelong, Vic: Faculty of the Reformed Theological College, 1962- . ISSN 0728-0912.

* *Women-church: an Australian journal of feminist studies in religion* (semi-ann.). Sydney, NSW: Women-Church, 1987- . ISSN 1030-0139.

* *Word in life: journal of religious education* (q.). North Sydney, NSW: Australian Catholic University, 26 -, 1978- . ISSN 0155-6894.

* *Zadok perspectives: quarterly journal of the Zadok Institute for Christianity and Society* (q.). North Fitzroy, Vic.: Zadok Institute for Christianity and Society, 1983- . ISSN 0810-9796.

   Zygon: journal of religion and science (q.). Cambridge, MA: Blackwell Publishers, 1966- . ISSN 0591-2385.

2. CLASSIFIED ORDER

Religion and religions

* *Australian religion studies review*
* *Gesher (Bridge): the official journal of the Council of Christians and Jews*
   Journal for the scientific study of religion
   Journal of feminist studies in religion
   Journal of religion
* *Journal of religious history*
   Journal of the American Academy of Religion
   Numen: international review for the history of religions
* *Prudentia: a journal devoted to the thought, literature and history of the ancient world*
   Religious studies review
   Reviews in religion and theology
   Soundings: an interdisciplinary journal
   Studies in religion/Sciences religieuses
   Zygon: journal of religion and science

Church history, including the Ecumenical Movement

Catholic historical review
Church history
The Ecumenical review
International bulletin of missionary research
International review of mission
Journal of early Christian studies: journal of the North American Patristics Society,
The Journal of ecclesiastical history
Journal of ecumenical studies

* *Lucas: an evangelical history review*
One in Christ: a Catholic ecumenical review
The Sixteenth century journal: the journal of early modern studies
Traditio: studies in ancient and medieval history, thought, and religion
Vigiliae Christianae: a review of early Christian life and language

Church and society

Christian century
Christianity today
Communio: international Catholic review
Concilium
* *Eureka Street*
* *Faith and freedom*
The Month: a review of Christian thought and world affairs
* *Nelen Yubu*
* *Pointers: bulletin of the Christian Research Association*
The Tablet: the international Catholic weekly
* *Women-church: an Australian journal of feminist studies in religion*
* *Zadok perspectives: quarterly journal of the Zadok Institute for
        Christianity and Society*

Bible and related literature

* *Australian biblical review*
Biblica
Biblical archaeologist
The Biblical archaeology review
The Catholic biblical quarterly
Interpretation: a journal of Bible and theology
Journal for the study of the New Testament
Journal for the study of the Old Testament
Journal of biblical literature
Journal of Near Eastern studies
New Testament studies
*Novum testamentum: an international quarterly for New Testament
        and related studies*
Semeia: an experimental journal for biblical criticism
Vetus testamentum

Theology

Anglican theological review
The Asia journal of theology
* *Australasian Catholic record*
* *Colloquium: the Australian and New Zealand theological review*
East Asian pastoral review
Evangelical quarterly
The Expository times
The Greek Orthodox theological review

    Harvard theological review
    Heythrop journal
    Journal of theological studies
    Journal of theology for Southern Africa
    Literature and theology: an interdisciplinary journal of theory and criticism
* *Lutheran theological journal*
    Modern theology
    PTCA bulletin: programme for theology and cultures in Asia.
* *Pacifica: Australian theological studies*
* *Phronema: an annual review*
    Quarterly review: a journal of theological resources for ministry
* *Reformed theological review*
* *St Mark's review: a journal of Christian thought and opinion*
    Scottish journal of theology
* *Stimulus: the New Zealand journal of Christian thought and practice*
    Theological studies
    Theology
    Theology today
* *Tjurunga: an Australasian Benedictine review*
* *Trinity occasional papers*
    Union Seminary quarterly review
* *Vox Reformata: Australasian journal for Christian scholarship*

Liturgy and worship

* *Australian journal of liturgy*
* *One voice: a magazine about church music*
    Reformed liturgy and music
    Studia liturgica: an international ecumenical review for liturgical research and renewal

Religious and theological education

    British journal of religious education: the journal of the Christian Education Movement
    Religious education
* *Religious education journal of Australia*
    Theological education
* *Word in life: journal of religious education*

Ministry, pastoral care and ethics

    Hastings Center report
    The Journal of pastoral care
    The Journal of religious ethics
    Journal of supervision and training in ministry
* *Ministry, society and theology*
    Pastoral psychology
    Second opinion
    Studies in Christian ethics

Theological librarianship

* *Australian and New Zealand Theological Library Association newsletter*

INDEXES TO RELIGIOUS PERIODICAL LITERATURE

The following general indexing services are listed and described in Part 1 - 'Indexing and Abstracting Services'. Full details, including frequency, related database information and CD-ROM formats, are noted in that section.

* *Australasian religion index, 1989-* .Wagga Wagga, NSW: Australian and New Zealand Theological Library Association and Centre for Information Studies, Charles Sturt University - Riverina, 1989- . ISSN 1033-2626.

The Catholic periodical and literature index, 1930- . Haverford, PA: Catholic Library Association, 1939- (Title and subtitle and composition vary). ISSN 0008-8285.

Religion index one: periodicals, 1949- . Chicago: American Theological Library Association, 1953- . ISSN 0149-8428.

Religious and theological abstracts, 1958- . Myerstown, PA: Religious and Theological Abstracts, 1958- . ISSN 0034-4044.

Indexes devoted to subject-specific periodicals, for example biblical journals, are cited in the relevant subject chapters.

Author and editor index

This index includes the names of

- the authors and editors of the works cited in this guide,
- corporate authors, that is organisations or institutions responsible for the text of a work,
- certain persons who contributed to particular works,
- persons responsible for significant translations.

Reference is usually to the *item* number as given in chapters 1-13, not to a page number.

Where a person or an organisation is referred to in an annotation or a related note, that name is indexed by *item* number with 'n' added for annotation or note, for example, Anderson, Robert, 166n.

Where an author, personal or corporate, is mentioned either in an introduction to a section or in separated note, that name is indexed by a bracketed *page* number, for example Berndt, Catherine H., (p. 123).

Abramson, Glenda, 135
Achtemeier, Paul J., 411n
Ackroyd, P. R., 455
Aharoni, Yohanan, 391
Aland, Barbara, 484
Aland, Kurt, 483, 499, 500n
Albrecht, Renate, 559
Ali, Ahmed (trans.), 99
Allen, R. E., 77
Allison, A. F., 253
American Theological Library
    Association, 35n
Ancient History Documentary
    Research Centre, 219
Andersen, Francis I., 434
Anderson, B. W., 416
Anderson, Gerald, 263, 265, 267
Anderson, Robert, 166, 166n
Anglican Church in Aotearoa,
    New Zealand and Polynesia, (p. 113)
Ansell, Leo J., 43
Apostolos-Cappadona, Diane, 606
Appleton, George, 576
Arav, Rami, 506
Arberry, A. J., 100n
Arnold, Denis, 584
Arns, Hans, 29
Ativa, Aziz S., 212
Atkinson, David J., 629, 654
Attridge, H. W., 143
Attwater, Donald, 191
Audi, Robert, 639
Augarde, Tony, 71
Australian Bureau of
    Statistics, (p. 32)
Australian Catholic Bishops
    Conference, (p. 110)
Australian Copyright Council, (p. 32)
Australian Institute of Aboriginal
    and Torres Strait Islander
    Studies, 114, 115
Aversa, Elizabeth, 5
Avery-Peck, Alan J., 6n
Avi-Yonah, Michael, 391, 393n

Bachmann, E. Theodore, 313
Bachmann, H., 500
Bachmann, Mercia Brenne, 313
Bagnall, Austin G., 17
Bailey, James L., 508
Balay, Robert, 2
Balz, Horst, 504
Barker, John, 349
Barnavi, Eli, 137
Bartlett, John, 68
Bauer, W., 496
Baumgartner, Walter, 429
Becker, Lawrence C., 647
Becking, Bob, 388
Beffa, Pierre, 277
Beinert, Wolfgang, 537
Benedictine monks of
    St Augustine's Abbey, 192
Bentley, James, 195
Bentley, Peter, 26, 113, 339
Berardino, Angelo Di
    see Di Berardino, Angelo
Bergin, Thomas G., 239
Berkowitz, Luci, 233
Berndt, Catherine H., (p. 43)
Berndt, Ronald M., (p. 43)
Bettenson, Henry, 186, 228, 229
Bieritz, Karl-Heinrich, 565
Bietenholz, Peter G., 241

Bilimoria, Purusottama, 94
Blackburn, Simon, 638
Blass, F., 487
Blazek, Ron, 5
Blombery, Tricia, 113
Bodensieck, Julius, 314
Bolton, Alexander, 176
Borchardt, D. H., 48n
Boswell, Jackson Campbell, 245
Botterweck, G. J., 448, 449
Bouma, Gary D., 102
Bowden, John, 529, 550
Bradley, James E., 182, (p. 66)
Brady, Thomas, 237
Bray, Gerald, 254
Breit, Marquita, 555
Breward, Ian, 57n, 337
Bria, Ion, 273
Brierley, Peter, 343
Briggs, C. A., 431
Bromiley, Geoffrey, 386, 503
Brook, A. E., 440
Brown, F., 431
Brown, George, 595
Brown, R. E., 403
Brown, Stuart, 641
Buckley, James J., 6n
Bullock, Alan, 640, 642
Burgess, Joseph A., 276
Burgess, Stanley M., 308
Burkhardt, Hans, 645
Burkhardt, Helmut, 548
Butcher, Judith, 79
Butler, Alban, 191
Buttrick, George Arthur, 385n
Bynagle, Hans E., 634
Byrne, Peter, 528

Cameron, Evan, 250
Cameron, Nigel M. de S., 352
Campbell, Alastair V., 657
Campbell, Antony F., 423
Campbell, Robert J., 625
Cannon, John, 177
Canon Law Society of America, 300
Canon Law Society of Great
    Britain and Ireland, 301, 302, 304
Capol, Cornelia, 552
Cargas, Harry J., 161
Carlen, Claudia, 298, 299
Carman, John, 646
Carson, D. A., 509
Caspi, Mishael Maswari, 363
Chadwick, Henry, 187, 226
Chadwick, Owen, 181
Chamberlaine, G., 441
Chamberlin, William J., 366
Charles, R. H., 452, 454n
Charlesworth, James H., 450, 452n,
    453, 454n, 465, 468, 518
Childress, James, 653
Chisholm, Alec H., 47n
Christian Research Association,
    108n, 113, 339
Chryssavgis, Militiades, (p. 102)
Ciarrocchi, Joseph W., 626
Clarke, Paul Barry, 652
Clifton, Chas. S., 200
Clines, David, 433
Coggins, R. J., 401
Cohen, J. M., 72
Cohen, M. J., 72
Cohn-Sherbok, Dan, 132, 167, (p. 58)
Collins, Mary, 538

Collinson, Diané, 641
Coogan, Michael D., 387
Coomler, David, 570n, 607
Coriden, James A., 303
Cornell, Tim, 216
Cornfeld, Gaalya, 146
Cornish, Graham P., 28
Corsini, Raymond J.,623
Cotterell, Arthur, 58
Council of Christians and Jews
    (Victoria), 170
Craigie, William A., 75n
Crim, Keith R., 385n, (p. 123)
Crittenden, Victor, 48n
Crocker, Lester G., 260n
Cross, K. E., 325, 326
Crossman, Richard C., 560
Croucher, Paul, 92
Crown, Alan David, 158, 159, (p. 56)
Cruden, Alexander, 378
Crumb, Lawrence N., 268
Crumlin, Rosemary, 602, 604, (p. 181)
Cully, Iris V., 598
Cully, Kendig Brubaker, 598

D'Aniello, Charles A., 174
Dacy, Marianne, 166
Daggy, Robert E., 555
Dahlitz, Ray, 65
Danby, H., 149
Danker, Frederick, 354, 418n, 488n, 496,
    (pp. 53, 122, 123, 129, 134, 148)
Dassmann, Ernst, 211n
Davidson, Allan K., 347
Davies, Rupert, 315
Davies, J. G., 564, 616n
Davies, W. D., 140
Day, Peter D., 569
de Greef, W.
    see Greef, W. de
de Lange, Nicholas, 138
Debrunner, A., 487
Delbridge, A., 76
Denzinger, Heinrich, 29, 291n
Devereux, Peter, 81
Devine, Elizabeth, 643
Di Berardino, Angelo, 210, 217
Dickey, Brian, 340
Diehl, Katharine, (p. 176)
Dillenberger, Jane, 605
Dindinger, P. Johannes, 262
Donaldson, James, 224
Donnachie, Ian, 353
Donnelly, Dorothy F., 234
Donovan, Peter, 124, 125, (p. 113)
Donzel, E. van, 96
Douglas, Leonora Mosende, 348
Downey, Michael, 592
Doyle, T. M., 295
Dozeman, Thomas, 579
Driver, S. R., 431
Duchet-Suchaux, G., 194
Dupuis, J., 290
Durnbaugh, Donald F., 311
Dutripon, Francois Pascal, 381

Edelheit, Abraham J., 160, 160n,
    161n
Edelheit, Hershel, 160, 160n, 161n
Edwards, Paul, 637
Efird, J. M., 489
Ehrlich, Eugene, 534
Einspahr, Bruce, 432

Eisenman, Robert, 462
Eliade, Mircea, 51, (pp. 23, 35, 43, 204)
Elliger, K., 419
Elliott, J. K., 520
Elwell, Walter A., 545, 551
Engel, Frank, 278, 279
Epp, Eldon Jay, 398
Epstein, Isidor, 152
Espinosa, Ricardo R., 476
Esposito, John L., 98
Evans, Craig, 514, 519, 525, (p. 140)
Evans, G. R., 187, 282
Even-Shoshan, Abraham, 438
Eynikel, E., 441

Fahey, Michael A., 269
Fahlbusch, Erwin, 547
Farmer, David Hugh, 193
Farmer, William R., 512n
Feldman, Louis H., 144
Ferguson, Everett, 209
Ferguson, George Wells, 609
Ferguson, John A., 14
Ferguson, Sinclair, 546
Field, Clive D., 315n
Fink, Peter, 567
Finkelstein, Louis, 140
Finson, Shelley Davis, 196
Fiorenza, Francis Schüssler, 537
Fischer, Boniface, 382
Fisher, Eugene J., 165
Fisichella, Rino, 536
Fitzmyer, Joseph A., 355, 403, 416n,
    456, 461, (pp. 123, 129, 140, 148)
Fitzpatrick, Georgina, 111, 335
Floyd, Wayne Whitson, 554
Forbes, A. Dean, 434
Forman, Charles W., 350
Francis, Fred O., 517
Frank, Francine H., 86
Frank, Ruth S., 129
Freedman, David Noel, 385
Freedman, Harry, 156
Frend, W. C., 230, 231
Fried, Jerome, 59
Fritze, Ronald H., 172
Froneman, C. J. J., 329

García Martínez, Florentino, 466
Garland, David E., 516
Garrett, John, 351
Gasque, W. Ward, 510
Gassmann, Günther, 275
Geden, A. S., 501
George, Leonard, 201
Gerardi, Pamela, 171
Gibb, H. A. R., 95n
Gill, Robin, 655
Gilling, Bryan D., 121
Gillman, Ian, 110, (p. 109)
Gilmont, Jean-François, 259
Gingrich, F. W., 496
Gisel, Pierre, 309
Glare, P. G. W., 497
Glasse, Cyril, 97
Glazier, Michael, 289
Goodrick, Edward W., 383
Goodwin, John, 263
Gordon, Peter, 52
Gorman, G. E., 7, (p. 66)
Gorman, Lyn, 7, (p. 66)
Grant, Michael, 208
Greef, W. de., 258

Green, Clifford J., 554
Green, Joel B., 505
Greenlee, J. Harold, 490
Griffin, Graeme M., 630
Griffiths, David B., 130
Grigg, Anthony R., 120
Gros, Jeffrey, 276
Grosvenor, M., 495
Gutman, Israel, 162

Hadidian, D. Y., 526
Hagen, Kenneth, 255
Hall, James, 610
Hamilton, Jeffries M., 428
Hansen, Eric C., 283
Hardesty, Nancy A, 88
Harris, D., 336 (p. 102)
Harris, John, 117
Harmon, Nolan B., 318
Harré, Rom, 624
Harrington, Daniel, 511
Hastings, Adrian, 324, (p. 107)
Hastings, James, 50, (p. 204)
Hatch, Edwin, 444
Hauser, Alan J., 400
Hauspie, K., 441
Hawthorne, Gerald F., 507
Hazell, Tom, 622
Hazlett, Ian, 206
Heller, Dagmar, 273
Hellwig, Monika, 289
Hennecke, Edgar, 521n
Henwood, John, 622
Herbert, A. S., 366n
Hewitt, George, 353
Hiley, David, 586
Hillerbrand, Hans J., 251
Historical Association, The
    (London), 175
Hofmeyr, J. W., 325, 326, 327, 328,
    329
Holladay, W. L., 430
Horst, Pieter W. van der, 388
Horton, David, 114
Houlden, J. L., 401
Houlden, Leslie, 528
Howard, W. F., 488
Hudson, Nicholas, (p. 32)
Hünermann, Peter, 291n
Hughes, Philip, 108, 113
Huiskamp, Harrie, 264
Hulbert, James R., 75n
Hultgren, Arland, 515
Humm, Maggie, 198
Humphreys, Robert, 109, (p. 109)
Hunter, Rodney J., 628
Husen, Torsten, (p. 183)
Hynd, Douglas, 336

Ingardia, Richard, 244
Institute for Antiquity and
    Christianity, 523, 524
Isichei, Elizabeth, 323
Ising, Dieter, 556

Jacobs, Louis, 134
Jacobs, Philip Walker, 203
James, M. R., 520n
Jay, Eric G., 491
Jedin, Hubert, 188
Jeffrey, David Lyle, 389
Jenkin, Coralie, 42

Jones, Charles Edwin, 307
Jones, H. S., 497
Jordan, Michael, 55
Josephus, Flavius, 146
Juergensmeyer, Mark, 646
Julian John, 587

Kadel, Andrew, 197
Kahn, Tamar Joy, 650
Kaldor, Peter, 341
Kaplin, Justin, 68
Kaske, Robert Earl, 243
Kasper, Walter, 287
Kassis, Hanna E., 100
Kazhdan, Alexander P., 213
Keck, Leander, 406
Kee, Howard Clark, 482
Kelly, J. N. D., 297
Kepple, Robert J., 12
Kim, Jaegwon, 644
Kirschbaum, Engelbert, 611
Kirwan, Lee, 41
Kittell, Gerhard, 502,503, (p. 139)
Klenicki, Leon, 165, 168
Klepper, Robert F., 589
Knight, Anthony, 602
Knight, Douglas A., 396
Koehler, Ludwig, 429
Köszegi, A., 8
Kohlenberger, John R., 384, 422,
Komonchak, Joseph A., 538
Kraft, Robert A., 397
Kramers, J. H., 95n
Krentz, Edgar, 10
Kümmel, W. G., 482

Lamb, Roger, 624
Lambdin, T. O., 425
Lampe, G. W. H., 498
Lane, Dermot A., 538
Laney, A. R. C., 455
Lang, Jove, 566
Lange, Nicholas de
    see De Lange, Nicholas
Langevin, Paul Émile, 358
Larson, Kenneth E., 257
Latourelle, René, 536
Lawton, Denis, 596
Leach, Maria, 59
Leach, Marjorie, 60
Lee, Sidney, 62
Lewis, Miles, 621
Léon, Domingo Muñoz, 476
Leonard, Bill J., 310
Levillain, Philippe, 296
Lewis, Donald M., 261
Liddell, H. G., 497
Lindboe, Inger Marie, 470
Lineham, Peter J., 120, 347
Linzey, Andrew, 652
Lippey, Charles H., 105
Lischer, Richard, 577
Lisowsky, Gerhard, 436
Livingstone, E. A., 184
Longstaff, Thomas R. W., 512
Lossky, Nicholas, 271, (p. 102)
Ludlow, D. H., 312
Lunden, Joel W., 256
Lust, J., 441
Lutheran Church of Australia, (p. 110)

McBrien, Richard P., 288
McCabe, James Patrick, 11, 12n
McCabe, Kendall, 579
McCarthy, Joseph M., 558
Macdonald, Charlotte, 67
McGee, Gary B., 308
McGrath, Alister, 527, 530, (p. 86)
Macgregor, Geddes, 54, 639n
MacInnis, Donald E., 118
McIntosh, Lawrence, 48n, 84, (p. 30)
Macintyre, Stuart, 171n
McKenzie, R., 497
McKim, Donald, 259n, 319
McKitterick, Rosamond, 236n
McKnight, Scot, 505
McLauchlan, Gordon, 49
McLean, N., 440
McLintock, A. H., (p. 21)
McManners, John, 180
McNamara, Martin, 451
Macquarrie, John, 653
MacRae, George W., 398
Maddock, Kenneth, (p. 43)
Maltby, William S., 249
Mandelkern, Solomon, 437
Mann, A. T., 616
Marshall, I. Howard, 510
Martin, James D., 426
Mason, Michael, 111, 335
Matthews, John, 216
May, David M., 469
Mayer, Cornelius, 235
Mays, J. L., 404, 411n
Mead, Frank S., 106
Meer, Frederic van der., 215
Melton, J. Gordon, 8, 61, 103, 104,
Metford, J. C. J., 185, 613n
Metzger, Bruce M., 370, 387, 478n,
        485
Mews, Stuart, 57
Meyendorff, John, (p. 102)
Migne, Jacques Paul, 220
Milgate, Wesley, 588
Millard, J. A., 329
Miller, Casey, 87
Miller, Patrick D., 411n
Miller, Robert J., 486
Mills, John J., 4
Mills, Watson E., 361, 475, 477, 478,
        479
Mir, Mustansir, 101
Mohrmann, Christine, 215
Moody, T. W., 344
Moore, Albert C., 615
Moulton, H. K., 501
Moulton, J. H., 488
Moulton, William F., 501
Moyles, R. G., 321
Müller, Gerhard, 549
Muether, John R., 12
Muller, Richard A., 182, 532, (p. 66)
Muraoka, T., 443
Murdoch, Norman H., 322
Murphy, Jillian, 632
Murphy, Roland E., 370, 403
Murphy-O'Connor, Jerome, 395
Murray, James A. H., 75n
Muse, Robert L., 360, 480
Musser, Donald W., 531
Musto, Ronald G., 544

National Council of the Churches
        of Christ in America, 331
Negev, Avraham, 394

Neil, Stephen, 263
Neirynck, F., 474
Nel, J. M., 327, 328
Neuner, J., 290
Neusner, Jacob, 6n, 148, 150, 151, 153,
        157, 157n,
Newsom, Carol A., 405
Nickelsburg, George W. E., 397
Nicol, Donald M., 214, 238n
Norman, Edward, 617
Norton, Mary Beth, 171
Nunn, H. P. V., 492n

Oberman, Heiko, 237
O'Brien, Mark, 423
O'Carroll, Michael, 539, 540, 541, 542,
        543
O'Farrell, Patrick, 338
O'Grady, Ron, 57n
Oliver, W. H., 66
O'Loughlin, F. T., 295
O'Malley, John, 248
Orange, Claudia, 66
Owens, John Joseph, 435
Ozment, Steven, 247

Packer, J. W., 455
Parrinder, Geoffrey, 73
Parshall, Linda B., 608
Parshall, Peter W., 608
Partington, Angela, 69
Pastoureau, M., 194
Pate, Larry D., 266
Pelliccia, Guerrino, 242
Pepper, Margaret, 74
Perret, Edmond, 320
Parry, Michael, 572
Peter, Rodolphe, 259
Peters, Melvin, (p. 136)
Peters, Pam, 83
Petuchowski, Jakob J., 169
Pfann, Stephen J., 463, 464
Pfatteicher, Philip H., 563
Pierce, Vivienne S., 631
Plaut, W. G., 447n
Polgar, László, 284
Posset, Franz, 255
Postlethwaite, T. Neville, (p. 183)
Poultney, David, 585
Powell, Mark Allan, 389
Prebish, Charles S., 91
Presbyterian Church of Aotearoa
        New Zealand, (p. 113)
Prevost, Ronnie, 599
Price, Joseph L., 531
Pritchard, James B., 392
Puglisi, James F., 270n
Purdy, Martin, 618
Purvis, James D., 139

Quasten, Johannes, 217
Queensland Catholic
        Education Commission, 90

Radice, Roberto, 142
Rahlfs, Alfred, 439
Rahner, Karl, 535
Ramsey, Boniface, 218
Randel, Don Michael, 583
Redpath, Henry A., 444
Reed, James E., 599

Reed, Stephen A., 460
Reed, T. T., 620
Rehkopf, Friedrich, 442
Reich, Warren T., 651
Reid, Daniel G., 330
Rengstorf, K. H., 145
Rice, Geoffrey, 123
Richardson, Alan, 529
Ricoeur, Paul, 60n
Riley-Smith, Jonathan, 240
Ringe, Sharon H., 405
Ringgren, H., 448, 449
Robbins, Vernon K., 70
Roberts, Alexander, 224
Robinson, James M., 462, 524
Robinson, Thomas A., 204
Rocca, Giancarlo, 242
Rogers, A. Robert, 5n
Rogers, D. M., 253
Rogers, Jeffrey S., 428
Ross, Leonhard, 436
Roth, Cecil, 131
Rousseau, John J., 506
Rowe, Kenneth E., 316, 317
Rubinstein, W. D., 163, (p. 42)
Rudolph, W., 419
Rüger, H. P., 421
Runia, David T., 142
Ryan, James G., 345
Rykheer, J. H., 327, 328

Sader, Marion, 6
Sadie, Stanley, 582
Sampley, J. Paul, 517
Schaff, Philip, 189
Schalit, A., 145n
Schiffman, Lawrence H., 457
Schiller, Gertrud, 612
Schmemann, Alexander, 569n, (p. 102)
Schmidt-Lauber, Hans-Christoph, 565
Schneemelcher, Wilhelm, 521
Schneider, Gerhard, 504
Schürer, Emil, 141
Schwartz, Marilyn, 85
Schwertner, Siegfried, 31, 549
Scott, R., 497
Scott, William A., 421
Senior, Donald, 375
Seow, Choon Leong, 427
Shamir, Ilana, 136
Shanks, Hershel, 458
Shavit, Shlomo, 136
Sheehy, Eugene, 1
Sherman, Mark A., 234
Shermis, Michael, 164
Simmons, Henry C., 631
Simpson, J. A., 75
Simpson, Jane, 122
Singer, Peter, 648
Slaby, W. A., 500
Slavens, Thomas P., 173, 635
Smart, Ninian, 107
Smeeton, Donald Dean, 252
Smith, Barry, 645
Smith, Jonathan Z., 53
Soards, Marion, 579
Society of Biblical Literature, 31n
Soggin, J. A., 417
Sosa, Ernest, 644
Soukup, Paul A., 581
Soulen, Richard N., 402
Southard, Samuel, 633
Sparks, H. E. D., 454
Speak, Graham, 207

Speake, Jennifer, 239, 613
Squitier, Karl A., 233
Stallybrass, Oliver, 640
Stamm, Johann, 429
Starkey, Edward D., 9, 130n, (p. 120)
Steeves, Paul D., 127
Stein, Gordon, 56
Steinberg, S. H., 178
Steinsaltz, Adin, 154, 155
Stelten, Leo F., 533
Stemberger, Günter, 147
Stephen, Leslie, 62
Stern, Ephraim, 393
Stevenson, J., 230, 231
Stone, Michael E., 143
Stover, Mark, 6n
Strack, H. L., 147
Strayer, James, 238
Streit, Robert, 262
Strong, James, 379
Suggs, M. Jack, 372
Sutcliffe, John M., 597
Sutton, Peter, 603
Swain, Tony, 116
Swarat, Uwe, 548
Swift, Kate, 87

Takenaka, Masao, 619
Tanner, Norman P., 190
Teichler, Paul A., 86
Thackery, H., 440
Thoma, Clemens, 169
Thomas, Page A., 512
Thomas, Terry, 255
Thompson, Bard, 561, 573
Thompson, Henry O., 359
Thompson, Roger C., 112, (p. 110)
Throckmorton, Burton H., 513
Thurian, Max, 574, (p. 172)
Thurston, Herbert, 191
Tice, Terrence N., 557, 635
Tierney, Helen, 199
Toms, C. E. H., 295
Toorn, Karel van der, 388
Tov, Emanuel, 463, 464
Tracy, James, 237
Trevor, Hugh, 346
Troyanovsky, Igor, 128
Tucker, Gene M., 396
Tudor-Craig, Pamela, 605n
Turner, Harold W., 126
Turner, Nigel, 488

Van Belle, Gilbert, 472
Van der Bent, A. J., 272
Van Segbroeck, Frans, 473
Vander Brock, Lyle D., 508
VanderKam, James G., 459
Vermes, Geza, 141, 467
Vickers, John A., 315n
Vine Hall, Nick, 44

Wagner, Günther, 471
Wainwright, Geoffrey, 574, 592n
Wakefield, Gordon S., 591
Walford, A. J., 3
Walker, Barbara G., 199n, 614
Walker, William O., 390
Walsh, Michael. J., 30, 292, 568
Walters, LeRoy, 650
Ward, Roland, 109, (p. 109)
Ware, Kallistos (Timothy), (p. 102)

Watson, Duane F., 400
Webber, Robert E., 571
Weber, Robert, 367
Weiner, E. S. C. 75
Welch, John W., 364
Weller, Paul, 119
Wenham, J. W., 492
Werner, Karel, 93
Whittaker, Molly, 493
Wiener, Philip P., 636
Wigoder, Geoffrey, 133, 168
Wild, Stephen A., (p. 43)
Wildi, Hans Markus, 553
Wilkinson, Robert, 641
Williams, Peter W., 105
Williamson, Raymond K., 280
Willimon, William H., 577, (p. 174)
Wilson, R. McL., 521
Wittstruck, Thorne, 362
Wollheim, William, 129
Wonneberger, Reinhard, 420
Woodings, R. B., 642
Wraight, Heather, 343
Wright, David F., 546
Wright, J. Robert, 282
Würthwein, Ernst, 418
Wybrew, Hugh, 570
Wyckoff, D. Campbell, 595

Yolton, John W., 260
Young, Robert, 380

Zerwick, M., 494, 495
Ziefle, Helmut W., 78,
Zitnik, Maksimilijan, 562

Title index

This index includes

- titles of all books and databases which are either cited in entries or referred to in annotations or notes,

- titles of series, identified by the addition of that word in brackets, e.g. Old Testament library (series),

- titles of periodicals which, because of their particular reference value, are referred to in the text, for example *Journal of biblical literature*.

This index, however, does not otherwise duplicate the periodical titles listed in Chapter 14.

Reference is usually to the *item* number as given in chapters 1-13, not to a page number.

Where a title is referred to in an annotation or related note, that title is indexed by *item* number with 'n' added for annotation or note, for example *Dictionary of Christian lore and legend*, 613n.

Where a title is mentioned either in an introduction or a separated note, that title is indexed by a bracketed *page* number, for example *Modern Australian usage*, (p. 32).

A common or similarly-sounding title is distinguished by the addition, in brackets, of an abbreviated form of the name of the author or editor, for example *History of Australian churches*, *A*, (I. Breward).

Lengthy titles have been shortened either by the omission of subtitles or, where the title is undivided, by the standard device of using ellipsis points (. . .).

Filing guidelines

- titles are filed in word-by-word order,

- acronyms and initialisms are filed as if they were single words,

- numbers, when beginning a title, are filed as though spelled out,

- articles, definite and indefinite, are ignored for filing purposes and, where part of title, are moved to the end of the entry.

For the sake of clarity, the bibliographic practice of italicising titles has been dispensed with in this index

Aboriginal art and spirituality, 602, (p. 181)

Aboriginal religions in Australia: a bibliographical survey, 116

[ABS] Catalogue of publications and products, (p. 32)

American Historical Association's guide to historical literature, 171

Amo, amas, amat and more, 534

Analytical concordance of the Bible, 380

Analytical key to the Old Testament, 435

Anchor Bible (series), 407

Anchor Bible dictionary, 385

Ancient Christian writers (series), 222

Ancient quotes and anecdotes, 70

Anglican Church in Aotearoa, New Zealand and Polynesia. Clerical directory, (p. 113)

Anglican tradition: a handbook of sources, The, 282

Annotated bibliography of Luther studies, 1984-1989, 255

Annual bibliography of the Australian Institute of Aboriginal and Torres Strait Islander Studies, 115

Annual bulletin of historical literature, 175

Annuarium statisticum ecclesiae, 306

Ante-Nicene Christian library (series), 224

APAIS: Australian public affairs information service, 32

APAIS thesaurus. 33

Apocrypha and Pseudepigrapha of the Old Testament, The, 452

Apocryphal New Testament: a collection of apocryphal Christian literature in an English translation, The, 520

Apocryphal Old Testament, The, 454

Archaeological encyclopedia of the Holy Land, 394

Archiv für Reformationsgeschichte. Beihefte: Literaturbericht, 246

Archivum Historicum Societatis Iesu, 284n

Art and the Reformation: an annotated bibliography, 608

Arts in the religion of the Pacific: symbols of life, 615

Asia journal of theology, The, 332

Atlas of the early Christian world, 215

Atlas of the Christian church, 187

Atlas of the Crusades, 240

Atlas of the Jewish world, 138

Atlas of the Roman world, 216

Atlas zur Kirchengeschichte, 188

Augustine's De Civitate dei: an annotated bibliography of modern criticism, 234

Augustinus-Lexikon, 235

Australasian religion index, 31n, 37, (pp. 18, 42, 45)

Australasian union list of serials in theological collections, 29

Australian and New Zealand Association of Theological Schools, Fact book, 342, 600

Australian books in print, 18

Australian Christianity in outline, (p. 111)

Australian Christians in conflict and unity, 278

Australian dictionary of biography, 64, (p. 110)

Australian dictionary of evangelical biography, 340

Australian education index, (p. 183)

Australian encyclopaedia, The, 47

Australian interlibrary resource sharing directory, 41

Australian lectionary for [1995], (p. 172)

Australian national bibliography, 13

Australian national bibliography, 1901-1950, 15

Australian public affairs information service, 32

Australian religious studies: a bibliography of post-graduate theses, 26

Australians: a historical library, 48

Babylonian Talmud, The, (ed. I. Epstein), 152
Baptism and Eucharist: ecumenical convergence in celebration, 574
Baptism, Eucharist and Ministry, (p. 172)
Beginning to read the fathers, 218
Beliefs and practices in New Zealand: a directory, 124
Bible and modern literary criticism, 399
Bible and the saints, The, 194
Biblia Hebraica Stuttgartensia, 419
Biblia patristica, 205
Biblia sacra vulgatam versionem, 367
Biblical bibliography, 358
Biblical Greek illustrated by examples, 494
Biblical law bibliography, 364
Bibliografia Joanica, 476
Bibliographia patristica, 202
Bibliographic guide to the comparative study of ethics, A, 646
Bibliographie biblique, 358
Bibliographie Jürgen Moltmann, 556
Bibliographie Karl Barth, 533
Bibliographie sur l'histoire de la Compagnie de Jésus, 1901-1980, 284
Bibliography of Australia, 14
Bibliography of bioethics, 650
Bibliography of British theological literature, 1850-1940, 526
Bibliography of Christian worship, A, 561
Bibliography of interchurch and interconfessional theological dialogue, 270n
Bibliography of new religious movements in primal societies, 126
Bibliography of Salvation Army literature in English, 1865-1987, 321
Bibliography of the periodical literature on the Acts of the Apostles, A, 477
Bibliography of the Samaritans, 159
Bibliography on Holocaust literature, 160n
Bibliotheca Calviniana, 259
Bibliotheca missionum, 262
Biographical dictionary of the Byzantine Empire, 214, 238n
Biographical dictionary of twentieth-century philosophers, 641
Blackwell companion to Jewish culture, 132n, 135
Blackwell companion to the Enlightenment, 260
Blackwell dictionary of evangelical biography, 1730-1860, 261, 340n, (pp. 110, 113)
Blackwell dictionary of historians, 177
Blackwell dictionary of Judaica, 132
Blackwell encyclopedia of modern Christian thought, 527, (p. 86)
Book list, 414
Book of Daniel: an annotated bibliography, The, 359
Book of Psalms: an annotated bibliography, The, 362
Book of Revelation: an annotated bibliography, The, 360, 480
Book of Ruth: an annotated bibliography, The, 363
Book of Jewish books, The, 129
Book of New Zealand women, The, 67
Book of the saints, The, 192
Books in print, 19
Books of the Bible (series), (p. 121)
Bonhoeffer bibliography, 554
Brethren encyclopedia, The, 311
Britannica book of the year, 46

Calendar and lectionary of the Uniting Church: [Year C - 1994-95], (p. 173)
Calendar of saints, 195

Cambridge Australian style guide, The, 83

Cambridge commentaries on writings of the Jewish and Christian world, 200 BC to AD 200 (series), 455

Cambridge dictionary of philosophy, 639

Cambridge history of Judaism, 140

Cambridge history of the Bible, 365

Canon Law abstracts, 304

Catalogue of English Bible translations, 366

Catalogue of publications and products [ABS], (p. 32)

Catechism of the Catholic Church, 292

Catholic almanac, 305

Catholic Church and community, The, 338

Catholic encyclopedia: an international work of reference . . . The, 285

Catholic periodical and literature index, The, 34, 179n

Catholic study Bible: The New American Bible, 375

Catholicism in early modern history: a guide to research, 248

Centro pro unione, 270

Chambers dictionary of beliefs and religions, 52

Chicago manual of style, The, 80

Christian communication: a bibliographical survey, 581

Christian faith in the doctrinal documents of the Catholic Church, 290

Christian theology reader, The, 530

Christianity in Oceania, 349

Christians in Australia, 279

Church and chapels: a design and development guide, 618

Church history: an introduction to research, reference works, and methods, 182, (p. 66)

Church in Africa, The, 324

Classics in Western spirituality (series), 593

Clerical directory (Anglican Church in Aotearoa, New Zealand and Polynesia), (p. 113)

Code of Canon Law: a text and commentary, The, 303

Code of Canon Law in English translation, 301

Code of Canon Law, Latin-English edition, 300

Collections of religion and theology in Australia and New Zealand, 42

Commentary on the Catechism of the Catholic Church, 294

Companion encyclopedia of theology, 528

Companion to ethics, A, 648

Companion to metaphysics, A, 644

Companion to Samaritan studies, 158

Companion to Scottish history from the Reformation to the present, 353

Companion to Sing alleluia, 588n

Companion to the Catechism of the Catholic Church, 293

Companion volume to the Dead Sea Scrolls microfiche edition, 464

Complete concordance to Flavius Josephus, A, 145

Complete concordance to the Holy Scriptures of the Old and New Testaments, 378

Complete Gospels: annotated Scholars Version, The, 486

Complete library of Christian worship, The, 571

Computer-Konkordanz zum Neuen Testamentum graece von Nestle-Aland, 500

Concise dictionary of national biography, The, 63

Concise dictionary of the Christian world mission, 263

Concise encyclopedia of Islam, The, 97

Concise encyclopedia of preaching, 577

Concise exegetical grammar of New Testament Greek, 490

Concise Hebrew and Aramaic lexicon of the Old testament, 430

Concise Oxford dictionary of current English, 77

Concordance of 'The Hymnal 1982', A, 589

Concordance of the Qur'an, 100

Concordance to 'The Book of Concord', 257

Concordance to the Septuagint and the other Greek versions of the Old Testament, A, 443

Concordance to the texts of the Greek New Testament, 501

Concordantiae bibliorum sacrorum vulgatae editionis, 381

Contemporary printed literature of the English Counter-Reformation between 1558 and 1640: an annotated catalogue, 253

Contemporaries of Erasmus, 241

Continental commentaries (series), 408

Coptic encyclopedia, The, 212

Coptic Gnostic library, The, 523

Copy-editing: the Cambridge handbook, 79

Corpus Christi: an encyclopedia of the Eucharist, 541

Corpus christianorum (series), 221, (p. 155)

Creeds, councils and controversies, 231

Creeds of Christendom, The, **189**

Crimes of perception: an encyclopedia of heresies and heretics, 201

Critical bibliography of writings on Judaism, 130

Critical guide to Catholic reference books, 11

Critical review of books in religion, 39

Crockford's clerical directory, 281

Davidson's introductory Hebrew grammar, 426

Dead Sea Scrolls catalogue, The, 460

Dead Sea Scrolls: Hebrew, Aramaic, and Greek texts with English translations, The, 465

Dead Sea Scrolls in English, The, 467

Dead Sea Scrolls: major publications and tools for study, The, 461

Dead Sea Scrolls on microfiche, The, 463

Dead Sea Scrolls today, The, 459

Dead Sea Scrolls translated: the Qumran texts in English, The, 466

Death and dying: a bibliographic survey, 633

Decrees of the ecumenical councils, 190

Dent dictionary of symbols in Christian art, The, 613

Dictionary of American English on historical principles, 75n

Dictionary of Baptists in America, 310

Dictionary of biblical interpretation, 401, 605n

Dictionary of biblical tradition in English literature, 389

Dictionary of Catholic devotions, 568

Dictionary of Christian art, 606

Dictionary of Christian lore and legend, 185, 613n

Dictionary of Christian spirituality, A, 591

Dictionary of Christianity in America, 330

Dictionary of classical Hebrew, The, 433

Dictionary of deities and demons in the Bible, 388

Dictionary of ecclesiastical Latin, 533

Dictionary of education (D. Lawton), 596

Dictionary of ethics, theology and society, 529n, 652

Dictionary of feminist theory, 198

Dictionary of fundamental theology, 536

Dictionary of hymnology . . . 587

Dictionary of Jesus and the Gospels, 505

Dictionary of Judaism and Christianity, 167, (p. 58)

Dictionary of Latin and Greek theological terms, 532

Dictionary of liturgical terms, 563

Dictionary of national biography, 62

Dictionary of New Zealand biography, 66, (p. 110)

Dictionary of pastoral care, 627

Dictionary of pastoral care and counseling, 628

Dictionary of Paul and his letters, 507

Dictionary of Pentecostal and Charismatic movements, 308
Dictionary of Qur'anic terms and concepts, 101
Dictionary of religion and philosophy, 54
Dictionary of religious education, 597
Dictionary of religious quotations, 74
Dictionary of religious and spiritual quotations, 73
Dictionary of Scottish church history and theology, 352
Dictionary of subjects and symbols in art, 610
Dictionary of the ecumenical movement, 271, (p. 102)
Dictionary of the history of ideas, 636
Dictionary of the Jewish-Christian dialogue, 168
Dictionary of the liturgy, 566
Dictionary of the Middle Ages, 238
Dictionary of theological German, 78
Dictionary of Western church music, 585
Dictionary of world mythology, A, 58
Dictionnaire d'histoire et de géographie ecclésiastiques, 183
Dictionnaire de spiritualité, 590
Dictionnaire historique de la papauté, 296
Dissertations abstracts international, 25
Dizionario degli istituti de perfezione, 242
Documentary history of Faith and Order, 1963-1993, 275
Documents of the Christian church, 186
Documents of the English Reformation, 254
Dreamings: the art of Aboriginal Australia, 603

Early Christian fathers (H. Bettenson), 228
Early Christianity: origins and evolution to AD 600, 209
Early church: an annotated bibliography, The, 204
Early Judaism and its modern interpreters, 397
East Asian pastoral review, 333
Ecumenical pilgrims, 273
Ecumenism: a bibliographical overview, 269
Elements of New Testament Greek, The, 492
Elenchus of Biblica, 356
Enchiridion symbolorum, definitionum, et declarationum . . . 291
Encyclopaedia Britannica, The new, 45, (pp. 65-66)
Encyclopaedia Judaica, 131
Encyclopaedia of Aboriginal Australia, 114
Encyclopaedia of Islam, 95
Encyclopaedia of religion and ethics, The, 50, (p. 204)
Encyclopedia of American religions, The, 103
Encyclopedia of American religions: religious creeds, The, 104
Encyclopedia of archaeological excavations in the Holy Land, 393n
Encyclopedia of bioethics, 652
Encyclopedia of early Christianity, 209
Encyclopedia of ethics (L. Becker), The, 647
Encyclopedia of gods, 55
Encyclopedia of heresies and heretics, 200
Encyclopedia of Jewish history, 136
Encyclopedia of Judaism, The, (ed. G. Wigoder), 133
Encyclopedia of Mormonism, 312
Encyclopedia of philosophy (P. Edwards), 637, 647n
Encyclopedia of psychology (R. Corsini), 623
Encyclopedia of religion, The, (ed. M. Eliade), 51, 592n, 616n, (pp. 23, 35, 43, 204)
Encyclopedia of the American religious experience, 105

Encyclopedia of the early church, 210
Encyclopedia of the Holocaust, 162
Encyclopedia of the Lutheran church, The, 314
Encyclopedia of the Reformed faith, 259n, 319
Encyclopedia of the Renaissance, 239
Encyclopedia of unbelief, The, 56
Encyclopedia of world art, 601
Encyclopedia of world Methodism, 318
Encyclopedic dictionary of psychology, The, 624
Encyclopédie du Protestantisme, 251n, 309
English key to the Latin words and abbreviations and the symbols of Biblia Hebraica Stuttgartensia, 421
English religion, 1500-1540: a bibliography, 252
Essay and general literature index, (p. 17)
Ethics index on CD-ROM, 649
European Reformation, The, 250
Evangelical dictionary of theology, 545
Evangelisches Kirchenlexikon, 547
Evangelisches Lexikon für Theologie und Gemeinde, 548
Everyman dictionary of religion and philosophy, 54, (p. 202)
Exegetical bibliography of the New Testament (series), 471
Exegetical dictionary of the New Testament, 504
Exhaustive concordance of the Bible, 379

Facsimile edition of the Dead Sea Scrolls, A, 462
Facsimile edition of the Nag Hammadi codices, 522
Familiar quotations, 68
Fathers of the church (series), 225
I Corinthians: an annotated bibliography, 479
Fontana dictionary of modern thinkers, 642
Fontana dictionary of modern thought, 640
Forms of Old Testament literature, The, 446
From every people, 266
Funk & Wagnall's standard dictionary of folklore, mythology and legend, 59
Future of our historic churches, The, 622

Genealogy of ecclesiastical jurisdictions, A, 264
Gospel of Luke (W. E. Mills), 475
Gospel of Luke: a cumulative bibliography, The, 473
Gospel of Mark: a cumulative bibliography, The, 474
Gospel parallels, 513
Grammar for biblical Hebrew, A (J. M. Hamilton), 428
Grammar for biblical Hebrew, A (C. L. Seow), 427
Grammar for New Testament Greek (J. M. Efird), 489
Grammar of New Testament Greek, A, (J. Moulton), 488
Grammatical analysis of the Greek New Testament, 495
Graphic concordance to the Dead Sea Scrolls, 468
Greek-English lexicon of the New Testament and other early Christian literature, A, 496
Greek-English lexicon of the Septuagint, A, 441
Greek-English lexicon of the Septuagint (Twelve Prophets), A, 443
Greek-English lexicon with revised supplement, 497
Greek grammar of the New Testament and other early Christian literature, A, 487
Greek New Testament, The, 484
Growing consensus, 276
Guide to reference books, 1, 2, (p. 24)
Guide to the gods, 60

Guide to the study of Greco-Roman and Jewish and Christian history and literature, 203
Guidelines for bias-free writing, 85
Guidelines on the use of inclusive language and non-discriminatory language, 90

Handbook of biblical criticism, 402
Handbook of Catholic theology, 537
Handbook of denominations in the United States, 106
Handbook of European history, 1400-1600, 237, 250n
Handbook of evangelical theologians, 551
Handbook of metaphysics and ontology, 645
Handbook of non-sexist writing, The, 87
Handbuch der Liturgik, 565
Handing on the tradition, 295
Hans Urs von Balthasar: Bibliographie, 1925-1990, 552
Harper atlas of the Bible, 392
Harper religious & inspirational quotation companion, 74
HarperCollins dictionary of religion, The, 53
HarperCollins encyclopedia of Catholicism, 288
Harper's Bible commentary, 404
Harper's Bible pronunciation guide, 390
Harper's encyclopedia of religious education, 598
Hebrew and Aramaic lexicon of the Old Testament, 429
Hebrew and English lexicon of the Old Testament, 431
Hebrew Bible and its modern interpreters, 396
Hermeneia: a critical and historical commentary on the Bible (series), 409
Hinduism in Australia, 94
Historic churches of Australia, 620
Historical atlas of the Jewish people, 137
Historical catalogue of printed editions of the English Bible, 1525-1961, 366n
Historical dictionary of Buddhism, 91
Historical dictionary of ecumenical Christianity, 272
Historical tables, 58 BC-AD1990, 178
History of Buddhism in Australia, 1848-1988, 92
History of Christian education, 599
History of Christianity (Owen Chadwick), 181
History of Christianity in Africa, 323
History of the Australian churches, A, (I. Breward), 337
History of the church in South Africa: a document and source book, 329
History of the church in South Africa: a select bibliography . . . 325, 326, 327
History of the Jewish people in the age of Jesus Christ, The, 141
History of the Methodist Church in Great Britain, 315
Holocaust: an annotated bibliography, The, 161
Holy Land: an archaeological guide from the earliest times to 1700, The, 395
House of God: church architecture, style and history, The, 617
Humanities: a selective guide to information sources, The, 5
Hymns and tunes: an index, (p. 176)

Icon handbook, The, 570n, 607
Iconography of Christian art, 612
Illustrated encyclopedia of New Zealand, The, 49
Images of religion in Australian art, 604
In our time, 165
Inclusive language in the church, 88
Inclusive-language lectionary, An, 89
Index to book reviews in religion, 40

Index to Brown, Driver & Briggs Hebrew lexicon, 432

Index to periodical literature on the Apostle Paul, 478

Index to the Code of Canon Law in English translation, 302

Index to the World Council of Churches' official statements and reports, 1948- 1994, 277

Information resources and services in Australia, 4

International bulletin of missionary research, 262n

International critical commentary on the Holy Scriptures of the Old and New Testaments (series), 410

International ecumenical bibliography, 270n

International encyclopedia of education, (p. 183)

International review of mission(s), 262n

International review of biblical studies, 357

International standard Bible encyclopedia, 386

Internationale Zeitschriftenschau für Bibelwissenschaft und Grenzgebiete, 357

Internationales Abürzungsverzeichnis für Theologie und Grenzbegiete, 31

Interpretation: a Bible commentary for preaching and teaching (series), 411

Interpreter's dictionary of the Bible, 385n

Intertestamental literature, 451

Interviewing for oral history at the National Library of Australia, 176

Introduction to biblical Hebrew, 425

Introduction to Rabbinic literature, 148

Introduction to the New Testament (W. G. Kümmel), 482

Introduction to the Old Testament (J. A. Soggin), 417

Introduction to the Talmud and Midrash, 147

Introductory bibliography for the study of Scripture, 355, 451n, 488n, (p. 122)

Irish church records, 345

Islamic desk reference, 96

Island churches of the South Pacific, The, 350

Japan's post-war Protestant churches, 346

Jerome biblical commentary, 403n

Jerusalem: the Holy City: a bibliography, 139

Jesus and his world: an archaeological and cultural dictionary, 506

Jewish religion: a companion, The, 134

Jewish world in modern times: a selected, annotated bibliography, 160, 161n

Jewish writings of the Second Temple period, 143

Jewish-Christian relations: an annotated bibliography and resource guide, 164

Johannine bibliography, 1966-1985, 472

Josephus and modern scholarship (1937-1980), 144

Josephus: a supplementary bibliography, 144

Josephus, the Jewish War, 146

Journal of biblical literature, 31n

JPS Torah commentary, The (series), 447

Judaism and Christianity, 9

Judaism in Australia, 163, (p. 42)

Key to the elements of New Testament Greek, 492

Konkordanz zum Hebräischen Alten Testament, 436

Koran. al Qur'an: a contemporary translation, 99

Koran interpreted, The, 100n

Language, gender, and professional writing, 86

Later Christian fathers (H. Bettenson), 229

Lexikon der christlichen Ikonographie, 611

Lexikon der Jüdisch-Christlichen Begegnung, 169

Lexikon für Theologie und Kirche, 287
Liberation theologies: a research guide, 544
Library of Christian classics (series), 225
Life of Jesus research: an annotated bibliography, 514
Literary forms in the New Testament: a handbook, 508
Liturgical dictionary of Eastern Christianity, The, 569
Liturgies of the Western Church, 573
Lives of the saints, 191
Living world of the Old Testament, 416
Lutheran churches in the world, 313
Lutherjahrbuch: Organ der internationalen Lutherforschung, 255n
Luther's works: index, 256

Macmillan Bible atlas, 391
Macquarie dictionary: the national dictionary, The, 76
Many faiths, one nation, 110
Matrology: a bibliography of writings by Christian women, 197
Medieval Christian literary imagination, 243
Methodist union catalog, pre-1976 imprints, 316
Midrash Rabbah, 156
Midrash reader, 157
Minister's handbook of mental disorders, 626
Mishnah: a new translation, The, 150
Mishnah: translated from the Hebrew, The, 149
Mission in the nineteen 90s, 265
Mission legacies, 267
Modern Australian usage, (p. 32)
Modern Catholic encyclopedia, 289
Modern encyclopedia of religions in Russia and the Soviet Union, The, 127
Mosques and Muslim settlement in Australia, 102
Multipurpose tools for Bible study, 354, 418n, 488n, (pp. 53, 122, 123, 129, 134, 148)

NAB (New American Bible), 373
Nag Hammadi Library in English, 524
Nag Hammadi texts and the Bible: a synopsis and index, 525
National Church HIV/AIDS: bibliography, 1993, 632
New Age encyclopedia, 61
New American Bible, 373
New American Bible: the New Testament revised edition, 374
New Cambridge medieval history, 236
New Catholic encyclopedia: an international work of reference . . . 286
New century Bible commentary (series), 412
New concordance of the Bible, A (A. Even-Shoshan), 438
New dictionary of Catholic spirituality, 592
New dictionary of Christian ethics (J. Macquarrie), 653
New dictionary of Christian ethics and pastoral theology, 629, 654
New dictionary of Christian theology, 529
New dictionary of liturgy and worship, 564
New dictionary of sacramental worship, 567
New dictionary of theology (ed. S. B. Ferguson), 546
New dictionary of theology, The, (ed. J. A. Komonchak), 538
New documents illustrating early Christianity, 219
New encyclopedia of archaeological excavations in the Holy Land, 393
New Eusebius, A, 230
New Grove dictionary of music and musicians, The, 582

New handbook of Christian theology, A, 531
New Harvard dictionary of music, The, 583
New history of Ireland, A., 344
New international Greek New Testament commentary (series), 510
New International Version, The Holy Bible, 377
New interpreter's Bible, 377n, 406, (p. 123)
New Jerome biblical commentary, 403
New Jerusalem Bible, 376
New Oxford annotated Bible with the Apocryphal/Deuterocanonical books, 370
New Oxford companion to music, The, 584
New Revised Standard Version, 369
New Testament abstracts, 481
New Testament and its modern interpreters, 398
New Testament apocrypha, 521
New Testament Christology: a critical assessment and annotated bibliography, 515
New Testament commentary survey, 509
New Testament Greek: an introductory grammar (E. G. Jay), 491
New Testament Greek: key, 491
New Testament Greek grammar (M. Whittaker), 493
New Zealand books in print, 21
New Zealand national bibliography, 16
New Zealand national bibliography to the year 1960, 17
New Zealand style book for New Zealand writers, editors, journalists, and students, The, 81, (p. 28)
Nil desperandum: a dictionary of Latin tags and useful phrases, 534
Nineteenth-century European Catholicism, 283
NIV (New International Version), 377
NIV exhaustive concordance, 383
NIV interlinear Hebrew-English Old Testament, 422
NJB (New Jerusalem Bible), 376
Noncanonical writings and New Testament interpretation, 451n, 519
Nova Vulgata bibliorum sacrorum editio, 368
Novae concordantiae bibliorum sacrorum iuxta Vulgatam versionem critice editam, 382
NRSV (New Revised Standard version), 369
NRSV concordance unabridged, 384

Official directory of the Catholic Church in Australia, 339n
Old Testament abstracts, 415
Old Testament in Greek according to the text of the Codex Vaticanus, The, 440
Old Testament library (series), 445
Old Testament Pseudepigrapha, The, 452n, 453
One blood: two hundred years of Aboriginal encounter with Christianity, 117
One hundred years of study on the Passion narratives, 516
Origins of the Salvation Army, 322
Orthodox liturgy: the development of the Eucharistic liturgy of the Byzantine Rite, 570
Oxford book of prayer, 576
Oxford companion to the Bible, 387
Oxford dictionary of Byzantium, 213, 238n
Oxford dictionary of modern quotations, 71
Oxford dictionary of philosophy, 638
Oxford dictionary of quotations, 69
Oxford dictionary of saints, 193
Oxford dictionary of the Christian church, 184
Oxford dictionary of the popes, 297
Oxford early Christian texts (series), 226
Oxford encyclopedia of the modern Islamic world, 98
Oxford English dictionary, 75

Oxford history of Christianity, 180, (p. 66)
Oxford history of New Zealand, 123
Oxford history of the Reformation, 251
Oxford illustrated history of Christianity, 180, (p. 66)
Oxford Movement and its leaders, The, 268
Oxford study Bible: Revised English Bible with the Apocrypha, 372

Papal encyclicals, 1740-1981, The, 299
Papal pronouncements: a guide, 1740-1978, 298
Parish registers in Australia, 44
Pastoral responses to older adults and their families, 631
Pathways to understanding, 166, 166n
Patristic Greek lexicon, A, 498
Patrologia cursus completus (Migne), 220
Patrology, 217
Paul Tillich: a comprehensive bibliography . . . 560
Pauline parallels, 817
Penguin dictionary of twentieth-century quotations, 72
Philo of Alexandria: an annotated bibliography, 142
Philosophy: a guide to reference literature, 634
Pierre Teilhard de Chardin: a comprehensive bibliography, 558
Place where God dwells, The, 619
Pointers: quarterly bulletin of the Christian Research Association, (p. 111)
Popular dictionary of Hinduism, 93
Preaching the revised common lectionary (series), 579
Preparing for worship: the essential handbook for worship leaders, 572
Presbyterian Church of Aotearoa New Zealand. Yearbook and directory, (p. 113)
Proclamation (series), 578
Prophets Nev'im, The, 424n
Pseudepigrapha and modern research, with a supplement, 450
Psychiatric dictionary (R. Campbell), 625
PTCA bulletin, 334
Pulpit resource, 580n

Reader's adviser, The, 6
Reallexikon für Antike und Christentum, 211
REB (Revised English Bible), 371
Reclaiming the Dead Sea Scrolls, 457
Reference sources in history, 172
Reference works for theological research, 12
Reformation Europe: a guide to research, 247
Reformation Europe: a guide to research, II, 248
Reformation guides to research (series), 246n
Register of church archives, 43
Religion: a view from the Australian census, 108
Religion in Australia: a history, 112, 338n
Religion in Australian life: a bibliography of social research, 111, 335
Religion in China today, 118
Religion in politics, 57
Religion in the Soviet Republics, 128
Religion index one, 35, 179n
Religion index two, 38, 179n
Religions in the UK, 119
Religions of Asia, 107
Religions of New Zealanders, 125, (p. 113)

Religious and theological abstracts, 36

Religious bibliographies in serial literature, 30

Religious bodies in Australia: a comprehensive guide, 109, (p. 102)

Religious books, 1876-1982, 24

Religious books in print, 23

Religious education, 1960-1993, 595

Religious history of New Zealand: a bibliography, 120

Religious information sources, 8

Religious periodicals directory, 28

Research guide to philosophy, 635

Responses to 101 questions on the Dead Sea Scrolls, 456

Revised English Bible with the Apocrypha, 371

Revue d'histoire eccésiastique, 179

Rhetorical criticism of the Bible, 400, 469n

Rightly dividing the Word of truth, 170

Sacra Pagina (series), 511

Sacramenta: bibliographia internationalis, 562

Sacramentum mundi: an encyclopedia of theology, 535

Sacred architecture, 616

Samaritans, The, p. (3: before 158)

Schleiermacher bibliography, 1784-1984, 557

Schlüssel zum Werke von Paul Tillich, 559

Secular who's who, 65

Select bibliography of periodical articles on South African church history, 328

Select library of Nicene and post-Nicene fathers of the Christian church (series), 227

Septuaginta: Vetus Testamentum graecum, 439

Septuaginta-Vokabular, 442

Shape of belief: Christianity in Australia today, The, 336, (pp. 102, 111)

Short-title catalogue of books printed in England, Scotland, & Ireland . . . 1475-1640, 245n

Shorter encyclopaedia of Islam, 95n

Signs and symbols in Christian art, 609

Simplified guide to BHS, 421

Sir Thomas More in the English Renaissance, 245

Sixteenth century bibliographies (series), (p. 84)

Sixteenth century essays and studies (series), (p. 84)

Social scientific criticism of the New Testament, 469

Songs of the people of God, 588

SPCK book of Christian prayer, The, 575

Stages on the way, 280

Sources chrétiennes (series), 221

Sources of information for historical research, 173

Sources of the Pentateuch: texts, introductions, annotations, 423

Statistical yearbook of the Church, 306

Style and content in Christian art, 605

Style manual for authors, editors and printers, 82, (pp. 30, 32)

Style manual for the presentation of papers and theses in religion and theology, A, 84, (p. 30)

Subject guide to books in print, 20

Synoptic problem: a bibliography, 1716-1988, The, 512

Talmud: the Steinsaltz edition, The, 154

Talmud: the Steinsaltz edition: a reference guide, The, 155

Talmud of Babylonia: an American translation, 153

Talmud of the Land of Israel, 151

Tanakh: a new translation of the Holy Scriptures according to the traditional Hebrew text, 424

Teaching bibliographic skills in history, 174
Text of the New Testament, The, 483
Text of the Old Testament: an introduction to the Biblia Hebraica, The, 418
Textbook of Christian ethics, A, 655
Texts for preaching (series), 580
Textual commentary on the Greek New Testament, A, 485
Theological and religious reference materials, 7, (p. 66)
Theological dictionary of the New Testament, 502
Theological dictionary of the New Testament (abridged in one volume), 503
Theological dictionary of the Old Testament, 449
Theological education, (p. 185)
Theologische Realenzyklopädie, 549
Theologische Realenzyklopädie: Abkürzungsverzeichnis, 31n, 549
Theologisches Wörterbuch zum Alten Testament, 448
Theologisches Wörterbuch zum Neuen Testament, 502n
Theotokos: a theological encyclopedia, 539
Thesaurus Linguae Graecae, (p. 77)
Thesaurus Linguae Graecae canon of Greek authors and works, 233
They came to care: pastoral ministry in colonial Australia, 630
Thinkers of the twentieth century, 643
Thomas Aquinas: international bibliography, 1977-1990, 244
Thomas Merton: a comprehensive bibliography, 555
To live among the stars, 351
Torah, The, 424n
Torah: a modern commentary, The, (series), 447n
Transplanted Christianity, 347
Trinitas: a theological encyclopedia, 540

UK Christian handbook, 343
Ulrich's international periodicals directory, 27
Understanding BHS, 420
Understanding the Dead Sea Scrolls, 458
Understanding the Old Testament, 416
United Methodist studies, 317

Veni creator Spiritus: a theological encyclopedia of the Holy Spirit, 542
Verbum Caro: an encyclopedia on Jesus, the Christ, 543
Veteris Testamenti concordantiae hebraicae atque chaldaicae, 437
Victorian churches [Australian], 621
Vocabulary of the Old testament, The, 434
Vollständige Konkordanz zum griechischen Neuen Testament, 497

Walford's guide to reference material, 3
What is Midrash, 157n
Western plainchant: a handbook, 586
Westminster dictionary of Christian education, 598n
Westminster dictionary of Christian ethics, 653
Westminster dictionary of Christian spirituality, 591
Westminster dictionary of Christian theology, 529
Westminster dictionary of liturgy and worship, 564
Whitaker's almanack, (pp. 65-66)
Whitaker's books in print, 21
Who's who in theology, 550
Winds of change, 341

Women and religion: a bibliographic guide to Christian feminist liberation theology, 196
Women in the New Testament: a select bibliography, 470
Women's Bible commentary, 405
Women's dictionary of symbols and sacred objects, 614
Women's studies encyclopedia, 199
Word biblical commentary (series), 413
World almanac and book of facts, (pp. 65-66)
World Alliance of Reformed Churches: general index, 1875-1992, 320
World Christianity: Oceania, 348
World Council of Churches yearbook, 274
World spirituality: an encyclopedic history of the religious quest (series), 594
Writings Kethubim, The, 424
Writings of John Calvin: an introductory guide, The, 258

Yearbook and directory (Presbyterian Church of Aotearoa New Zealand), (p. 113)
Year book Australia, (p. 32)
Yearbook for Australian churches, 108n, 113n, 339, 347n, (p. 111)
Yearbook of American and Canadian churches, 331
Yearbook of Australian religious organisations, 108n, 113, 338n, 339n, (pp. 111, 173)
Yearbook of the Lutheran Church of Australia, 339n

Zadok papers, (p. 111)
Zadok perspectives, (p. 111)

Subject index

This index includes the key resource-types, subject areas, concepts, terms, persons, areas and organisations covered in this work. There are three sorts of entries:

1. Types of reference resources, that is bibliographies, encyclopedias, language dictionaries and so on. These are sub-divided by the subjects covered. The headings for resource-types are printed in bold:

   bibliographies
   > Bible
   > biblical criticism

2. Subjects which have received more than cursory notice. A subject may be divided by a type of reference resource, or by a subject-subdivision:

   Judaism
   > atlases
   > Holocaust

3. The names of organisations mentioned in the text.

   The preface and introduction are not indexed.

References in this index are to page numbers, not to item numbers.

abbreviations
    biblical writing, 15
    of periodical titles, 14-15
Aborigines
    see Australian Aborigines
abstracts
    see indexing and abstracting
    services
Acts of the Apostles
    bibliographies, 146
addresses, postal
    theological libraries, 18-19
    theological schools, 111, 185
        in Australia , 185
        Canada, 108
        Great Britain , 44, 112
        New Zealand, 185
        United States of America, 108
Africa
    Christianity, 106-108
    histories, 106-107
aged persons, pastoral care of
    bibliographies, 197-198
agnosticism
    see unbelief
AIDS (Disease)
    bibliography, 198
American Theological Library
    Association (ATLA), 16, 17, 18
Americas, the
    Christianity, 108
    religious movements, 39-40
ancient world, 72-73
Anglican Communion, 96
    directory, 96
    documents, 96
antisemitism, 56-57
apocryphal literature
    Hebrew, 139-141
    New Testament, 154-156
Aquinas, Thomas, 80
Aramaic language
    concordances, 136
    lexicons, 134-135
archaeology
    biblical, 127-128
architecture
    see church architecture;
    religious architecture
archives, 18-19
art
    see Australian Aborigines; art and
    religion; Christian art; religious art;
    religious symbolism
art and religion, 188-193
    Christianity, 189-193
arts, the
    encyclopedias, 188
Asia
    church architecture, 193
    Christianity, 108-109
    religious movements, 40
Association for Theological Schools
    in South East Asia (ATESEA),
    108-109
atheism
    see unbelief
atlases (major subject areas)
    Bible, 127
    Christianity, history of, 68
    crusades, the, 79
    early Christianity, 74
    Judaism, 50-51
    Middle Ages, 7
    Roman world, 74

Augustine of Hippo, 78
Australasian
    book reviews, 18
    indexing systems, 17
    periodicals, 207-218
    theological education, 111,
        185
Australia
    see also Australasian;
    Australian Aborigines
    archives, 19
    bibliographies, 4, 9,
    biographies, 25, 110
    books in print, 10
    Buddhism in, 37
    Christianity in
    bibliographies, 109-110
    biographies, 110
    statistics, 111
    yearbooks, 110
    church architecture, 193
    church history
    copyright, 32
    dissertations, 13
    ecumenism, 91
    encyclopedias, 20
    evangelicals, 86, 110
    Hinduism in, 37
    indexing services, 15, 17
    Islam in, 39
    Judaism in, 57
    language dictionaries, 28

    libraries, 18-19
    parish registers, 19
    pastoral care, 197
    periodicals, 207-218
    reference books, guides to, 4
    religious movements, 40-43,
        45-46
    research organisations, 111
    secularists, 25
    statistics, 32
    style manuals, 29
    theological education, 111, 185
    union lists of periodicals, 14
Australia and New Zealand
    theological education, 111, 185
Australian Aborigines
    art, 188-189
    bibliographies, 42-43
    encyclopedias, 42
    religions, 42-43
    spirituality, 181
    surveys, 43
Australian and New Zealand
    Association of Theological Schools
    (ANZATS), 111, 185
Australian and New Zealand
    Theological Library Association
    (ANZTLA), 17
Australian Association for the Study
    of Religions, 41

Balthasar, Hans Urs von, 163
baptism, 103, 169-172
Baptist churches, 103
Barth, Karl, 163-164
Bible, the whole
    see also Hebrew Scriptures;
    intertestamental literature;
    New Testament; New Testament
    apocryphal literature

abstracts, 131-132, 146-147
archaeology, 127-128
art, 189
atlases, 127
biblical criticism,
        bibliographies, 128-129
        dictionaries, 129
bibliographies, 120-122
commentaries, 129-131
concordances, 124-125
criticism
        see biblical criticism
dictionaries and encyclopedias,
        125-126
guides to the literature, 120
histories, 122
periodicals, 216
pronunciation, 126-127
versions
        bibliographies to, 122
        ancient, 122
        Catholic, 122-123,
        modern, 123-124
        English, modern, 123
        evangelical, 124
        Vulgate, 122-123
            concordances to, 125
Bible and literature, 126
biblical criticism and interpretation,
    128-129
bibliographies
    (Bibliographies of types of
    reference resources are followed by
    bibliographies of major subjects.)

    types
        book reviews, 17-18
        dissertations, 12-13
        indexing and abstracting services,
            15-17
        national bibliographies, 8-10
        periodical literature, 13-14
        reference books, guides to, 6-8
        trade bibliographies, 10-12

    subjects, major
        Australia, religions, 41-42
        Bible, 120-122
        biblical criticism, 128-129
        Christian theology, 158
        church history, 66, 71-72,
        ecumenical movement, 89
        feminism, 70
        Hebrew Scriptures, 131
        historical research, 64-65
        Jewish-Christian dialogue, 58
        Judaism, 49, 56-57
        missions, 86
        New Testament, 144-146
        New Zealand, religions, 44
        patristic period, 71-72
        philosophy, 201
        Reformation, 81-82, 84, 85
        religious education, 184
        religious movements, Australia,
            41-42
        theologians, 163-165
        theology, Christian, 158
        worship, 169
bioethics, 205
        bibliographies, 205
        encyclopedias, 205
biographies
        Australia, 25, 110
        ecumenical movement, 89-90

evangelicals, 86, 110
Great Britain, 24
missions, 88
New Zealand, 25-26
philosophers, 202
Renaissance, 79-80
secularists, 25
theologians, 163-165
Bonhoeffer, Dietrich, 164
book reviews
        indexes to, 18
        published reviews, 17-18
books in print, 10-12
Brethren, the, 104
Buddhism, 37
        in Australia, 37
Byzantine civilisation and churches,
    74

calendars
        church, 172-173
        perpetual, 65-66
Calvin, John, 85
Canada
        churches, 108
        theological schools, 108
canon law, Catholic Church, 100-101
catechesis, Catholic Church, 99
Catholic Church and Catholicism,
    96-102
        bibliographies, 96
        canon law, 100-101
        catechisms, 99
        dictionaries and encyclopedias,
            97-98, 160-161
        doctrines, 161
        documents, 98-99
        liturgy, 170
        missions, 87
        papacy, 99-100
        statistics, 102
        theology, 160-161
        yearbooks, 101
Catholic Library Association, 16
Catholic Reformation, 81-82
Catholicism
        see Catholic Church and
        Catholicism
charismatic movement, 102-103
China
        religious movements, 43
Christian art, 189-190
Christian churches
        see Christianity; church history:
        denominations
Christian ethics, 205-206
        dictionaries, 205-206
        documents, 206
Christian Research Association
    (CRA), 41, 42, 111
Christian theology,
        see theology, Christian
Christian-Jewish dialogue
        see Jewish-Christian dialogue
Christianity, history of, 66-91

        see also church history;
        ecumenical movement;
        Jewish-Christian dialogue

    resources
        atlases, 68, 74
        bibliographies, 66, 71-72, 89
        biographies, 86, 88, 89-90

databases, 77
dictionaries and encyclopedias,
    67, 72-74, 86, 87, 89
documents, 67-68, 83, 90
guides, 66-67, 74-75
periodicals, 215-216
texts, 75-77

periods
    early period, 71-78
    medieval and renaissance, 78-81
    Reformation, 81-85
    enlightenment and modern periods,
        85-91

countries
see also more detailed entries
under the following countries:
    Africa, 106-107
    the Americas, 108
    Asia, 108-109
    Australia, 109-111
        ecumenism, 91
    Great Britain, 112
    Ireland, 112
    Japan, 112-113
    New Zealand, 44-45, 113
    Oceania, 113-114
    Scotland, 114-115
    South Africa, 107-108

subjects
    Aquinas, Thomas, 80
    Augustine of Hippo, 78
    Calvin, John, 85
    creeds, councils, 68
    ecumenical movement, 88-91
    evangelicalism, 86
    feminism, 70-71
    Luther and Lutheranism, 84-85
    medieval learning, 80
    missions, 86-88
    More, Thomas, 81
    Oxford Movement, 88
    religious orders, 80
    saints and saints' days, 69-70
    women, role of, 70-71

Christology, 153, 161

chronologies, 65
church and society
    periodicals, 216
church architecture, 192-193
    guides, 192
    Asia, 193
    Australia, 193
church calendars, 172-173

church councils, 68
church fathers, early
    see patristic period
church history, denominations
    see also Christianity, history of;
    more detailed entries under the
    following denominations:
        Anglican Communion, 96
        Baptist, 103
        Brethren, 104
        Catholic Church, 96-102
        Church of Jesus Christ of the
            Latter-day Saints, 104
        Lutheran churches, 104
        Methodist churches, 104-105
        Orthodox churches, 102
        Pentecostal and charismatic,
            102-103

        Presbyterian and Reformed,
            105-106
        Protestant denominations, 103
        Salvation Army, 106
church history, periodicals, 215-216
church music, 174-177
        dictionaries, 175
        hymnology, 176-177
        plainchant, 175
Church of Jesus Christ of the Latter-
    Day Saints, 104
Church unity
    see ecumenical movement
Churches
    see Christianity; church
    history; and individual
    denominations
Codex iuris canonici (1983)
    see canon law
commentaries, biblical
        whole Bible, 129-131
        Hebrew Scriptures, 138
        New Testament, 152
communication, Christian, 174
concordances
        Bible, 124-125
        Dead Sea scrolls, 144
        Hebrew Scriptures, 136
        New Testament, 150
        Septuagint, 137-138
copyright, 32
Coptic church, 73
councils (church), 68
counselling, pastoral
    see pastoral care
Counter-Reformation
    see Catholic Reformation;
    Reformation
creeds, Christian, 68
crusades, the, 79

Dead Sea scrolls, 141-144
        bibliographies, 142
        concordances, 144
        guides, 141-142
        texts and translations, 142-
            143
death and dying
        bibliographies, 198
deities, 22, 126
dictionaries
    see encyclopedias and
    dictionaries; language
    dictionaries
directories
        churches and clergy
            Australia, 110
            Great Britain, 96, 112
            New Zealand, 113
dissertations
        general, 12-13
        religious, 13
Dreaming, the, 188-189

East Asia, 108-109
Eastern churches
    see Coptic church
Eastern Orthodox church
    see Orthodox churches
ecumenical movement
    see also World Council of
    Churches
        in Australia, 91
        bibliographies, 89
        biographies, 89-90

dictionaries, 89
periodicals, 215-216
ecumenism
see ecumenical movement,
education,
see religious education;
theological education
**encyclopedias and dictionaries
(major subject areas)**
arts, the, 189
Australian, 20
Bible, 125-126
biblical interpretation, 129
Catholic theology, 160-161
Christian ethics, 205-206,
church music, 175
ethics, 204
general, 20
Hebrew Scriptures, theology
of, 139
heresies, 71
Judaism, 49-50, 58-59
Middle Ages, 79
music, 175
mythology, 23
New Age movements, 23-24
New Testament - theological,
150-151
New Zealand, 21
pastoral care, 196-197
philosophy, 201-202
preaching, 173
Protestant theology, 162-163
psychiatry, 196
psychology, 196
religion, religions, 21-24
religion in politics, 22-23
religious education, 184
Renaissance, 79
spirituality, 180
theology, 158-159, 160-161,
162-163
unbelief, 22
worship and liturgy, 169-171
England, Reformation in, 83
English literature and Bible, 126
Enlightenment, the, 85-86
Erasmus, Desiderius, 79-80
ethics, 203-206
see also bioethics; Christian ethics
bibliographies, 203-204
bioethics, 205
companions, 204
encyclopedias, 204
indexing services, 204-205
periodicals, 217
Eucharist, 161, 169-172
evangelicalism, 86
evangelicals
biographies, 86
Australian, 86, 110
New Zealand, 86

feminism
see also women
bibliographies, 70
dictionaries, 70-71
Festschriften, indexes to, 17
fundamental theology, 160

gender and language, 31
German, theological, 29
Gnosticism, 154-155
see also New Testament

apocryphal literature
gods and goddesses, 22
Gospels, the
bibliographies, 145-146, 152
Jesus research, 153
parallels, 153
synoptic problem, 152
Great Britain
biographies, 24
Christianity, 112
religious movements, 44
Greek language
see also Septuagint
grammars, 148-149
lexicons, 149-150
texts, NT, 147
Greek theological terms, 159

Hebrew language
biblical texts, 132-133
concordances, 136
grammars, 134
lexicons, 134-135
Hebrew Scriptures, 131-139
bibliographies, 131
commentaries, 138-
concordances, 136
grammars, 134
indexes and abstracts, 131-132
introductions, 132
lexicons, 134-135
Pentateuch, 133
Septuagint, 136-138
texts and textual criticism,
132-134
modern Jewish, 133-134
theology of, 139
Torah, 138
heresies
encyclopedias, 71
Hinduism, 37
in Australia, 37
historical Jesus, 153
historical research
see history, research in
historiography, 65
history, research in, 64-66
bibliographies, guides, 64-65
chronologies, 65-66
historiography, 65
oral history, 65
Holocaust, the, 56-57
holy days, 173
Holy Land
archaeology, 127-128
Holy Spirit, 161
homiletics
see preaching
hymns, 176-177
companions, 176
concordances, 176-177
dictionaries, 176

icons, 190
inclusive language, 30-31
gender and language, 31
religious usage, 31
indexes and abstracts
see indexing and abstracting
services
indexing and abstracting services
Australasian, 17,
Australian, 15
book reviews, 18

canon law, 101
education, 183
ethics, 204-205
Hebrew Scriptures, 131-132
multi-author works, 17
New Testament, 146-147
religious periodical literature,
15-17, 218
interlibrary loans, 18-19
intertestamental literature, 139-144
see also Dead Sea scrolls
Apocrypha and Pseudepigrapha,
140-141
guides, 140
texts, 140-141
Ireland
Christianity, 112
Islam, 38-39
in Australia, 39
Koran, 39
Israel
atlases, 50-51
history, 50

Japan
Christianity, 112-113
Jerusalem
bibliographies, 51
Jesuitica (Society of Jesus), 96
see also religious orders
Jesus Christ
see Christology; Jesus research
Jesus of history, 153
Jesus research, 153
Jewish-Christian dialogue, 57-59
Jewish theology, 49-50, 139
Jews,
see Judaism; Holocaust;
in Australia, 57
Josephus, Flavius, 52-53
bibliographies, 52-53
concordances, 53
Judaism, 49-59
ancient period, 51-52
atlases, 50-51
in Australia, 57
bibliographies, 49, 56-57
culture, 50
dictionaries, 49-50, 58-59
encyclopedias, 49-50, 57
histories, 50-51
ancient, 51
Holocaust, 57
intertestamental period, 139-144
literature, 50
modern period, 56-59
rabbinic literature, 53-56
rabbinic period, 53-56
theology, 49-50

Kant, Immanuel, 199
Koran, 39

language dictionaries
current usage
Australia, 28
New Zealand, 28
historical, 27-28
theological, 29
Latin theological terms, 159-160
law, biblical teaching
bibliographies, 121-122

lectionaries, 172-173, 174
Liberation theology, 161
libraries
Australian, 18-19
New Zealand, 18-19
interlibrary loans, 18-19
religious and theological, 19
Lima liturgy, 172
liturgical texts, 171-172
liturgy
see also worship and liturgy
calendars, 172-173
Catholic, 170
Christian, 169-172
dictionaries and encyclopedias,
169-171
Orthodox, 170-171
periodicals, 217
texts, 171-172
Luther, Martin, 84-85
bibliographies, 84
indexes, 84
Lutheran churches, 104
Lutheranism
concordances, 84-85

Mary, Mother of Jesus, 161
medical ethics,
see bioethics
medieval period
atlases, 79
Christianity, 78-81
dictionaries, 79
literature, 80
history, 78-79
religious orders, 80
Merton Thomas, 164
metaphysics, 203
Methodist churches, 104-105
bibliographies, 104-105
documents, 104-105
encyclopedias, 105
Middle Ages, 78-80
Midrash, 55-56
ministry, 172, 196-197
periodicals, 217
Mishnah, 54
missions, Christian, 86-88
bibliographies, 87
biographies, 88
dictionaries, 87
directories, 87-88
Mohammed the Prophet
see Islam
Moltmann, Jürgen, 164
More, Thomas, 81
Mormon Church
see Church of Jesus
Christ of the Latter-Day Saints
multi-author works, indexes to, 17
music
see also Church music
general works, 175
Muslims
see Islam
mythology, 23

Nag Hammadi material, 155-156
see also NT apocryphal literature
relation to Bible, 156
texts, 155-156
national bibliographies
Australia, 9

New Zealand, 9-10
New Age movements, 23-24
New Testament
        see also Gospels
                bibliographies, 144-146
                commentaries, 152
                concordances, 150
                dictionaries, 150-151
                Gospels, the, 152-153
                grammars, Greek, 148-149
                indexes and abstracts, 146-147
                introductions, 147
                lexicons, Greek, 149-150
                literary forms, 151
                Pauline material, 154
                textual studies, 147-148
New Testament apocryphal literature,
        see also Nag Hammadi codices
                guides, 154-155
                texts, 155
New Testament pseudepigrapha,
        154-155
New Zealand
        see also Australasian; Oceania
                bibliographies, 9-10, 44
                biographies, 25-26
                book reviews, 18
                books in print, 11
                Christianity, 113
                        documents, 113
                church history, 44-45, 113
                directories, 113
                encyclopedias, 21
                evangelicals, 86
                histories, 44-45
                indexing services, 17
                language dictionaries, 28
                libraries, 18-19
                periodicals, 207-218
                religious movements, 44-45,
                        45-46
                secularists, 25
                style manuals, 29
                theological education, 111, 185
                union lists of periodicals, 14
                women and religion, 44
New Zealand Association of
        Theological Schools (NZATS),
        111, 185

Oceania,
                arts in, 192
                bibliographies, 45-46
                Christianity, 113-114
                        histories, 114
                religions, symbolism, 192
                religious movements, 45-46
Old Testament
        see Hebrew Scriptures
oral history, 65
Orthodox churches, 102
                Byzantine churches, 74
                icons, 190
                liturgy, 170-171
                theology, 162
Oxford Movement, the, 89

Pacific islands
        see Oceania
papacy, 99-100
                biographies of popes, 99-100
                dictionaries, 99-100
                encyclicals, 100

papal statements, 100
parish registers, Australian, 19
pastoral care, 196-198
                dictionaries, 196-197
                histories
                        Australia, 198
                periodicals, 217
                specialised areas, 197-198
patristic period, 71-78
                atlases, 74
                bibliographies, 71-72
                dictionaries and encyclopedias,
                        72-74
patrology, 74-78
                collections, 75-77
                databases, 77
                guides, 74-75
Paul and Pauline material
                bibliographies, 146
                parallels, 153-154
Pentateuch, 133, 138
Pentecostal and charismatic churches,
        102-103
                bibliographies, 102-103
                dictionaries, 103
periodical literature
                abbreviations of titles, 14-15
                bibliographies in, 14
                directories, 13-14
                recommended titles, 207-218
                union lists, 14
periodicals
                Australasian, 207-218
                religious and theological,
                        207-218
Philo Judaeus, 52, 72
philosophers, 202-203
philosophy, 199-203
        see also ethics; metaphysics
                bibliographies, 201
                dictionaries and encyclopedias,
                        201-202
                modern thought,
                        biographies, 202-203
                        dictionaries, 202
plainchant, 175
popes
        see papacy
postal addresses
        see addresses
prayer, prayers, 173
preaching
                communication, 174
                encyclopedias, 173
                lectionary, 174
Presbyterian churches, 105-106
Protestant denominations, 103
Protestant theology
                dictionaries and encyclopedias,
                        162-163
pseudepigrapha, New Testament,
        154-155
psychiatry
                dictionaries, 196
psychology
                dictionaries and encyclopedias, 196

quotation sources
                ancient, 26-27
                general, 26
                modern, 27
                religious, 27
Qumran community,
        see Dead Sea Scrolls

Quran
  see Koran

rabbinic Judaism, 53-56
rabbinic literature, 53-56
reference books, guides to
  general, 6-7
  religious and theological, 7-8
Reformation, 81-85
  art and, 190
  bibliographies, 81-82, 84
  Catholic, 81-84
  encyclopedias, 82-83
  in England, 83
    bibliographies, 83
    documents, 83
    guides, 81-82
    reformers, 84-85
Reformed churches, 105-106
Reformed faith, 105
reformers, 84-85
religion
  bibliographies, 7-8
  dictionaries and encyclopedias, 21-23
  indexing and abstracting services, 15-17
  multi-author works, indexes to 17
  periodical literature, 13-14

  in the Americas, 39-40
  Asia, 40
  Australia, 40-43
    statistics, 32
  China, 43
  Great Britain, 44
  New Zealand, 44-45
  Oceania, 45-46
  Russia and the Soviet Union, 46
religious architecture, 192-193
  church architecture, 192-193
    Asia, 193
    Australia, 193
  surveys, 192
religious art, 188-189, 190-192
  Australian Aborigines, 188-189
religious education, 184-185
  bibliographies, 184
  dictionaries, 184
  histories, 185
  periodicals, 217
religious orders, 80
  see also Jesuitica
religious symbolism
  guides and dictionaries, 190-191
Renaissance, the, 78-79
rituals
  see liturgical texts
Roman Catholic Church,
  see Catholic Church
Roman world, atlas, 74
Russia, Soviet Union
  religious movements, 46

sacraments, 169-171
saints, saints' days, 69-70
Salvation Army, bibliographies, 106
Samaritans, 56
Schleiermacher, Friedrich, 164
Scotland
  Christianity, 114-115
secularists, 25

Septuagint, 136-138
  texts, 136-137
  lexicons, 137
  concordances, 137-138
Society of Jesus,
  see Jesuitica
source collections, early Christianity, 75-77
South Africa
  Christianity, 107-108
Soviet Union
  religious movements, 46
spirituality, 179-181
  Australian Aboriginal, 181
  dictionaries, 180
  documents, histories, 180-181
statistics
  Australian, 32
  Catholic Church, 102
style manuals
  Australian, 29
  biblical writing, 15
  general, 29
  New Zealand, 29
  religious, 30
symbolism, religious, 190-191
synoptic problem
  see Gospels

Talmud, 54-55
  Babylonian, 55
  Palestinian, 54
Teilhard de Chardin, Pierre, 164-165
terms, Greek and Latin, 159-160
textual criticism
  Bible, 128-129
  New Testament, 147148
theologians
  biographies, 163
theological education, 185
  Australasian, 111, 185
  Australian and New Zealand, 111, 185
  periodicals, 217
theological librarianship, 18-19
  periodicals, 218
theological libraries, 18-19
theological schools, 111, 185
  postal addresses in
    Australia , 185
    Canada, 108
    Great Britain , 44, 112
    New Zealand, 185
    United States of America, 108
theology of
  Hebrew Scriptures, 139
  New Testament, 150-151
theology, Christian, 157-165
  bibliographies, 158
  Catholic, 160-161
  dictionaries, encyclopedias, 158-159
  documents, 159
  fundamental, 160
  handbooks, wordbooks, 159
  liberation, 161
  Orthodox, 162
  Protestant, 162-163
  periodicals, 216-217
  terms, 159-160
  theologians, 163-165
theology, Jewish, 49-50
  see also Jewish-Christian dialogue
theses,

see dissertations
Thomas Aquinas
   see Aquinas, Thomas
Tillich, Paul, 165
Torah, 138
trade bibliographies
   general, 10-11
   religious, 11-12
Trinity, 161

unbelief, 22
union lists of periodicals, 14
United States of America
   Christianity, 108
   religious movements, 39-40

Vermigli, Peter Martyr, 84
Vulgate Bible, 122-123

women
   see also feminism
   bibliographies, 70
   dictionaries and encyclopedias,
     70-71
   in the New Testament, 144-145
   in New Zealand, 26, 44
   symbolism, 191
   writers, before 1500, 70
World Council of Churches, 90
worship and liturgy, Christian, 169-173
   bibliographies, 169
   church calendars and lectionaries,
     172-173
   dictionaries and encyclopedias,
     169-171
   handbooks, 171
   liturgical texts, 171-172
   periodicals, 217
   prayers, 173

Zadok Institute for Christianity and
   Society, 111